The Boom Boom Retreat

A MEMOIR

Talya Lewis

ISBN: 1495377334
ISBN-13: 9781495377334
Library of Congress Control Number: 2014905867
CreateSpace Independent Publishing Platform
North Charleston, South Carolina

To my parents:
They were supportive of my writing this book and are the best parents I could ask for. Their strength in acknowledging that, like all of us, they were not perfect is an inspiration for me.
Thank you, Mom and Dad. I love you.

ACKNOWLEDGMENTS

*M*emory has a strange way of working. There are things we remember with such clarity, and there are things that are lost to us forever. In between are those vague recollections that may be marred by wishes, desires, fears, and time. In this memoir I put together my memories of my youth, a time when anguish dominated my experience. I did this with honesty and integrity, to the best of my ability, to define my traumatic experiences. What was not shared—places where questions from the reader remain unanswered—is due to the many memories that may be in indeed lost to me forever.

What is important to remember now are all those people who stood by me during the writing of this book. First and foremost, I want to thank my family: my parents, who sat through dinner after dinner reliving excruciating memories that they had separated themselves from as much as possible, only to relive them once again, and my husband and children for their unflagging support and encouragement. At times I appeared more immersed in my writing than I did in them. I also would like to thank Robin Needleman, who got me on the right track, helping me think about writing in a way I had not known before. I would like to thank Richard P. Kluft, MD, PhD, for his assistance along the way as I wrote and prepared this book. Dr. Kluft was my mentor in the fellowship program of the Psychoanalytic Center of Philadelphia and was generous in sharing his knowledge and experience about the process of writing and about managing the often frustrating journey from first rough draft through publication. Lastly, I would like to thank Martha Rinehart, who was indispensible in the editing of this book. Martha edited the pages of this extraordinarily personal manuscript with great skill, sensitivity, and love. Martha, I could not have done this without you.

Doodling images from my mind was a distraction
that I did frequently. This doodle is from 1979.

DR. TAMMY ROGERS

*H*er words shocked me. They caught me off guard. They triggered me. I looked up at her. I glared. *Are you insane? Have you lost your fucking mind?* Rage and fear stirred violently within me as I tried to understand her intentions, the insanity, the craziness, the ludicrously outrageous inappropriate suggestion she had made. Frenzied thoughts racing violently through my mind, I shot my blue daggers at Dr. Rogers*.

With my past gripping my back, its claws digging in like those of a rabid animal, I could not shake it off. My body swelled with memories of a history long buried, filling me with fury, and I spat it all over Dr. Rogers.

"Don't ever suggest anything like that! How dare you suggest that! I would never send a child away!"

As quickly as the rage set upon me, there was Control.

"Don't ever suggest anything like that again."

Dr. Rogers stared at me. A full minute went by. I think.

"Talya, can we talk about it?"

"No."

"I think we need to talk about it. I know it can be scary to hear a suggestion like that regarding one's child, but I feel there's more to it than that. Your reaction is extreme."

You think?

---

* All names, except that of the author, have been changed to protect privacy.

I folded in upon myself, keeping my organs safe from attack. Suddenly I felt small, dwarfed in my chair. Danger. She saw it. She suspected.

"I can see this is difficult for you."

The need to pull away from Dr. Rogers while staying physically present began to overwhelm me. I searched for distraction: Overstuffed bookshelves. *Psychotherapy and the Adolescent Patient, DSM-IV, Behavioral Techniques, Autism and Its Spectrum.* The wallpaper textured, rippled. A blue frame, a child holding a balloon, a yellow butterfly. A top lying without motion, crayons on a table, plastic and small; two chairs comparable in size. *Adolescent Disorders, Play Therapy and the Abused Child.*

"Talya?"

Pulled back by her words, my blue eyes locked onto her brown eyes.

"I really think we need to talk about it."

"No!"

After a sigh of resignation, Dr. Rogers spoke.

"OK, we'll table it for now."

I knew what this meant—that she would come back to it—but in my disconnect from life as I was growing up, I was lost to the meaning of many of our language's idiomatic phrases. The first time Dr. Rogers had used this colloquial term I had to ask my husband what it meant.

"Rogers says, 'Let's table it for now' a lot. What's she talking about? What does it mean?"

His blue pools of warmth pulled me in and embraced me, making me feel safe, not judged.

"It means she'll get to it later, at some point. I'll bet she has a lot she has to table with you."

Matching creases at the corners of our mouths united us in sarcasm.

I was pulled away from my thoughts as the space between Dr. Rogers and me diminished. I dropped my eyes to protect the space she was invading as she pulled her chair close to mine. Lost in the gray industrial carpeting, the speckles in its fibers dancing as I stared long enough, allowing each speckle to pull me in and take me away.

Dr. Rogers spoke softly.

"Let's talk about your feelings and your difficulty with following through on the behavioral techniques we're working on for you to use at home. I know it's hard for you. I know you have some very intense feelings about this. What concerns me is that other parents with children that have similar issues also have a hard time with their kids. They're not easy children to parent. But it seems as though your difficulty is extreme. It makes me wonder what else is going on. It makes me wonder if your daughter's eliciting old feelings, maybe feelings from a time that was difficult for you. Can we spend some time looking at that notion at some point?"

"Maybe."

Shame hung over me, making me want to hide. I knew if Dr. Rogers continued to search, she would find what I had hidden. A sudden shift in focus brought my eyes to hers, my blue piercing her soft brown with magnetic force. Suddenly Powerful. Feeling large in my chair, I put forth an air of superiority, a shield to prevent her from seeing. My treasure had been hidden and static, and I did not expect someone to start digging now. I had come to Dr. Rogers only to help my daughter. The threat of exposure created a wall, a facade, forcing my body to grow large and intimidating, for if I didn't, she would hate me, judge me, banish me, reject me. If the lid of my treasure opened, the sleeping demon would awaken and rise in the light of day, where up to that point it had haunted me only in my dreams, my sleep interrupted by the touch of the demon, taunting and mocking.

"Talya, there's something strong and intense that she's triggering in you. Can we talk about it?"

"Maybe."

Dr. Rogers had suggested I explore what lies behind the walls, the protective layers I had built up through the years, and she suggested I do it with her as part of the treatment for my daughter, until...

"I've been concerned about you. I'm concerned about the intensity of your feelings toward your daughter, as well as the nature of those feelings. It's too much for us to work on here, but you need to find their source so you can help yourself and in turn help your daughter. I'd like to suggest that you see someone. There are good therapists out there who can help you get past some of the inner conflict. Then you can better help your daughter."

"I can't come back here?"

"I'm saying I think you need therapy. I'm not the one to be able to do it with you."

"What?"

Salt burned the skin on my cheeks. The cruel taste—the enticing flavor—reached my lips. Pressure from my elbows bore into my thighs. The smell of my hands permeated my nose. The friction on my face of skin rubbing against skin was replaced by piercing blue meeting soft brown.

"I thought we were working together."

"I would continue to see you, Talya. We would keep working on the behavioral techniques. Each time you come in to see me, you could give me the thumbs-up or thumbs-down so we can keep connected with how your therapy is going."

"You said *you* would help me. I can't believe you're doing this to me. I can't believe you're pushing me out of your practice. I have to find someone else? I'm Done, Dr. Rogers! I Am Done!"

"I didn't say you couldn't come back. I just said that I feel as though you need some more intensive therapy and that I can't provide it."

I stood. Her words brushed against my ears, Misunderstood. I heard, "I don't want to help you. Go find someone else." I put on my navy-blue Montgomery duffle coat, the weight pushing down on the fibers of my sweater, itching my skin, and picked up my bag. I never would be able to find another Dr. Rogers. She knew the intolerable pain that consumed me as I'd attempted to mother a child who triggered me to my core. She knew the guilt I had shared with her, the fear of never being able to recover the maternal instinct that created an unbreakable bond. Then to kick me out! Left to shiver like a starving dog...abandoned. Head down, tail sadly protected between his legs, slinking between people unnoticed and uncared for. *I have nowhere to go!*

My hand touched the cold doorknob. I wanted to turn it and run. I wanted to stay, locked in union with Dr. Rogers. The creak coming from the hinges seared into my thoughts, while the friction under my shoes as I walked across the carpeting—the ugly industrial carpeting—prevented my speedy getaway. How could she? Standing alone in the elevator, I welcomed the isolation. Images passed like a movie reel through my mind, images with no home, with no place. Outside the cold blast of winter air sent shivers through me as I pulled the hood of my Montgomery coat over my head. How could she? I pushed against the wind as I turned the corner, my car beckoning me. I slid in. The black leather interior held the cold from the outside, but as the engine ignited, the heat quickly filled the inside. A moment of silence followed by salty moisture moving down my cheeks, my lips receiving the wetness. *Dr. Rogers, how could you?*

ATTITUDE

"Why do I have to be back here? Why? I don't want to. Why do I have to stay back here?"

"Well, you have a choice. You can show us that we can trust you, and you'll be able to come off runaway precautions or you can continue to behave the way you have been and stay on precautions. Once your behavior changes and we can trust you, you'll be put on level zero, and you'll be allowed more freedom."

The putrid sulfur of an active volcano precedes its eruption when hot angry lava is spat violently from its mouth. Thick, hot, fiery goo rolls rapidly down its side, covering all living things in its wake, flattening and burning them with its touch. The eruption was instantaneous and impulsive as my rage spewed from my core.

"Level zero! What the fuck? Level zero! What's that going to do? What the fuck is that going to get me? What do I care about level zero? I hate you. I hate you. I hate you!"

I stood in front of the staff member, the pores of his skin large and gutted with scars of acne from his youth, and twisted my interlocked hands together, my skin reddening with the friction. I had no choice but to keep my teeth clenched in an effort to cage words that carried sheer hostility, until the flood held too much pressure and pushed through again.

"Level zero sucks! I still won't be able to go outside! I'll still have to sit in this fucking building all day while everyone else gets to go outside! It's not fair, not fucking fair! What did I do?"

The weight of my head pushed my chin to my chest. I felt exhausted as the anger sucked all the energy from my body.

"It's not fair."

"Since you've been here, you haven't given us reason to trust you."

"What am I supposed to do?"

"Change your attitude."

"What?" *Are you out of your fucking crazy mind?*

His girth took up space, compromising the quantity of air that was left for me to breathe. I couldn't grasp the notion of "change" he was suggesting. What was there to change? Why should I have to change? What was I even doing in this terrifying place?

"What do you mean *change* my attitude? I didn't ask to be here. I don't *want* to be here! Why do I have to be on runaway precautions?"

Opposing statements went unnoticed by my unskilled mind. I was unaware of my words, their meanings, how they would be perceived and interpreted. My life was shifting and changing, frightening and out of my control. The freedom that was expected and that was a right had been stripped away like skin from the bodies of Roman martyrs, and I was left to face my days in the most terrifying of circumstances.

"I don't care! Keep me on runaway precautions. Keep me on them. I don't fucking care. Level zero isn't anything so fucking great. I still don't get to go outside. I still don't get anything, so I don't give a fuck!"

"It gets you closer to level one, where you can go outside."

"I don't care! I want it now! I don't wanna wait! I didn't do anything! I didn't do anything! I want it now! Now! Now! *Now!*"

THE SEARCH

*I*t was the Christmas season when I called Blue Cross for a list of names of therapists in private practice. Not because Dr. Rogers suggested it but because I wanted to help my daughter. Not because it was difficult being me but because I wanted to help my daughter. Not because I had a past that haunted my dreams but because I wanted to help my daughter. Not wanting to burden my husband with the expense of a private-pay therapist, I went through my insurance company. What I had gone through—what I had to deal with from my past, what terror gripped me—was not his problem, nor was it his responsibility.

Once the list arrived in the mail and I opened it, I saw names— name after name, seven pages long. They meant nothing to me. I knew I wanted to see a woman, so I crossed off all the men. I knew I wanted a woman who looked like Dr. Rogers, so I started to search by calling therapists whose names sounded like "Dr. Rogers." Dr. Anna Loretti, PhD, Ann Rice, PsyD, Ann Evans, MSW. They all sounded caring on the phone, but none of them had any space in their practice, they were not taking on new patients. They would have been perfect, but I couldn't see any of them. None of them had space for me. I finally found a woman, Dr. Roberta Smith. We talked on the phone twice before our appointment, and she seemed caring and sincere during these brief conversations—emotionally available. On January 5, I arrived at her suite for our first appointment.

Her waiting room was warm and inviting, with soft lighting and an enticing coffee machine on the table, though I dared not move. I sat reading *Glamour* magazine, admiring the thick full lips of the model on the page, the confidence in her pose, as I waited for this unknown woman, this woman I hoped would be the twin of Dr. Rogers. As I sat and waited, my eyes were riveted to the page, my heart beating rhythmically against my chest. A door opened.

"Hello. Talya?"

Disappointment.

"Yes."

"I'm Dr. Smith. It's nice to meet you. Would you like to come into my office?"

I smiled. Her dark-brown eyes did not change expression as she returned the smile. She did not look like Dr. Rogers. I got up and followed her in. The minimal decor in her office seemed to mirror her personality. She motioned for me to sit on a Laura Ashley–designed sofa, the flowers faded by the sun. At her desk she turned her chair around to face me.

"Why are you here?"

"I have some issues with my daughter that I have to work through."

"OK. Before I ask you more about that, I would like to take a history. Is that OK?"

No, you idiot, it's not OK.

"I guess."

"OK, so where did you grow up?"

"I grew up in the Midwest, until we moved here when I was thirteen."

"Are you married?"

"Yes."

"How's your relationship with your husband? Do you get along?"

"Yeah. My relationship with my husband is great. We're very close. I love him."

I began to feel her prying, screwdriver in hand, forcing off the lid from a can that wanted to remain shut.

"Do you have children?"

"Yes, I have three."

"How old are they?"

"Nine, eleven, and thirteen."

"What are they?"

"One of each."

Silence.

I waited for the flat, humorless exterior of Dr. Smith to soften. Her face remained smooth. No wrinkles dotted the corners of her eyes. No wrinkles encased her mouth. She had no laugh lines.

Clearing my throat I responded.

"They're girls."

"How close is your family?"

"We're close. I love my kids. I love my husband. I mean, the kids have their issues—all kids do—but we're close."

"How about pets? Do you have any?"

Wrapping my head around the urgency of these questions became impossible. The relevance of the different species that shared the same roof somehow didn't seem as important as what had brought me to therapy in the first place, yet I continued to answer to appease her curiosity.

"Yes, cats. I have two of them. One is a Siamese. He's incredibly needy and dependent. He lives through me. He exists through me. I define him, his identity, you know? As a matter of fact, he's so unsure of my existence that he needs to be touching me, his paw on some part of me, whenever he gets the chance, which is usually once I'm in bed for the evening."

Though my description of Oliver, my vocal and loving Siamese, was accurate, dead-on, I unsuccessfully prodded for a reaction other than blank.

"I also have a Ragdoll. Do you know Ragdolls?"

"No."

"Well, they're called Ragdolls because they're soft and floppy like a ragdoll. When you pick them up, they actually flop. It's weird. They feel like putty, like they have no bones. And their fur—it's great. It's so soft, like rabbit fur, and nonmatting, so we only have to groom him once a week, even though his fur is long."

My description of my feline companions excited me more than it interested her. Again there was silence that lasted for only a moment before Dr. Smith realized, with her highly therapeutic and skilled mind, that questions regarding my family and my animals were done. Then, with expertise, she transitioned with a savvy that surpassed the naked eye.

"Have you ever been in therapy before?"

The pressure to smile was insurmountable and reflexive, so tight my muscles hurt. This was a smile I knew well. This was a smile I hated. It was the smile of secrecy, guarding emotions that were dark and threatening. I pulled my eyes away from Dr. Smith and gazed toward the window, trying to leave the space where I found myself trapped.

"Have you ever been in therapy before?"

"Yes."

"How long ago?"

"A long time ago."

"Can you tell me about it?"

"No."

"No?"

As I spoke, Dr. Smith held a notebook firmly in her lap, pen in hand diligently writing down every word I said causing me to speak v e e e r r r r y y y   s l l l o o o w w w l l l y y y and pause every so often so she could keep up. It was this I used to change the direction of our conversation.

"Do you have to write everything down? It's making me uncomfortable."

"I have to. It's for the insurance. I have to keep a very careful log. It's their requirement."

"So you'll always do this? You'll write down everything I say during every session?"

"Yes. At least in the beginning."

Dr. Smith looked nothing like Dr. Rogers. Dr. Rogers was at least my age, if not a little older, and dressed as though she cared more about other people than she did about herself. Dr. Smith, by contrast, appeared younger, and as I was not comfortable with this, I asked an important question.

"So you're asking me a lot of questions. Can I ask one?"

Dr. Smith nodded.

"How old are you?"

"I don't reveal my age to patients."

An instant sense of inferiority struck me, the lesser position of patient to therapist. Though my question accomplished nothing but shame for me, it jogged her mind for more superficial questions for her history-taking agenda.

"Let me ask you, do you have any siblings?"

Back to the family.

"I have a sister."

"Older? Younger?"

"Older."

"Does she live locally?"

"No."

"Where does she live?"

"Out of the country."

Dr. Smith rested the pen in her notebook.

"OK, we're done for today. Are you ready to schedule our next appointment?"

"Huh?"

"Are you ready to schedule our next appointment?"

I found myself scurrying to catch up with the abrupt transition.

"I have to check my calendar at home. I'll call you."

I did call her. I got her voice mail.

"Dr. Smith, thank you for seeing me the other day. However, I don't feel ready for therapy right now. Thank you for your time, though."

Several days later I received a letter in the mail.

Dear Talya,

I want to let you now that my door will always be open for you. When you feel you are ready to start therapy, let me know.

It was a pleasure meeting you.

Sincerely,
Dr. Roberta Smith

Once again I told the next therapist I met with that I was looking for someone to help me work through some issues with my daughter, as I had done with Dr. Smith. Her name I did not retain, but the question she began with remained firmly embedded in my memory.

"Have you ever tried to kill yourself before?"

"What?"

"Have you ever tried to kill yourself before?"

Again, as with Dr. Smith, an uncontrollable, greatly unwanted smile smeared my face. I tried with futility to wipe it away, knowing it was answering her question without any words.

"Why do you have to ask me that?"

"It's a question the insurance company wants me to ask all new patients."

Though this woman didn't write every word down verbatim that came out of my mouth, she asked a very personal question that Dr. Smith did not find necessary to ask—a confusion of rules, a contradiction in expectations. I answered because I already knew I was never going back.

This woman never smiled. Her thin skin covered her bones with a papery translucence, her fragility continuing past her sheath to her skinny frail body, slightly curved and supported by a cane as she walked with a tentative pace. White hair, as wiry as her frame, sprang out of her scalp with no rhyme or reason. As I looked at her, my mind drifted to stories young children hear about witches, her scraggy physique depicting them to perfection. She made me uncomfortable.

"So what is it you've come to therapy for?"

"Well, I have some issues with my daughter."

"What issues?"

"Typical kid stuff that I'm just finding to be a bit more of a struggle than I think it should be."

The fact was my daughter was fine. She wasn't struggling with any deep personal problems. She wasn't showing signs of mental illness or developmental delays. She was active—too active, the ADHD kind of active.

"I can't help you with that. A lot of parents have a hard time with typical kid stuff. You have to be patient—that's all."

Two opposing ideas slapped me with force: *How dare she get rid of me in such a manner! Thank God she was not suggesting I come back to see her.* When the session was over, I politely got up and ran out of there as fast as I could without looking like I was running. Once outside, with the cool air wrapping itself around my face, I could breathe. I walked to my car, slid into its shelter, and drove home.

I saw a few more therapists in consultation, but none seemed quite right. None of them made me feel that they would provide me with the warmth and caring that Dr. Rogers had. I wanted Dr. Rogers. I hated Dr. Rogers.

MEREDITH

The motto "Good things come to those who wait" was appropriate in this case. My search through the seven-page directory of helping professionals was long. With patience and perseverance, I finally seemed to land in the hands of the therapist I was looking for. She had only a master's degree, with which I was not impressed. She went to Harvard, with which I was. On the phone her secretary had a sweet, caring, patient tone.

"I know she doesn't have a PhD, but she's been in practice for thirty-five years. She's good. She knows what she's doing."

"What am I supposed to call her, 'Ms. Barner'?"

"No. She has her clients call her 'Meredith.'"

"OK. Does she have any available appointments?"

When I arrived at her office, I entered the small waiting room, where two receptionists sat behind a pane of glass. They smiled, and one of them asked to see my Blue Cross card and requested my thirty-dollar copay. The chairs were closely spaced in the small area, leaving me suffocated, uneasy, exposed as I read the latest issue of *People* magazine. I sat and waited, wondering what Meredith Barner would be like. I sat and waited with the same anticipation I'd had with each therapy appointment before this one. I was already experiencing the disappointment I was bound to feel with this session, as I had with all the previous sessions before hers. After a few minutes, I was asked to come around to Meredith's office.

I looked around her office, another small space but cluttered with objects. She had a jade plant by the door, bookshelves, a desk, and two big chairs—one sitting with its back to two big windows, the other facing them. It struck me right away that she had the demeanor of Dr. Jones, my daughters' pediatrician. I could not find the clone of Dr. Rogers, but I had found a cousin of Dr. Jones. I knew right away that Meredith was right for me.

The first several sessions with Meredith were very superficial, as we talked about movies and some of the people in *her* life. I wasn't ready to tell her anything, and she wasn't pushing me. Relaxed in her manner, she did not write down everything I said, and she did not ask me if I had ever attempted suicide, so I guess there were different rules for different therapist, or perhaps they simply each chose which ones they wanted to follow.

THE SECRET

A month into our time together, Meredith left for a three-week vacation abroad. When she returned from her trip, it felt as though she had been gone forever, her existence tenuous, as her presence was necessary for me to keep a grasp on her role in my life. I was on the brink of exposing a secret I had sustained for twenty-five years. Sitting in her office, my arms crossed over my body to keep the anger of her departure and then her return from tearing through my core, I made a decision not to give in to my insanity, to behaviors that were reminiscent of my past. I chose to open up to Meredith instead of bash her for the abandonment.

"You know, it's really hard for me to come into your waiting room."

"Why is that?"

"I feel so uncomfortable."

"What's uncomfortable about my waiting room?"

"Well, it's not your waiting room in particular. It's any therapist's waiting room. I'm just really embarrassed. I don't want anyone to see me here."

"What's embarrassing about it?"

"What if someone sees me?"

"Who would see you?"

"I don't know, just anyone. Your receptionists' seeing me embarrasses me. I'm so uncomfortable being here. Not just here but any therapist's office."

I looked at the gift bags she had in a corner, Santa Claus smiling cheerfully on one of them. The vessels in my face widened, allowing my blood to freely rush in excess—the red cells, the white cells, the platelets, the plasma racing to my cheeks. An internal inferno flared up inside me, pulling my attention inward. The more I focused on it, the more intense the experience became. It was the first time I had shown any emotion in her office, and she wanted to know where these feelings were coming from, from what decayed cavity.

"I know it's hard for many people to come to see a therapist. That first move, that first step can be difficult, but you've made it. What is it at this point that has you feeling so embarrassed? What makes this so very difficult for you?"

My gaze remained firmly attached to Santa Claus.

"I don't know."

"Were you ever in therapy before?"

I took in all the chaos in her office: the mess, papers piled high in one corner, bags lying stacked in another. On the white wall, scuffed with age, a picture hung, a boat aimlessly floating down a river, no direction, a man sitting alone steering to nowhere. The sun on the canvas tried to peer through, inhibited by a cloud, threatening rain and danger to the man. Her bookshelves, lined with therapeutic literature, caught my attention. I read the titles: *The Treatment of Multiple Personality Disorder, EMDR in Trauma, Hypnosis and Psychotherapy, Borderline Personality Disorder in Adolescence.*

"Yes."

"When?"

"A very long time ago."

"How long ago?"

"When I was sixteen."

"Can you tell me about it?"

In a moment of panic, my breath stopped. Her deep-brown eyes, hiding behind spectacles to aid her vision, were pressing heavily into mine. Images of a young girl lying in a room far from her home teased my thoughts. Fluorescent lights beating down, door closed, freedom seized, muscles contracting. I held my breath. I held my breath until I no longer could. I exhaled and inhaled, drawing air deeply into my lungs. The image of the girl began to fade, and I looked at Meredith.

"Well, when I was sixteen, I ended up in therapy. What more is there to tell?"

I knew I had chosen to see Meredith, and therapy was no longer being forced upon me, but I felt as if I would be giving in to this looming authority figure if I gave too much. My gaze dropped into my lap—submission or avoidance?

"Can you tell me a little about that experience? Maybe we can see why you are so uncomfortable now."

Meredith sat, watching and waiting for me to give some information, something she could go on. My blue, gray, and black scarf, which I kept loosely draped over my shoulder, offered me protection and comfort. I played with the fringes, braiding and unbraiding them as I planned my approach. I played with the fringes to *avoid* talking. I played with the fringes to distract myself so I *could* talk. The pressure of my secret was pushing against my chest, frantically trying to find a way to escape. I wasn't sure whether it was trying to escape being known or trying to escape being hidden, but I didn't stop long enough to find out. Meredith's patience finally paid off.

"When I was sixteen years old, I was put in a hospital."

"What kind of hospital?"

"A private psychiatric one."

Aug. 8, 1482   1

Dear Mom and Dad,

██████████████ and I are friends
again. We're both pretty happy
about that.

██████████████ is out of the
boom boom retreat and has
her own apartment. ███████ and
█████ called me one night.

The three of us will spend
time together when I get home.
They can't wait. It's nice to
feel wanted.

I'm glad dad lost weight and
it's a shame mom got fat. How
much did she gain, 5 pounds?

I bounce from 108 - 111 pounds.
So when mom gets home we'll
diet together.

            I love you both
            XOXO

                    Love,
                        Lilli

BETRAYED

*A*s I walked home from my revealing session with Meredith, my mind wandered. I began to remember people who influenced my life, for better or worse. I could not shake the memory of Nicole.

Nicole was really tall, which I guess at the time made me feel quite small—the contrast so perceptible—and she was also kind of pretty, with an exotic aura that rarely went unnoticed, stirring feelings of jealousy in me that were difficult to tolerate. The reality of our relationship was that she loved me more than I loved her. Nicole scared me. She had a strong, opinionated personality, which she let flow freely. She was also serious in her outlook, with no room for humor. Anger was always on the surface of her skin. When Nicole was angry—and you never knew when you might trigger her—the pain oozed from her pores. Her face contorted like a newborn experiencing severe distress, red and wrinkled, with tightened muscles as she cried her words, wetness spitting from her mouth, dripping from her nose, falling from her eyes. I did not feel very comfortable around her, but you couldn't escape people in the enclosed confinement of institutional life. When you became friends with someone, there was no place to go, no place to hide, trapped within the walls of insanity.

Community meeting was a daily gathering in which the whole unit—all the kids, all the staff who worked that evening, and the director of the unit, the psychiatrist in charge—came together in the lounge and, well, met. We discussed things that were happening on the unit—patients' behavior (confronting those who had been acting out) and upcoming events (like the trip that was planned for Friday evening). On this night a list of names of those who had earned the privilege of going to the mall was called out.

"Mark, Sara, Ann, Brian, Jim…"

Through good behavior and my having met expectations, I was now on level three, which afforded me the opportunity to grab a soda at the food court and window-shop with my fellow mental patients. The anticipation built with each name—the excitement—as my heart ran a happy race. For the first time since I had arrived at The Hospital several months prior, I was going on the trip.

"Pam, Ken, Glen, Marcy, Riley…"

Sitting and waiting, leg shaking with anticipation.

"Wendy, Nicole…"

Name after name—ten, eleven kids, a few more but not me. I didn't understand. Nicole was called. Others were called. I was on level three. I was full of anticipation and excitement, ready to go to the mall, to be free, to be a teenager, just for one night, but it was to be a precious night. I had earned it; I was following the program; I wanted to go. I was confused, looking around, piecing together what had just happened—or what had failed to happen—waiting for them to realize they'd forgotten. The names were called. The meeting was finished.

The weight of my sadness and disappointment was crushing. Slowly the lounge emptied as the kids and staff headed back to their rooms or the rec room or the nurses' station, where a large table, maybe five feet by ten feet, was a meeting point to sit and talk, or to ready themselves for the trip. The lounge, which had been bustling with the activity of twenty-four adolescents and the staff who was there to oversee them, was now deserted.

In a surrealistic fog, I got up and went into my room to find some comfort. Security in hand I walked out and headed back to the lounge holding tightly on to a photograph—green grass, a tree with leaves, sun and warmth and blue sky, my house as the backdrop. Sitting on the lawn was my dog, Gaia, with me next to her, my arm draped lovingly, holding her close. She was a white springer spaniel mix with dark-brown markings on her head. I loved her, the fourth and last dog of mine that my parents had given away. I sat again in the big, orange, comfortable chair where I had been sitting during the meeting, picture in hand. Disappointment and reality were intermingling, two like-charged ions, swirling around my head, ricocheting off each other but never making contact.

ICannotBelieveIt!
ICannotBelieveIt!
IAmNotGoingOnTheTrip!
IAmNotGettingOut!
ICannotBelieveIt!
ICannotBelieveIt!

My self-pity and confusion were interrupted by a voice, lunging at me from the door of the lounge.

"Lee, you gonna sit there all night?"

Bruce spoke in a burly, intimidating voice that matched perfectly his intimidating presence. He was one of three staff members at The Hospital who was a Vietnam veteran. In an attempt to create an atmosphere of a family—strict father, loving warm mother, protective big brother, cool older sister—the head of the adolescent unit had handpicked his staff. The vets served a purpose. They stood large through their demeanor, so intimidation became their tool. I did not look up when he approached me, concealed and safe by denying his presence.

"Lee, you gonna sit there? You're upset about the trip, are you?"

Meg, accompanying Bruce on his mission, was a female staff member of what I suspected was Irish descent. She had an impatience for my behavior. I felt as though Meg would prefer the cattle prod to me, finding my actions to be manipulative, attention seeking, and difficult—typical false perceptions from those around me. Alone in the lounge, feeling vulnerable, disappointed, the blanket weighing heavily, I was trapped with two staff members who had the power of intimidation on their side. Bruce spoke in a mocking tone.

"Lee, you didn't think you were going to be able to go on the trip, did you?"

"Yeah, of course I did! Why can't I? I'm on level three. It's not fair!"

"Not fair? Not *fair*? What would be not fair about it? I would like to hear it."

"I'm on level three."

"Not anymore."

Eyes widened as though to better take in what I was hearing, head spinning as though to toss it back out again, I tried to grasp this new reality: no trip, no level three. I looked at Bruce and Meg, the whites of my eyes proportionately larger than the blue.

"Why not? What do you mean 'not anymore'? What did I do?"

"You told your roommate you've been cutting yourself. That's not level three behavior."

"What're you talking about?"

My gut tightened, pushing acid into my chest. I clenched my teeth to keep the toxic substance from spraying all over Bruce and Meg. I had told my roommate Nicole, my best friend, that I was feeling like cutting or perhaps that I had. I had confided. She had betrayed.

"You've been cutting, and you're not going anywhere."

As the rage and disappointment percolated, I sat frozen by overwhelming emotion. My leg shook vigorously as it rested on a ledge in front of me. With my hands protecting my face from seeing, from knowing, I suddenly heard the picture of my dog being ripped.

"Say good-bye to your picture."

Pressure swelling, pushing against me, riding up higher and higher, I continued to clench my teeth, attempting to prevent the rage from spilling out until the force within became too strong to withstand.

"I Can't Believe You Fucking Did That!"

A flood of tears drained from my eyes like a dam bursting from the pressure, while my hands continued to shelter my face, hiding me from my reality. Bruce came around the back of the big, comfy, orange chair. He took my arms. He pulled them behind the back of the chair. He held me still—open, vulnerable, exposed. Then he spoke.

"Don't you know that trick? I didn't rip your picture. I just made the sound. You know that trick."

Gut tightening, acid, teeth clenching, toxic substance. I struggled against him, trying to get my arms free from his grip, trying to hide my face, my reality, once again, to feel sheltered from the horrors that were my life. I struggled but could not get free. I spent that night in seclusion, tethered to the bed. That night I was taken off level three and put on self-injury precautions two, nicknamed "SIP 2," with fifteen-minute checks from staff as I spent my days sitting at the nurses' station, the big table, maybe five feet by ten feet, and my nights sleeping in seclusion, imprisoned, alone, abandoned.

THE MEETING

I tried to keep my secret safe in an unpredictable world. It was big and powerful, towering over me like a skyscraper in an earthquake, ready to crash down and crush me. With each seismic wave that threatened its stability, I ran and hid for cover—my husband looking through my phone book, finding a significant name and number, threatened its stability twenty years ago, shortly after we had met. A phone call from my past threatened its stability eighteen years ago, shortly after my wedding. And then there are the scars: daily reminders and daily threats. I so feared the escape of my secret, its oozing into my environment, permeating all that I held dear, all that I was protecting. My Pride. My Self-Respect. My Shame. I never allowed my parents or my sister to speak of my secret, forbidding them to ever utter a word—not one word—of my degrading and humiliating past. It was my secret, and I always planned to keep it my secret until the day I died. Then, as hard as I held it, I let it go, one day, in one instant, it was no longer a part of my private world. After twenty-five years, it was no longer my secret. After I told Meredith, I told my husband; I told my friends; I allowed my family to discuss it; I had become thirsty—unquenchably thirsty—for anyone's memories to fill my gaps. I had gone from one extreme, complete secrecy, to the other: total, unrelenting openness.

Every Wednesday evening I have dinner with my parents, a tradition that started several years ago, giving me a chance in my busy life as a wife and mother to spend some time with them. Despite my issues with my parents—that I always felt my mother needed a mother more than she wanted to be a mother, that my father became a father not because he wanted to but because of the threat of loss, fearing my mother would leave if he did not "give" her children, that they had children not to make us part of a cohesive unit but to serve as objects to fulfill their own needs for love and for preventing abandonment—I enjoy chatting with them. I know they love me.

One night, sitting at the table with them, enjoying a Bombay on the rocks as my mother sipped her wine, along with a beautiful plate of angel hair pasta with my mother's rich homemade red sauce, succulent and delicious, I told my parents I had finally shared my past with my husband. I now wanted them to share their memories of the past with me.

Silence.

The room became still, as if movement would make my words true. In a confused tone, my mother responded.

"Talya, I thought you had forgotten about what you went through."

Forgotten?

"I thought, since you never talk about it, that you pushed it down inside yourself and that you had forgotten about it."

"Well, Mom, pushing something down inside oneself doesn't mean forgetting. It just means you've buried it where it can sneak out and haunt you in the night. Do you realize I wake up at night frequently and cry myself back to sleep, thinking about my past? Thinking about what I went through?"

"No, baby. I had no idea."

"Well, I do. Now I want some of your memories. I want some answers."

Her eyes, fixed on the burgundy colored wine she delicately swirled in her glass, blinked three for four times, preventing a display that would reveal her sadness.

"OK. I'll see what I can remember."

As I talked about a time when I was sick and utterly dependent, a painful sensation of vulnerability threatened my well-being. The discomfort was potent, but getting the information was too important, and the benefits (the knowledge I was going to acquire) outweighed the risks (the negative emotions I was going to experience in the process).

As I sat at the dining-room table, my dinner greeting my nose with mouth-watering smells, my attention was drawn to the heavy expression that pulled on my mother's face, dragging it down by its sheer weight. She did not want to remember. She did not want to talk about this. She did not want to relive the past—the horrifying, anguished past—but I did not care because I *did*.

A soft, wet warmth glossed over my mother's eyes as she stepped back into her mind. She pursed her lips and sent them to one side, gazing my way and using her childhood nickname for me as she spoke.

"I don't remember much either. You know, Lilli, it was a very long time ago. I have a hard time remembering things from that far back. It was a difficult time for us. I do remember your school calling Daddy and me. They wanted to meet with us. They called us in, and I was shocked at what they told us."

The reflexive, unwanted smile of nervousness deceptively crossed my face. Anticipation, curiosity, and a morbid thrill came from hearing about the hellish things I had forgotten.

"Oh, my God. Shocked? What did they say?"

"Well…"

My mother paused, her eyes becoming unfocused and distant, as though she were seeing the past floating through the air right before her, and then continued.

"One day we got a call.

"'Mrs. Wasserman?'

"'Yes.'

"'This is Mrs. Stein. I'm calling from The High School.'

"'Yes?'

"'We would like to set up an appointment for you and Dr. Wasserman to come in.'

"'Is there a problem?'

"'Well, the principal asked that you come in. He would like to have a meeting regarding Lee.'"

"Lee" was the name I went by in my youth. I hated my name. Talya. I hated the queerness of my name. Talya. I hated how it made me—a child who already felt different, isolated, and odd—feel different, isolated, and odd, so I went by "Lee."

"'Is she in some kind of trouble? Has something happened?'

"'When would it be a good time for you to come?'

"'I'll have to talk with my husband, but mornings are usually good.'

"'Can we say tomorrow morning? If there's a problem, you can call.'

"'That should work.'

"'How about tomorrow morning at nine?'"

As my mother recalled the remnants of this conversation, a dark shadow of pain gently passed over her face, caressing her with its evil, unforgiving presence. She was no longer wondering what the problem was. She knew, in that moment, during our Wednesday-night dinner, she knew. Time had answered all her questions. Time had shown her all her fears. She continued.

"The next day your father and I went to the school. When we got there, we were asked to sit and wait, that the principal would be ready for us in a few minutes. I remember sitting feeling nervous, wondering what this could be about. We knew that you were having a hard time, that things in junior high had not been easy for you, and that things weren't going well in high school either, but we were not prepared for what we were about to be told. Finally we were brought back to a room."

— 29 —

"Do you remember what the room looked like? Was it big or small? Do you remember any of the details of the room?"

"Not really. Not too many. I do remember it wasn't a very big room, and there was a conference table in the middle. What surprised me was that there were others in the room waiting to meet with us."

I could see from my mother's eyes, as they appeared to be seeing things that I was not, and from the tension she was holding in her face, that she was being transported, as we spoke, to that very room, to that very day, to that very moment, so long ago.

"'Mrs. Wasserman, Dr. Wasserman, please come in. Have a seat. We're meeting today with [Mr. Eminence] the principal, [Mr. Annoying] the vice-principal, as well as [This Fine Gentleman] the school psychologist, [Mrs. Here to Help] Lee's guidance counselor, and [Mr. Professor] Lee's homeroom teacher.'"

My mother moved swiftly between past and present, remembering details long forgotten.

"Your father and I walked into that room feeling very nervous. I re-member your principal's voice: 'We are all very concerned about Lee.' At that point I remember my heart going up into my throat. I felt the lump sit there, and I couldn't get it down. I couldn't swallow it. To see all those people in the room and to hear those words—'We are all very concerned about Lee'—made my blood run cold. Daddy spoke first.

"'What's the concern?'

"'Well, she's having a very hard time at school. First, as you are aware from her report card, she is failing literally all of her classes.'

"'Yes, we are aware of this.'

"'Second, we have reports from all Lee's teachers that she is very disruptive in class, very impulsive. She makes faces at the teachers when they're conducting class and has been known to get up and simply walk out in the middle. She actually curses and laughs at them in class and in the hallways, and when she's given work, she refuses to do it. As a matter of fact, she hasn't handed in a single assignment since the school year began, and it's now December.'"

My mother looked at me after she recounted this memory, as she re-lived the information delivered to her and my father from the principal of my high school, with a roomful of people judging her daughter, judging her. As though straps were holding her in place to suffer the pain of fifteen hundred spikes emanating from her chair, penetrating her skin, she attempted to reestablish comfort. She took a sip of the wine left in the bottom of her glass. A gust of air, sweet and sad, exited my mother, and for now her remembering was done.

PLAY

My childhood memories tease my conscious mind like a sour, dissolving tablet resting on one's tongue—hard to tolerate then gone within seconds. Holes, dark and empty, take up the space where there should be color and noise and people—laughter, tears, angst, anything. My body, a shell, stands alone and empty as my mind hovers close by, two distinct and separate entities, with emotions that are strong but barely connected to fleeting memories or to none at all. What I do know from those few glimpses into my past that I retain—or from what I've been told—is that I was not an easy child, perhaps not even a happy child.

In the house where I grew up, the basement was dark and scary. Of the four rooms that made it up, only the playroom's stucco walls were covered with the fake, brown, wood paneling common in the 1960s. The cement floor was untouched, as was the ceiling, where pipes ran the width and curved around the length. I would sit, when I had the courage to tackle my fears that lurked about in the dungeon atmosphere, and play a solitary game.

After gathering my dolls from where they were stored, I brought them to the dungeon and laid them gently on the floor. Knowing they would not attempt to flee, I left them alone to get my supplies and returned with a ball of rope and scissors. I would sit down next to my helpless victims, the hard floor offering little comfort, with the ball of rope held firmly in my fist. Unraveling the perfect length for my game, one by one, I would cut the rope and lay each piece by my side. Each doll got a noose firmly placed around her neck. Placing my dimpled hands flat on the cold cement floor to support my body, I pushed myself to standing and picked up my dolls one at a time. Climbing up on a chair—arms stretched, supported by tippy toes—I tied the other end of the rope to the pipes. Their glassy eyes open, they stared blankly into the distance, looking at nothing as they dangled helplessly, powerlessly. One day, as I watched them suspended motionlessly, one of the dolls succumbed to the pressure, the workmanship of her body weakened by the constant hanging. Her soft pink body, stuffed with fluff, held on to her hard plastic limbs but could no longer hold on to her head, the two parts falling separately to the floor. I walked over, picked her up, and carried her parts to the laundry room, where there was a closet with supplies to clean and tools to repair. I forced her head back onto her body, working diligently, my tongue protruding between my lips. I took nails—many, many nails—and hammered them all around the doll's neck until she was once again intact and ready to be hung again.

I would lie in bed at night, my head up toward the window, my room dark as the call to sleep whispered in my ear. Every couple of minutes, a glow from the lighthouse on the lake would shine in and caress the walls with its softness. Eerily, in the distance, the sound of a foghorn would call out and echo through the misty night. I would lie in bed and wait. Some nights it wouldn't come because the sky was too clear and the ships could come in on their own, Navigating the Shores Unassisted.

Searching for comfort, I listened to the cars pass along my street, at times with long intervals in between with no sound from their engines to assure me that others were there, when my mother's voice would bring hope.

"I'll be up in five minutes to kiss you good night."

With patience, and my blanket pulled up to the tip of my chin, protecting me, leaving no part exposed as fear of little monsters hiding under my bed ravaged my mind, I would wait. I would wait for those five minutes, which turned to ten, twenty, fifty, sleep, sleep, sleep.

Our family life revolved around my parents and their activities and their wants and their needs. The droning repetition of living their lives, living in an adult world, spurred an unwanted expression of boredom in me.

I was told to stop.

I would express it more.

I was told to stop.

More.

Stop.

More. More. More.

Stop.

Tantrum.

In an effort to control the unwanted behaviors of a lonely child, the impulsive words that would come to mind flowed freely in my house.

"You rotten kid! How did we get stuck with a kid like you!? Keep it up and I'll smash your head up against the wall! Why can't you be more like your sister?"

When I was a kid, I had a very hard time connecting to my peers, not knowing how to relate to them, how to be playful, how to be talkative, how to be natural, how to *be*. And they knew it.

I have a memory. I was standing by my desk—blond, blue eyed, skinny. My sense of who I was and who I was allowed to be was immersed in murky waters. The skin covering my bones was toxic, like that of a leper, making me want to outrun myself so as not to further contaminate my already defeated self-perception.

Mary was the popular girl, with blond hair, blues eyes, freckles, the perfect nose, and confidence, the type that radiates out, and other children come running over to soak in it.

Standing at my desk, the popular girl swept past me with a playful stride and pulled at my shirt, tugging me to respond.

"I got you, Talya. I got you!"

The joyous flutter of my heart was rapidly replaced by a thud. The sound of blood rushed through my ears, my eyes turning inward as I scrambled helplessly, searching my memory for a modeling event of how I could best respond to this frolicsome gesture. Digging frantically as though searching for a buried bomb with seconds until detonation, I searched. Relief. I realized I was supposed to chase Mary, and sure enough, as I turned I saw her run across the classroom.

"I'm coming, Mary! I'm gonna catch you! I'm coming!"

Mary ran across Mrs. Smith's second-grade classroom. Awkward, hating my body in movement, I ran after her. Mary was laughing. I began to laugh. Mary was having fun. I was trying to have fun but with little success. I still had another image, an important one, that I needed to find. Once again the frantic digging resumed. What was I to do once I caught up to Mary? I used all my energy, scraping at the dirt, fingers bleeding, in an effort to find a treasure that simply was not there. I could not get an image of what other children did once they caught up to the person they were chasing. My instincts as to how to respond came up even more empty handed.

Runningpanickingrunningpanicking. I caught up to Mary.

Runningpanickingrunningpanicking. I grabbed Mary.

My fear held me captive like a platoon of angry soldiers. My emotions ran down my arm, across my hand, through my fingers, bursting out and grabbing Mary, Hard. My fingers, my fear, my Shame dug into her skin. I do not recall the teacher seeing this. I do not recall getting into trouble. What I do recall is that the other kids saw it, and Mary saw it. Well, Mary *felt* it.

What I do recall is the Shame.

PROFESSIONAL REJECTION

*M*y mother and I were sitting at her kitchen table, and once again we embarked on our excursion to the past. Trapped between vivid memories and amnesia, reminiscing became an obsession, one I hungered for: *What happened? Why did it happen? Did it really happen?* I needed to know. My heart felt as though a viselike pressure were squeezing hard on it until the pain from the force shot through my body like pus from a zit and spread wildly through me. I was more equipped than I had been when I was young, now able to master my emotions, an internal steel canister containing all the pressure. With each detonation I sucked it back in, holding it tightly inside as my mother and I sat at the table and ransacked what had been left dormant for so many years.

"Mom, this is important for me to hear. I'm trying to make sense of that time in my life. I know it was hard for you, but how about me? I had to live it firsthand. I had to experience it firsthand. It was my life. I need to hear everything that you remember."

I didn't know who was being more selfish: my mother for focusing on how it affected her life as opposed to mine, or me for focusing on how it affected my life as opposed to hers, but I knew we had to meet in the middle, with no clear idea where that middle was. I wanted to know what happened so I could make sense of my past, and I needed her memories to accomplish my goal, so I decided it was about me, not her. She is the mother. I am the child. And so I pursued.

"Go on, Mom. Tell me more. I want to hear everything you remember."

I settled back in my chair, the taste of gin gliding over my tongue. The sins of my past evoked feelings of guilt as I pushed my mother into a dark frightening cave, where she preferred not to go, where she would never go if it were not for me holding the proverbial knife. It is animal instinct to avoid dangerous places. A battle within me—a twisting turmoil beating heavily on my conscience—threatened to interfere with my digging for my mother's memories. Things that had been buried were now floating on the surface, buoyant so they could not be pushed down, like a dream I once had—a garage standing alone, not attached to a house, was filling with dirty, murky water. As the water filled the garage, all the trash stored within its confines surfaced and began to soil the inside space, even spilling out. I listened intently to my mother, like someone hearing the recounting of a suspenseful novel. I listened to my life.

"Go ahead, Mom. I want to hear what else happened when you and Dad were called into my school."

A small gust of air from the depth of her belly escaped between her lips. She continued to recount the day she and my father were called into a meeting at my high school.

"While we were sitting in that darn conference room, the principal turned to us after telling us about the behaviors you were exhibiting and said…"

My mother's lips stopped moving. Her breath seemed to cease. The wrinkles, soft and deep, intensified between her brows, and then her lips resumed.

"'We have to expel your daughter.'"

"What?"

A wave of electricity rushed through me so unexpectedly that my sense of balance was momentarily compromised. Expel me? I had no memory of this. It was so many years later—so much time stood between then and now—but the pain felt fresh, a dagger from the past piercing my flesh, penetrating my heart. I found myself sitting at my mother's kitchen table as an adult, raw and exposed, rejected by my past.

"What are you talking about?"

"They told us to find a doctor for you. If you could get yourself under control, I suppose they planned on keeping you. They said, 'We want to expel her, but first you can try to get her help,' so I brought you to three different doctors. There was one in the city."

As my mother talked about this man, he slowly began to appear in my mind, as vivid an image as he once had been in reality. His large presence took up space in my mind's eye as he sat across from me wearing a brown tweed jacket, looking at me softly and speaking, his lips cradled by a mustache and beard. His office was on the second floor of an urban townhouse. Eerily, as I drive past it today, chauffeuring my children to their numerous engagements, the same bamboo blinds, ragged with age, cover the first-floor window. Across from him was a big soft chair where I would sit, protected by my navy-blue pea jacket, keeping me warm, safe, and prepared to flee. My eyes worked the room, taking in and sending out all the signals that were necessary to communicate. His soft voice asked questions as he administered the psychological test I had been sent there for. He handed me a Rorschach card, eager to hear what I "saw." I took the card and sat with it, my eyes glaring, thin slits showing only the dark pupils, dilated in the dimly lit room, the soft lighting coming strictly from table lamps and one floor lamp.

"You can throw the card if you want."

He picked up one of the cards from the pile that he had placed neatly on the coffee table between us and threw it across the room, showing me how it was done. I sat frozen in my seat, my expression remaining unchanged. I did not move; I did not speak. I clung to the card as I clung to my anger. If I had moved, I may have unleashed a wave that would have grown into a tsunami, the impossible. As my mind now wandered through the office of the psychologist I had seen so many years ago, my mother's words pulled me back to the present.

"He did the testing over several sessions, and when it was finished, he met with Daddy and me and told us you were experiencing some very difficult feelings and needed therapy, but he couldn't provide it."

"Why?"

"He said you were very difficult and refused to talk with him. He didn't feel he could handle someone like you."

My blood raced feverishly to my face, my heart racing to keep the pace while my diaphragm expanded and contracted with the same velocity. Thoughts scrambled to make sense of what I was hearing: *Couldn't handle someone like me? What the hell does that mean? Was that not his job? Who could* he *handle?* The angry, vulnerable feelings I'd experienced so long ago shot out of me like fire and lava from an erupting volcano.

"What the fuck? What an asshole!"

The effort it took for me to relive my painful, tumultuous past with my mother was exhausting, as the vulnerable feelings I had always hidden from my parents threatened to emerge. A brick wall needed to be quickly constructed to protect and hide them from view. How dare anyone see me suffer? Even though the past was what it was—she knew; she had been there; it was hers as well as mine—I found her knowing invasive. I knew, however, that this was the only way I could come to terms with it, to get it out of my head and out of my dreams. The only way was to talk about it and let her talk about it and remember it and let her remember it.

My mother shifted in her seat. With each episode she recalled, a puff of air escaped her lips, preparing them to form the words she dreaded.

"Well, after him we brought you to another man, a doctor in the suburbs. I remember he had an office in his house. I brought you to him three times, and after the third one, he told me he couldn't see you anymore either. He also told me you were very difficult and weren't cooperative with him. He said people like you are very difficult to treat."

People like me. A fact, frustrating and unnecessary: Many therapists are afraid. They are afraid for their time. They are afraid for their boundaries. They are afraid for their sanity. Though I can't say that I entirely blame them, as they may find themselves caught in the transference like a riptide, pulled out to sea. Their life preserver is to turn "people like me" away. It's far easier and far safer.

"Lilli, I don't really know what was going on in his mind. I don't remember much except he didn't want to treat you. It was a long time ago. I remember him talking about your anger. I know after the third time with him he wouldn't take you back."

"I can't believe it! These guys were doctors! What did you and Dad do after that?"

"We found a woman. I don't remember her name or very much about her either, but I do remember you lasted even less time with her."

"I remember her! She was in the Medical Pavilion Building, wasn't she?"

"Yes."

"I can see her. I remember her as clearly as I remember the other guy from the city. I can't remember the doctor from the suburbs, but I remember the other two. The woman—she had blond hair, and I remember sitting in her office, and she would just sit there and stare at me."

The image of the woman slowly faded, replaced by that of a small child being pulled from museum to museum, trekking through Europe, mesmerized by paintings that recorded medieval tortures. She stood four feet tall, with silky blond hair and gray-blue eyes, looking up at *torture*. A martyr lay on a grill, flesh burning, open wounds, gaping and raw, searching for an escape but tied down hard and fast, unable to move. The image of the martyr, breasts exposed, thrust me again to the present only to be greeted by the memory of sitting with another therapist with whom I could not connect: *You bitch! Are you just going to sit there? Get me the fuck out of here! Say something, bitch!*

I relayed to my mother my memory of this woman, this doctor who made use of the psychoanalytic technique of letting the patient do all the talking, as the patient felt moved to. Well, I was not moved.

In a tone that revealed the experience of a rebellious fifteen-year-old, I continued.

"I remember telling her that I wanted her to talk, that I didn't know what to say, and she said something like, 'That's OK. Just say whatever you want.' What a bitch."

These memories grabbed me with large, strong hands and pulled me, powerless, to my past. At fifteen years old, I didn't want to talk to an older woman, a therapist, reinforcing the idea that I was defective, different, sick. I wore a protective cover that most teens wear, I was not the one with the problem. I was not the one who needed help. My family did. The stork had delivered me into the wrong household. There was no hope in ever being able to repair the rift that separated me, the alien creature, from my family.

Referring to the woman who once again had failed her daughter, my mother spoke.

"Hmmm. I remember that, Lilli. I remember that was a problem. That was what made it difficult for her to treat you. I think you saw her twice, and then she also refused to have you come back."

My perception of my parents' dining room changed. The lights that had seemed warm and welcoming when I had arrived were casting an ominous light, cold and forbidding. Those old feelings buried deep inside me were spilling out. Not wanting my mother to see them, I frantically scooped them up like a child gathering water from the ocean in her small, plastic bucket. Waves crashed back up on the shore. I gathered. They crashed. I gathered. Then I remembered some more.

"There was actually something else about that woman. This is something that I never forgot and that was eerily insightful."

"What?"

"I remember she told you guys, 'Whatever you do, don't put your daughter in a hospital.'"

The pressure of my mother's lips pressing hard against each other made them appear pencil thin, whitening the skin around them. The cold, hardened lips contrasted sharply against the wet warmth in her eyes, holding back guilt and fear that was threatening to erupt.

"Yes, Lilli. She said that. She did."

"How did she know? I almost want to find her and tell her, let her know she was right."

Soft hands, fragile with age, hid my mother's face.

"Yes. She did. She did say that."

Soft moisture caressed her cheeks.

"Yes. She did."

THE REARVIEW MIRROR

*I*t was always difficult for me the closer I got to Meredith's office. I left my house and walked through Piper Square, up Beech Street, past people, past dogs being walked by people, past the hustle and bustle of a large city. When I first started seeing Meredith, it was February, and I wore my coat, gloves, and scarf, protecting against the strong wind and bitter cold. As I arrived and waited for the elevator, I would scan the environment, on the lookout for familiar people seeing me, catching me going to the office of *my therapist*. Shame rose in my body as the elevator rose in the shaft. Once I would arrive, I would open the door like a ninja, walk in, pay, and wait to be summoned for my session, leafing through magazines—*Self, People, Time*—trying to look interested in what I was reading, trying to look absorbed, trying to disappear.

"Talya, you can come back now."

I got up and went into Meredith's office, eyeing a poem that hung on her wall that shared an approach to life, in her mind, worthy of framing. I read it and reread it, looking busy, looking interested, until Meredith came in and sat, giving me my greatly anticipated cue that I was to sit as well. Off came my coat, which I would rest neatly on the floor beside me, but the scarf stayed protectively around my neck.

"How are you doing this week?"

"OK."

"Did anything happen that you would like to talk about?"

I was unable to maintain eye contact with Meredith, distracted instead by the blue, black, and gray plaid pattern of my scarf. I braided and unbraided the tassels that decorated its ends. I played with the tassels to *avoid* talking. I played with them to distract myself so I *could* talk. Like exploding little pellets, memories popped up in my head that made me uncomfortable, ashamed, angry, detached, isolated. They were memories that only I had of events that only I endured. Stealthily I looked back at Meredith, trying to catch her gaze and noticing that her eyes were catching the light from outside.

"Meredith, are you bored?"

A force pushed against my insides like flames trying to storm their way through a home. *She must be bored with me!* I know she felt as if she were pulling teeth talking with me, having expressed this in previous sessions. However, the things she wanted me to say were too toxic to flow out of me without the antivenom readily available, and it was not.

"What?"

"Are you bored with me, Meredith?"

"Why do you say that?"

The laugh that escaped me held little humor.

"Well, you're distracted. You're looking over there."

I gestured over my shoulder, using my head to indicate where her glance had been. I was sensitive to every shift she made. Her eyes, her sighs, her hand gestures—every movement became like words in a novel that I read with focused attention.

"I know you're bored with me."

A look of concern was the facade that hid dangerous feelings for a therapist. Meredith was beginning to struggle with her own inadequacies. I was becoming a danger to the perspective she held of herself as competent.

"Talya, no. No, I'm not bored."

To express my disbelief, to confront her concealment, would mean I would have to give up seeing Meredith. How could I see someone so disinterested in me? This realization was pushed down quickly. I needed her, so I allowed it.

"OK."

"So tell me—how did you end up in The Hospital?"

Without pause, for fear that with any hesitation I would freeze in the moment, I blurted out my response.

"Just after I turned sixteen years old, I overdosed on twelve sleeping pills in the lobby of my high school."

"Go on."

It was hard for me to talk about this, to admit it, yet my past was putting pressure on me, and it was seeping out, so I continued, braiding and unbraiding the tassels on my scarf, my distraction so I could talk.

"Well, one day I brought a bottle of sleeping pills to school and took them during a break or something. I was standing in the lobby after I did it, and I remember my girlfriend Francis coming up to me and asking what was wrong, so I told her what I'd done. I don't know why I told her. Maybe I was scared. Maybe I wanted help. Maybe I wanted someone to save me. Anyway, she walked away. The next thing I remember is the school nurse coming out to get me and bringing me to her office. I remember sitting in a chair, and then the police came. They said I had to go with them, but I didn't want to."

As I sat with Meredith, a vivid image came to mind: a big bright space, the sunlight coming from a row of glass doors with the high school office to the right as I looked outside, the nurse's office to the left. The lobby of my high school was quickly replaced by the image of me sitting on a cold metal chair while the nurse talked.

"Lee, if you don't cooperate with the police and walk out to their car with them, they'll put you in handcuffs and carry you out."

"I don't want to go."

"You don't have a choice."

The two policemen stood silently, looming over me like giant Sequoias hiding sunlight from the plants trying to grow beneath them.

Their presence served its purpose: intimidation. Their presence served its purpose – I was getting noticed.

"I don't want to go."

"Lee, this is your last chance."

Under duress I got up and walked between the two policeman, now not as towering as they had been moments ago. Out of my awareness began the rumors, in the moment, as the students watched my police escort. My desperation numbed by the aide of the sleeping pills, I quietly walked out of the warmth of the school building into the freezing temperatures outside and got into the police car, the school nurse climbing in beside me. With what little dignity I had left, my posture took the pose of the rebellious teen, leaning low in my seat with my knees pressing into the back of the one in front of me. The school nurse spoke, anxiety dominating her tone.

"She's getting tired. We have to hurry."

In the rearview mirror, two eyes peered back at me.

"When's your birthday?"

I did not answer the policeman.

"When's your birthday?"

I did not answer.

"Do you have pets at home?"

I did not answer.

The anxiety released by the school nurse moved through the air with palpable force.

"She's getting tired. Are we almost there?"

The eyes reappeared in the rearview mirror.

To the nurse: "Just a few more minutes and we'll be there."

To me: "Can you talk to me?"

I did not answer.

As we pulled up to the front of the [medical] hospital and came to a stop, the nurse and I sat there, imprisoned in a car that had no door handles on the inside. We waited for the policeman to release us, the innocent nurse eager to get out with the guilty teenager.

"Come on."

Feeling pressured by his command, I pushed myself reluctantly out of the car, the nurse following like a terrified dog pursuing its master. I turned and walked away from the emergency-room door, a weak attempt at fleeing. Though I tried to walk fast, I was tired, weighed down heavily by dissolved tablets that brought on sleep.

"No, no. This way. You have to go in."

The policeman took my arm as he would that of a criminal, twisting it gently behind my back, and though it didn't hurt, I knew he would twist harder if I resisted. I hesitated as we approached the sliding glass doors, feeling as though they may take off my nose as they opened, my visual perception manipulated by the intoxicating effects of what I had ingested. We walked—the policeman, the nurse, and I—to a desk where a lady was sitting, as though she were expecting me. Feeling pressured yet again by a command from the cop, I sat in a chair to the side of the desk.

"Watch her. She doesn't want to be here." And then he walked away.

I did not see him again. I did not see the school nurse again.

THE DEMON THAT LAY WITHIN

They took me immediately, unlike the others sitting in chairs that had come into the emergency room willingly and wanting. As I sat isolated in a small room, my heart flittered between twinges of excitement and the viselike sensation with which I had become so familiar. Every noise pulled my attention, the surge of adrenaline masking my exhaustion. Finally the doctor came in, a woman with dark hair and dark eyes and, in a punishing, warden-like voice, spat out three simple phrases. "I need you to drink this. It's going to make your stomach upset. It's going to make you throw up."

She handed me a little plastic cup filled with a syrupy liquid. Not willing to test her authority, I drank it, and then I sat and waited, again alone. Eventually my mother walked in. A flush of heat passed through my body with intense force. My soul exposed and vulnerable, I hated my mother, her hazel eyes. I began to chatter, my words my vehicle to escape my emotions.

"They gave me this gross stuff. They said it would make me sick. Fortunately I have a strong stomach."

My mother, not hearing my words, spoke.

"Baby, why?"

The pity in her voice unlocked my fury.

"Don't call me 'baby'!"

Unwilling to allow her to see me, I turned away. Facing the door, I saw the doctor with the dark hair and dark eyes steal her way back into the room. She spoke to my mother with little more compassion than she had used with me.

"You can wait in the seating area. We'll let you know when you can see your daughter again."

Relieved because I did not want my mother there, and terrified by the militant doctor, I attempted to distract myself from these polarized emotions before they tore me down the middle. I took in the white walls. The white sheets on the bed where I was imprisoned by chrome bars pulled up on either side so I wouldn't fall off should I drift into sleep, the lights, bright and fluorescent, an insult to my eyes and skin tone. A set of drawers made out of a durable metal was pushed against the wall, where staff could easily access the supplies safely housed inside. The doctor's voice, soft but with no compassion, pulled my eyes to hers. Her quiet tone was not without an agenda: to keep the peace, making her task easier, faster, safer.

"The medicine didn't work. It was supposed to make you throw up. Since it didn't, I'm going to have to help."

To my horror, she came at me with a tongue depressor. It did not take much for my muffled mind to figure out what her intent was. Dreading her barbaric plan, I cried out.

"*No!*"

"The choice isn't yours."

Looking away I protected the entrance she was trying to infiltrate. Her tone shifted from soft yet lacking in compassion to dark and heavy.

"If you don't cooperate, we'll put you in hard leather restraints, put a tube down your nose, and pump your stomach. It *will* hurt."

A yellow, plastic, square bucket, not too deep, became the receptacle for all my pain. With each retch, over and over, a piece of the demon that lay within me was pushed out of my body. With each breath of air I took to fill my lungs, the demon rushed back in. My nostrils were plastered with the sweet smell of the substance that coated the outside of each pill, still intact, the same way they had appeared when I had ingested them.

Eventually the doctor faded from my view. The weight of my body seemed to triple as I dropped back on the bed, the room taking on a surreal feel, the forms of the objects no longer making sense. I lay on the bed exhausted when the psychiatrist assigned to my case came in to talk with me. He was an average-size man with brown hair and a mustache, his voice soft as he spoke.

"Hi, Lee. I'm going to be your doctor while you're here. I'm a psychiatrist. Do you know what that is?"

My eyes caressed him sleepily, only a small amount of blue visible.

"Yeah."

"You had a rough time of it, I'm told. How are you feeling now?"

Devoid of energy, my tone conveyed whatever emotion was left awake within me.

"I don't know."

"OK. Well, you look very tired. It's OK for you to sleep now. I'm going to admit you, and when you're feeling more awake and up to talking, we'll talk."

The psychiatrist walked out.

My mother walked in.

And I slept.

I was put in a private room. Though the room was private, my life was not. A nurse sat with me while I ate, slept, showered, and took a shit. Within a few days, though, I had proven to be responsible for my own safety, and the nurse was released from her post. On this day, sitting in my room waiting for the psychiatrist to pay his daily visit, I remembered a movie that excited my imagination, *Harold and Maude*. Harold had a habit that I liked. He would feign his death, and he did so brilliantly. Thinking this may be an intriguing and rewarding use of my time, I decided to feign mine, for the pleasure of the psychiatrist of course. Once he arrived, there I lay, motionless in the big chair in my room, eyes closed, my breath obvious only to me. I felt the psychiatrist's presence displace the air that stood between him and me. The silence, the stillness, sent the clear message that he was not amused, and for this I paid the price.

I always have wondered whether my life would have taken the same path had I not done *that*.

FLOWER POWER

*F*lashbacks from my childhood invaded my consciousness, flittering about and enticing me to listen, tempting me to reach up and grab each intruding memory. Some were more distant, buried deep in the dungeon of my mind, far from my awareness and in need of being salvaged. Digging for memories had become my goal during my Wednesday-night dinners with my mom and dad. Sitting at the table, eating and drinking, my parents and I talked a little about their day, a little about mine. Slowly the conversation shifted gears, a fork in the road that came upon us almost unnoticed. Standing before us was my past.

"Do you remember when I was in kindergarten, and I needed glasses?"

My mother nodded.

"Did you know I was faking it?"

The up-and-down bobble of my mother's head stopped abruptly with a forward tilt and a furrowed brow.

"What do you mean, 'faking it'?"

Eyes squinted, the corners of my mouth raised, I had taken a liking to shocking my mother with my past.

"Yeah, I was faking it. I remember telling my kindergarten teacher I couldn't see. I remember telling her, standing in the coatroom, that I saw everything blurry."

The hardwood floors, golden brown and shiny, became clear in my mind's eye. I could almost smell the classroom, crayons and paper leaving their scent. My mother's words snapped me back to the moment.

"I remember when she informed us. That's when I made an appointment for you with an eye doctor."

"Well, I didn't need it. I can still see how the floor looked the first day I wore my glasses to school. Everything looked slanted, like when you put on glasses that belong to someone else. I remember sitting in my little wooden chair and looking down. Since I really didn't need those glasses, everything looked distorted."

My mother's face held an expression that may have frightened me as a child.

"Now I understand why you needed glasses only for the four or five months that you did. I could never understand that before. If I had known you were faking it! And I had to drive all the way out to Lakeside for those eye doctor appointments for you."

"You can't be mad. I was in kindergarten. It was the beginning of your kid getting into emotional trouble. How about asking, 'Why would my six-year-old need to get attention in that way?'"

In that moment my mother appeared sunken in, suddenly small.

"Hmmm."

"Can I tell you a more shocking one?"

Her eyes quickly met mine. Small but a moment ago, her posture took on that of a peacock. Like a wounded animal whose fur or feathers fluff to make it look bigger, my mother was ready to ward off her attacker...the past.

"What did you do?"

The memory was like a slide, thrusting me to my past, putting me face-to-face with my best friend Ann.

"You wanna know what I'm gonna do?"

"What?"

"I hate my front teeth. They're ugly."

"Why are they ugly?"

"I don't know. I was born with ugly teeth. I want teeth like yours."

"Why?"

"I don't know. I like your teeth. I hate mine. They're ugly. You know what I'm gonna do?"

"What?"

"Wait here. I'll show you."

Swiftly I ran downstairs and made my way into the laundry room. The sunlight could not brighten the mood, the windows in the basement too small to allow it in. To create a false sense of welcome, my mother had made orange-flower-patterned curtains to cover the small windows, an illusion that all was cheerful. I walked to the laundry room and into the closet, where my parents kept tools for little home-repair jobs: hammers, nails, screwdrivers. I got the hammer. I got the screwdriver. As though the boogeyman were on my back, I raced for the stairs and back up to Ann, who was patiently waiting for me.

"OK. Are you ready?"

"Yeah, but what are you gonna to do?"

When I opened the door to the powder room, the mirror held the reflection of a skinny little girl with short blond hair, gray-blue eyes, and pale skin. Above my head and below, at the corners of the mirror, flower-power stickers clung, serving the same purpose as the orange-flower-patterned curtains in the basement. My eyes reflected my pain and my determination. I looked at myself, at nine years old, and did not like what I saw.

"Talya, what are you doing?"

"You'll see."

Like a loyal soldier, Ann stood waiting, her blue eyes catching mine in the reflection. Screwdriver and hammer in hand, my reflection mocked me. *Destroy.* The hard metal rested on enamel. My muscles tightened, pumping courage in the form of adrenaline through my system. Contact, hammer to screwdriver. Fear jumped in front of me, and I hesitated then pushed it aside. Contact…again. Again. Again. Hammer to screwdriver. The thrill. The reward. With each strike came confidence.

Eyebrows raised, gray-blue projecting into the mirror. A realization as confusing as it was exciting, the pain felt good.

Success.

"Look, Ann. I broke the tooth I hate."

Ann stood, eyes riveted, more white showing than blue.

A shadow camouflaged my mother's face, blending her in with the darkness of my past. Her eyes moistened.

"Why, baby? Why would you have done that? I remember when you broke your tooth. I had no idea you did that to yourself."

The pity that came from my mother was fuel for my fury, leaving me no choice but to fuel her agony in return.

"There's more, Mom. If only you knew. There's more."

DEPARTURE

*A*s I lay in bed after an evening of reminiscing with my parents, my mind was loud. I could not still the scenes that kept playing over and over. I closed my eyes, shutting out the present, and began to drift, but sleep lasted for only a short time. I relinquished control of my thoughts and let my mind wander.

The day came; finally I was to leave the [medical] hospital. The boredom had lasted for seven days. The pressure of my body barely made a dent on the hard hospital mattress, but my mother's gaze weighed on me heavily, detaching from me as my psychiatrist entered my room. As her eyes moved toward him, mine went to the few belongings I had packed, ready for my trip back home. My friends also were there, Theresa and Brian, helping me get ready to go. My psychiatrist sat in the big chair in my room, the one I had used to feign my death. His eyes joined mine with a stern gaze.

"Lee, you're being discharged today."

"Yeah. I know."

"But we can't let you go home."

I jumped off the bed, as though a bolt of electricity had passed through the mattress and shocked my body, so intense that it propelled me forward.

"*What are you talking about?* What do you mean, I can't go home?"

"We can't allow you to go home. We don't feel you'll be safe. You're going to a hospital where you'll get some therapy."

Venom spewed from my lips.

"What do you mean, I can't go home! What the fuck do you mean! I am too going home!"

"I can't let you. The arrangements have been made, and your parents are going to bring you there today. Your friends can go with you too."

"What the fuck do you mean? I am too going home! You can't make me go anywhere!"

The nod of his head sent me running out of my room. My racing steps echoed in the sterile hallway of the [medical] hospital. Off the psychiatric unit, down another hallway, I ran. Standing like a queen's guard at Buckingham Palace, a man from security became a barrier to any further progress. I stood trapped between a nightmare and a soldier. The security guard walked toward me, pushing me with his presence. As he left me no choice, I moved back toward the nightmare, and Theresa grabbed my arm.

"Get the fuck off me, Theresa."

As I shook her off like a bug on my sleeve, a nurse came toward me, big and powerful, and with her weight she pressed against me, wedging me between her and the wall. I stood rigid. In a deep, controlled voice, low and shallow, I spoke the last words to her, my last memory of the [medical] hospital.

"Get the fuck off me! *Now!*"

MISS MARY MACK

*D*eciding my past was something that made more sense to share with those close to me than to keep guarded and secret, as I had done for twenty-five years, I chose to allow a dear friend to see what I was harboring inside. Welcoming her into my past, I told her a story that may have been relatable to our own daughters, still young and innocent, playing Barbie and learning how to read. We sat in my dining room, about a foot apart, my friend leaning toward me, resting her elbow on the warm cherrywood dining room table, supporting her head with a curious tilt. Creating distance between my present and past, I leaned back in my chair in a resting posture, my legs pressing against the side of the table with my knees creating a protective wall, a kind of approach-avoidance dance between wanting to tell and wanting to bury my secrets back into the grave from which they had been exhumed.

"I used to play this game. I called it 'TP.'"

"What did 'TP' stand for?"

"Taking pills."

My friend smiled.

"What did you do?"

"Well, I'd rummage through my parents' medicine chest and take pills. I can't remember why. I wasn't trying to kill myself, because I don't think I knew about suicide when I played this game, and I don't think I was trying to get high either—I wasn't old enough."

"Why? How old were you?"

"Around eight."

"Ohhh, that's young. Still playing Barbie and learning how to read."

She shifted in her seat as though a new position in her chair would allow her to better hear what I had to say.

"When I was a kid, I hated myself, starting when I was pretty young. I hated my body; I hated my skin; I hated everything about me. I guess because of this I would let people do bad things to me. I would almost invite it or walk into traps."

"What do you mean?"

My friend's blue eyes became soft and concerned, creating a sense of safety juxtaposed with a feeling of vulnerability that was reminiscent of so much pain. My thoughts cascaded back in time, seventh grade, the end of the day. Chatter and laughter filled the space. Hands clapping on each other. "Miss Mary Mack Mack Mack, All Dressed in Black Black Black." The linear pattern of children evident a few minutes before had now lost its shape as restless kids awaited the dismissal bell. From the front of the line, I saw her approach.

"Hey, Talya. Can we do something?"

"What?"

"We're playing this game. I scratch the other person's arm. I do it hard, and we see how long you can take it. Wanna play?"

I knew this game was intended to hurt me, and no other kid had played—the fool they thought I was, the fools I knew they were. It was my plan to invite the pain that I was still too naïve to know that I could implement myself. The control they thought they possessed was only because I was gifting it to them in an illusion of torturer and victim.

"Yeah."

"OK. Good."

Her white teeth peered through her full lips, an appearance of friendship with the Devil hiding behind it.

"Give me your arm."

My eyes bore into her then dropped to the floor. I knew she would break before I did. I wanted to be tortured. I wanted to be punished. I wanted to be inflicted with pain. My skin reddened as her nails broke through flesh, the friction of the back-and-forth tearing into me. I stood. She scratched. I stood. Pulled and ragged, my fair skin showed signs of trauma. The girl's teeth disappeared behind her full lips.

"How about you meet us when the bell rings? We'll be at the end of the playground on the Chestnut Avenue side where the swings are. We can hang out."

A tornado swirled chaotically, savagely invading my internal space. My wretched soul pleaded for deliverance.

"OK."

When she returned to her place, the hum of chatter and laughter filled the space once again. Hands clapping. "Miss Mary Mack Mack Mack, All Dressed in Black Black Black." I stood still, alone among my peers. I could smell the deceit, the booby trap that awaited me. Torn in half, ripped down the middle, I wanted to run and hide. I wanted to be tortured. Shame and pride fought for attention. Should I run and escape my fate or tackle it head on and face my nemesis, me?

The bell rang.

The cool air brushed against me. My pace was labored, like an animal moving through a swamp suctioned by mud, I made my way toward Chestnut Avenue. I saw the swings move gently in the wind and beside them the group of girls, standing intertwined, leaving no space between them. Having set their trap, they waited for their prey. My chest fought to hold in my heart, beating at a speed inversely proportioned to my step. At first they appeared small but gradually became larger until their breath intermingled with mine in the cold Midwestern air. They greeted me with a bottle of glue. Slowly my blond shoulder-length hair bonded to itself, white stickiness dripping over me. As I spun around, my eyes met glares from all angles, white teeth showing between lips, full and thin, voices echoing in my ears. I was surrounded but alone. Suddenly an impact, and my body folded, the hard ground my bed. My body was still. I did not fight. I wanted to hide. I wanted to disappear. I wanted to be tortured. I wanted to be punished. I wanted to be inflicted with pain.

"Leave her alone."

My savior came to rescue the fallen maiden, the eighth-grade boy who had more conscience than all the kids put together. His name was Al. All the eyes that had been boring into my skin were now casting their glare onto him. The laughter and shouting that had just a moment ago permeated my ears was hushed.

The weight on my hands supported me as I rose. My pace took on speed as I crossed the rest of the playground. The creaking of the swings, metal chains against metal hooks, brushed past my ears. I walked home. I showered. I never told. It became one of many secrets.

ORNAMENTS

*C*oming into my parents' home, I had become sensitive to the brightness of the lights, which created a frosty, cold atmosphere. I would set the dimmer lower, producing a soft glow—warm, safe and inviting. Placed religiously in my hand was a Bombay gin, the clanking of the ice cubes signaling my taste buds of the pleasure to come while the smells of my mother's cooking shared in the dance of culinary expectations. We would settle into our seats, uplifted by food and conversation, moving from their day to my day to my kids to my husband to my past.

"Do you guys remember when I used to shoplift?"

My mother's eyes shut, her chin slowly meeting her chest in response to the inevitable intrusion of all things old. A soup of emotions swam chaotically within her as I began to reminisce, my insatiable hunger for reliving what once was.

"Do you remember when I used to shoplift?"

"Yes, I remember."

I was eleven years old, walking home from school with two friends and a deep sense of insecurity. The frigid Midwestern temperatures were softened by our Eskimo parka jackets with hoods pulled up over our heads, jutting past our faces like the noses of aardvarks, protecting us from the harsh wind that slapped our cheeks. Walking on Upper Avenue, the shopping street in the community where I lived,

I looked at my friends and offered a suggestion I knew they would enjoy.

"Let's go to the gift shop and see what we can take."

"OK. I dare you to take as much as you can."

"You dare me?"

"Yeah, see how much you can get into your coat."

With the urge to squelch my insecurity through the rush of endorphins that accompanied shoplifting, the dare was difficult to refuse. My friends and I walked into the little gift shop and ambled around. Then we split up, all going in a different direction. I headed toward the Christmas ornaments, looking at them, touching them. I wanted them to be mine. My eyes shifted suspiciously from the ornaments to the two women who owned the shop, busy at the cash register, not paying attention to me. With my eyes held tightly on to the women, my hand felt its way around the pile of Christmas cheer, like that of a blind girl, searching. With a stealthy maneuver, a little train, then a Santa Claus, a rocking horse, and a candy cane all made their way into the large pockets of my heavy jacket. Endorphins rushed through my body, coating me inside and washing away all that felt wrong. Hungry for more, I made my way to the section where they had record albums, seasonal ones for Christmas. My eyes once again searched for the two women, and with my confirmation that they were engaged elsewhere, a record album found its way securely into the body of my jacket. With my heart pushing against my chest in rapid succession, I found myself feeling a slap of cold air and a sense of accomplishment. I had satisfied my impulse. I had quieted the beast.

My loot stashed away, I sat in my bedroom engaged in whatever activity suited me at the time. Enter my mother.

"Talya."

"Yeah?"

"The woman from the gift shop on Upper Avenue called me this afternoon."

I heard my blood rush past my ears.

"She said you were there with your friends."

Blood rushing.

"Were you?"

Blood rushing.

"Yeah."

With my hands interlocked, I watched my thumbs rotate around each other in an attempt to distract her. I could not allow my mother to look into my soul, or she may see what I was hiding.

"She said they saw you shoplifting."

Blood rushing.

"What?"

"She said they saw you shoplifting."

"I wasn't."

My father came into my room. In his hands were the prizes that had been in my hands earlier that day. I still have no idea how he had found them.

"Where did you get these?"

"They belonged to my friends. They gave them to me."

"We were called by the woman from the gift shop on Upper Avenue."

The blue of my eyes disappeared beneath my upper lids.

"I know. Mom told me!"

"She said you were shoplifting."

Searing heat rushed through my body.

"I wasn't!"

"Are you sure?"

"Oh, my God. *No*, I wasn't! My friends gave me those ornaments. I wasn't shoplifting!"

"OK, because if they came from the gift shop, you should return them."

"They didn't! I told you! My friends gave them to me! Man."

My parents' eyes met, and then they turned and left. Defeat? Resignation? Apathy?

"Lilli, we didn't know what to do."

"So you just let me get away with it?"

"We suggested you take the things back."

"You suggested, but you didn't make me. You were the parents."

"I know. But you said the ornaments came from friends. We wanted to believe you. We didn't know what to do, and we had worked it out already with the woman at the gift shop. She just asked that you not go in her store anymore."

"Oh, great. Thanks, Mom."

My mother's focus shifted to her lap, her hands twisting her napkin. The drawn look on her face exposed her guilt. She had betrayed the rule that a parent should guide her child. She had betrayed the child by not protecting the rules.

"It's OK, Mom. As parents we all make mistakes."

TIME MOCKING ME

*W*hile I was growing up, my family and I spent our summers in Europe, each year packing up our suitcases, boarding a plane, and leaving the most valuable thing behind, my life. My sister and I had no friends in Europe since we weren't there during the school year, which would have provided us the opportunity to meet other kids, so she made books her companion, and I made boredom mine. At twelve years old, no longer agreeing to this intolerable situation, I decided to experience America for a summer, be with my friends, go to overnight camp, sleep out by myself, and feel less different, less isolated, less alien.

My sister's friend Barbara spent her summers in America but wanted to go to Europe, so an agreement was made between our families – Barbara would go with mine, and I would stay with hers.

Separation, the intolerable torture, had the potential to unleash emotions that were beyond my capacity to cope. With a heart saturated with pain and simply too weak to carry it alone, I would displace it—I the projector, my mother the screen. I imagined her desperately needing me, tears streaking her cheeks, longing for her child with passionate pleas—"Talya, Talya"—echoing through my empty soul. Consuming every ounce of my being, the despair would take hold and squeeze, devouring me and leaving me unable to escape its grip. My best friend Ann lived next door with only my driveway dividing our homes. Sleepovers at her house predictably ended prematurely, as I would flee for the suffocating embrace of my mother.

North and east, on the lake, a small fishing community had been settled. The houses were quaint, just large enough to hold the fishermen's families. Several grungy boats lining the dock bobbed up and down with the soft movement of the frigid water, their silhouette barely visible against the night sky. This was our setting for a dinner out, the best seafood in the area, approximately one hour from our home. The plan was that I would eat out with my family, and then once home, I would pack my overnight bag and go next door…to sleep. Away From My Family. This idea saturated my every thought throughout the meal. As I ate I had to push the food past the lump that lay heavily in my throat like a cork. The cork held the flood of emotions that were applying pressure from bursting out and spewing my pain over the delectable fish that had been served in mouth-watering fashion.

Time has a way of mocking us, tricking us into thinking there is a lot then suddenly pulling the rug out, and the time is gone. The engine hummed quietly as I sat silently in the backseat. The streetlights appeared to run past our car, interrupting the darkness. The motion was soothing. I never wanted it to stop. Once home, I was repeatedly pulled away from my packing by heart-wrenching pain crashing down like angry waves on the shore. *I want to sleep over desperately. I know it is the normal thing to do. I know other kids do it. But tonight I'm the only kid in the world doing it.* The task finally complete, I picked up my bag, the weight magnified by loneliness as the waves hit me hard and repeatedly. I kissed my mother; waves hit me hard and repeatedly. I kissed my father. I kissed my mother one last time; waves hit me hard and repeatedly.

With all the lights on—casting a blanket of safety, alive and welcoming—I lay on my side on the soft carpeting, Ann lying next to me, with the glare of the television reflected in our eyes. The Friday-night movie had us entranced, and the smell of popcorn met our nostrils with pleasurable anticipation. Ryan, Ann's older brother by eleven months, joined us. Three bowls of homemade popcorn were eventually placed in front of each of us, our fingers quickly grabbing several kernels at a time and shoving them into our mouths. Fizzy Coca-Cola, the ice crackling inside the glass as the warm soda cooled, tickled my nose. I drank, calming my thirst and replacing the salty flavor of popcorn with sweetness. Then, once again, time mocked me. The evening, filled with entertainment, noise and life, suddenly came to a halt. The credits from the movie, replacing the actors, moved up the television screen just fast enough so you could read the names. Our popcorn bowls were now empty. The ice in our glasses, the soda gone, had turned to water. Ann, Ryan, and I pushed our tired bodies off the floor and headed upstairs, Ryan going his way, Ann and I going ours. The noise quieted in the house, with only the soft murmur of Ann's parents talking as they cleaned up from the evening. The house would soon be dark. Salty moisture caressed my cheeks and moved softly over my lips.

"I wanna go home."

Ann's sister Karen, twelve years older than I, came into the room looking at me with intensity in her eyes, her head cocked forward like an angry peacock.

"What?"

"I wanna go home."

"Why?"

The taste of salty wetness touched my lips.

"I wanna go home."

A gust of air pushed out between Karen's lips as the brown of her eyes rolled up behind her upper lids. I can't blame her. I was disappointing her sister.

"Why do you have to go home? You live right next door. Ann was excited about you sleeping over."

"I miss my mom."

The taste of salty wetness burned my lips. Karen's eyes rolled. Shame coated me like thick paste and desperation held me captive.

"Fine. Get your things."

I gathered my overnight bag, this time its weight magnified with shame. Clashing emotions hit head on, and the battle raging within me shook my foundation as each sigh of relief brought on the crushing force of failure. I left the safety of Ann's house and stepped into the darkness, the streetlights my only companions, giving me temporary comfort as the crisp night air cut into me and the darkness surrounded me. The sound of my footsteps jumped into my ears faster, faster, faster, *faster*! My heart pumped fear rapidly through my body. My eyes scanned. Shadows followed me, forcing me to outrun them. My heart pumped faster; my feet moved faster; my eyes scanned faster. The shadows crept up behind me. The distance between my home and Ann's grew greater and greater. The sound of my steps jumped into my ears—faster, faster, faster, *faster*! Home. I lay in my bed, just me and my failure.

I was pleased with my decision to stay with Barbra's family while Barbra went with mine, until the day came. I was unable to think ahead, plan for the future, take one step at a time, learn to sleep over next door first, then down the block, then everything in between, then enforce a three-month, three-thousand mile separation from my family. My thinking—extreme, flawed, and in the moment—had made sense to me at the time. I was unable to plan ahead, and no one had helped me do this, so my decision was made. The separation was inevitable.

The anticipation had been building, with ripples of anxiety moving quickly through me like little bolts of electricity repeatedly shocking me and from which I could not escape. Out my window a car made its way up our driveway, honking its horn, sending my heart plummeting to the depths of my belly. The *beeeep beeeep* severed my hold on my family, my hands tingling, my mind escaping into a dense fog. A moment of silence in my house was once again replaced by the frenzied excitement of travel—the last-minute check of the windows and doors, the extinguishing of lights, the gathering of suitcases, and the hustling out the door to our vehicle of separation. We all piled in, my dad sitting in the front seat, while my mother, sister, and I shared the back. This was our last moment of intimacy. I was to be dropped off at Barbara's house, and then my family was to be taken to the airport. With each rotation of the wheels, my nerve endings pulsated. With each bump in the road, my limbs seemed increasingly weighted and heavy. With intolerable pain overwhelming my capacities, I started to leave myself. My nerves severed from my body, the signals not reaching my brain. My mind's focus became the movement. I was detached from my body. The experience, the inevitable, was lost in motion. As the houses rushed by, my eyes adjusted rapidly, streaks of color swishing past the window, *woosh, woosh.* Stop. The sound of the taxi changed, once in motion but now hovering, still, waiting. The softness of my mother's lips felt so warm, so loving that I wanted to hang on to her forever, to grip her and stop time. In that moment I was with my family, alone. The air hung heavy, wrapping around us like a blanket. I curled up in that blanket, lost in the love I had for my family and in the fear I had of being abandoned, until suddenly the sound of the trunk slamming shut jolted me into reality. My mother handed me two Matchbox cars, a sports car and a tractor. Though I was twelve years old, I clung to my childhood with clenched fists and slid out of the taxi. The weight of my suitcase put pressure on my arm, forcing me to lean to one side to compensate as I pulled myself heavily up the steps that led to Barbara's front door. I dropped the suitcase and straightened my posture before knocking hard. As I waited for the door to open, I turned to face the family I so desperately needed, to send one more kiss to keep them safe, to tell them I had changed my mind. I wanted to be with them. I turned around to give them one more kiss.

The empty space where the taxi sat just a moment ago rushed toward me like a tidal wave and crashed into me. My gut wrenched tightly. I was unable to breathe. I stood on the porch, my soul naked. I was alone.

Within moments the door opened, and I went in, bringing my suitcase upstairs into the room that I was to share with Barbara's younger sister, who was my age, twelve. She wasn't there, so I put my clothes in the dresser that had been emptied for me. As I moved from suitcase to drawers, moisture caressed my cheeks, as soft and warm as my mother's kiss. With each caress came anguished pain. The moisture became streams, running down my face, and the pain escaped through sobbing and howling, like that of a dying, wounded animal. My cries tore through the house, chasing after anyone who would listen, but each person seemed successful in outrunning them.

During my stay at Barbara's house, I wrote to my family, frequently asking them to please send me an airline ticket so I could join them. I let them know how sad I was, how lonely I was, how badly I wanted to be there with them, my family. I said I had made a mistake. I was not ready for the separation I had imposed on myself. *Please, Mom and Dad, send me a ticket so I can come be with you.*

Eventually things got better as the summer progressed. Though I continued to write letters to my family begging them to bring me to Europe, I did settle in, becoming accustomed to the routines at Barbra's house. In the middle of the summer, I went to an overnight camp with Ann, my best friend, and had an experience that would be expected only from a child entering the throes of a mental illness.

YES, HORSES CAN SMELL FEAR

*A*t this point I had been with Meredith for many months, getting more comfortable with her and starting to trust her a little more. I opened a door, allowing her to peek in, and lying just beyond the threshold was the big blue sky opening up over two weeks of my youth. Warm air, tents, bugs, mud, kids, counselors, bonfires, songs, giggles, late nights, marshmallows, chocolate, graham crackers of course, sailboats, a lake. There were eight girls in a group, four to a tent. The tents had wood floors and a front door, more like cabins with a tarp roof and siding, and thin mattresses covering metal-framed beds. Ann and I picked beds right next to each other. Though Barbara's family was my host for the summer, Ann was my companion at camp. Our group had two counselors, one male and one female. On the first day, already my cravings began, strong urges from inside pushing against me while the pressure to let them escape became unbearable.

"I have an idea."

Several sets of eyes converged on me like a swarm of mosquitoes.

"What? Tell us."

"OK. Just to have fun, I'm gonna go in the cabin of the guy counselor, right? Then I'm gonna take all his things. I'm gonna hide his stuff under my bed, and we can see what he does. Let's see how long it takes him to find his things. OK?"

Giggles of agreement fueled me.

"You guys look out for the counselors. I'm gonna go into the cabin and grab all I can."

Rivers of adrenaline surged through my veins, making the anticipation overwhelming. I knew what the outcome would be, and I could not wait. The girls stood outside of the cabin as I giggled and quietly slithered my way in. I saw the treasure, the belongings of the counselor with the dark hair. Another surge of adrenaline revved me, and I grabbed and grabbed and grabbed and grabbed. With my arms stretched around my treasure, I stepped cautiously out of the cabin, and my eyes met those of the other girls, signaling them of my success. With a slick speed, like a soldier defying the enemy, I escaped into my tent and stashed the treasures under my bed, and then I went back for more. I went back again and again and again. When the job was done, I awaited my reward.

"OK guys. Let's see how long it takes him to figure it out. Shh, you can't say anything."

I was giddy with excitement, proud of my accomplishment.

I saw him approaching.

I was giddy with excitement.

He was walking toward his cabin.

Giddy with excitement.

He went in.

Giddy.

Echoing through our corner of the camp, his voice flung through the sky and met us head on.

"Girls! Come over here! I need to talk with all of you."

Eager to please, our bodies surrounded his.

"My stuff's gone."

Giddy with excitement.

"Where's my stuff?"

Giddy.

"All right, I know you guys think this is funny, but I would like my stuff."

The girls and I exchanged glances, with little snickers escaping from some of them. Expecting betrayal I was surprised, very surprised, by their loyalty to *Me*. Perhaps it was because they didn't know me yet— their opinion of me was still virgin—but for the time I relished in the bond we shared. Then I blurted it out, like vomit from a drunk, starved for the negative attention that I was about to be fed, the hair of the dog.

"I have it!"

With stiff, deliberate movements, the counselor with the dark hair took a stance that mirrored mine.

"You have my stuff?"

"Yeah."

"Where is it?"

"I'm not telling."

His posture sent the other girls away.

Giddy with excitement.

"What do you mean, you're not telling?"

"I'm not telling you where I put your things. You have to find them."

"Why are you doing this? What kind of game are you playing?"

His voice controlled, the volcano still quiet, he was giving all his attention to me.

"I want my stuff. Tell me, or I'm taking you with me everywhere I go until you do tell me." A light bulb…"Hmm. I know. How about we have a look in your tent?"

His sense of control gradually was being replaced with exasperation as the volcano came closer to eruption, but I was experiencing what I had set out to. Positive interactions never quenched my thirst for contact with the opposite sex, even at a very young age, as I responded with pleasure to negative attention.

His strong hand wrapped itself firmly around the soft white flesh of my upper arm, making escape impossible. My heart pushed heavily, repeatedly, against my chest. My breathing was shallow and fast.

He guided me toward my cabin, his strength steering the way and his breathing mimicking mine. Our eyes met. He spoke to me with his look. I answered with mine. I knew what he wanted, and I wanted it too. His desire...to lash out, yell at me, "You crazy child, where the hell is my stuff?" My desire...for him to lash out, yell at me, "You crazy child, where the hell is my stuff?" Leaning for support, his hand resting on my thin mattress, he looked under my bed and found his belongings.

"Great, now your job is to bring it all back to my cabin. I'll watch you do it."

His belongings, or at least as many of them as I could carry, were cradled in my arms as I brought them back to his cabin, one hundred yards from my tent. It took me as many trips to put them back as it had to put them there in the first place, and when I was done, I went and met up with the other girls.

Camp continued. I took sailing and learned to dive off the pier into the lake and to ride horses.

Can Horses Smell Fear?

I was drenched with fears, many of them irrational. I kept them neatly tucked away where no one knew they were there, except perhaps a horse. Tandar was white with black spots, a beautiful horse—big, proud, and unpredictable. He was in control.

"OK, kids. Today we're going on trail rides. Everyone has to tack up their horse and be ready."

Laughter and chatter followed us as we walked toward the barn. I tried to catch some of the excitement, but my fists were tightly clenched. Once in the barn, as everyone scrambled to ready the horse that had been assigned to them on the first day of camp, I cautiously approached Tandar's stall. As I moved toward him, my steps sluggish, the sensation of pinpricks covering my face, he threw his head back in warning, his ears pinned flat. Following instructions I got Tandar out and put on his tack. His large nostrils stretched bigger as he smelled the stench of fear. Timidly I held the lead line against his resistance, his whinnying echoing through the barn and spinning me around in search of assistance. Once everyone was tacked up, all the kids led their horses out of the barn, and Tandar and I followed. Instructed to mount and sitting high on our horses, the other kids seemed miles away from me. I turned my head toward my counselor's voice.

"You can run your horses. We'll run them until we reach the woods, and then we'll take the trails to the picnic area and have lunch."

I looked around at all the kids, their heads nodding in agreement. With smiling faces as they anticipated the pleasure of cantering their horses across the fields, they followed the counselor, beginning with a trot. My body moved rapidly up and down, exaggerated and uncomfortable. Were all eyes on me, laughing at my shameful figure in motion? I held on, sure I was going to drop off with the next bounce until we moved into a canter. Suddenly my body was still as the action became smooth, carrying me along in gliding motions, breezing across the ground. *I'm OK. I'm doing it.* As my body made less movement, I felt more contained, less shameful. *I'm OK.* Then the counselor brought her horse back down to a trot and then a walk, and all our horses followed. A scent passed through the air. Tandar picked it up, like a whistle with a pitch so high only a dog can hear.

"Counselor. Counselor, help! My horse. I can't control Tandar. He keeps walking into the trees."

"You need to relax. If a horse senses you're scared, it'll try to get you off its back. Just take a deep breath and relax. Enjoy yourself."

Woman, you have forsaken me. My utter abandon to an animal so tuned into the fear that dripped out of my body, invisible to the naked eye, made me desperate for salvation. At the mercy of Tandar, knowing there was nothing I could do—knowing I could not control my fear, relax, and enjoy myself—I just held on and let the horse take control as he walked into trees, brushing my leg against them, in an effort to get me off. A horse felt my emotions, felt my anxiety, felt my fear, and did not want me on his back, but I stayed on because I did not have a choice. He walked on because he did not have a choice. We were prisoners together, responding to the most basic, primal urges: escape from fear, escape from anxiety, escape from me.

Yes, Horses Can Smell Fear.

The adults at camp, for the most part, were no more than eighteen or nineteen years old. They were unskilled at dealing with my behavior, which was strange and frustrating to them. Grimaces, a tongue sticking out, an inappropriate burst of laughter, a finger directed toward an innocent recipient, soft murmurs to others about others, being caught in the act, others' belongings mysteriously appearing in my possession. Within me was a desire to be responded to with anger, to be punished… *to be liked.*

The Episcopalian minister who ran the camp had a son, blond and good-looking, who was one of the counselors. I taunted the minister's son: grimaces, a tongue sticking out, an inappropriate burst of laughter, a finger directed toward him, soft murmurs to others about him. I did whatever it took to make him aware of me—whatever it took. I pushed and pushed. I taunted and taunted. He cracked. I pushed. I taunted. He cracked.

The path from the lake, a dirt road soft beneath one's step, was bound on either side by woods. The only breath I heard was mine. As my legs carried my thin frame rapidly up the hill, I sensed my space being invaded. Suddenly a hand on my back exerted such a force that I landed in a bed of leaves within the boundaries of the woods, surrounded by tall foliage, invisible to anyone who may pass by. Each time the large foot met my stomach, a grunt escaped my mouth. Each time a fist met my body, instinct took over, and the fetal position became my protection. He continued to hit me, blow after blow, and to kick me, strike after strike. As I cowered in that protective position, relief and joy were juxtaposed against pain and fear. I enjoyed the pain from the blows, over and over; the blows that kept bombarding my body. With each blow a dark fog left me, the evil that lived within being banished. With each kick and the piercing sensation of physical pain came a little relief from the suffocating, overwhelming nature of my emotions. I enjoyed every minute as this eighteen-year-old boy, the son of the minister, beat up on this twelve-year-old little girl.

Suddenly all ceased. His shadow stood large over me, blocking the rays of the sun that strategically made their way between the branches of the trees.

"There you go, you little fucked-up bitch."

Three girls in a row, we sat on a log with the sun, strong and hot, beating down on our backs. I had told them what the minister's son had done.

"Did you tell one of the counselors what happened?"

"Yeah."

"What did they do?"

"They told me I don't have to horseback ride since I'm in pain."

"Does it still hurt?"

"Yeah."

The hurt was in my bones, my muscles, my Heart. The attention I was getting was the narcotic I was looking for, what I always searched for everywhere I went. No sacrifice was too great for the narcotic.

Camp continued uneventfully, with swimming, sports, and on the final night, a dance and marshmallow roast. It was during this event, as camp was coming to a close, that the minister's son approached me. My chest wall struggled to contain the pressure of the rhythmic knocking as the distance between us shrank. The corners of his eyes turned up, matching the corners of his mouth. His voice soft, he whispered to me.

"I'm sorry."

I sat by the fire, the heat softly touching the skin on my face. I soaked up the warmth from the flames and from his words.

STORY TIME, SEVENTH-GRADE STYLE

The rays of the sun went from warmth beating down on my back to the cold crispness of autumn, the trees shedding any sign of summer. The sense of bareness one feels when looking at naked branches, devoid of the green life that grows on them, was the sense of bareness I carried within. With the beginning of the school year came the hope for new opportunities. I arrived to school on the first day of seventh grade to find that Barbra's younger sister, with whom I had developed a friendship over the summer while I stayed with her family, had saved me a seat. Me. There I was, sitting with the other girls I wanted be friends with while my internal world was riddled with demons attempting to sabotage my life.

The soft white flesh with blond fuzz gently running up and down my arm felt foreign to me, a parasite growing on my bones. My place within my family felt equally foreign and parasitic. My existence was only to feed off my host for survival. It was impossible to grab on to a sense of belonging, so with the girls showing an interest in me, I had to keep them hooked. I turned my mind's eye inward and saw emptiness, a vacuum, entirely void, so to keep them hooked, I had to have bait. To do this I filled the emptiness with stories, lies that would make me appear more exciting.

"Do you guys know what happened once when I was at the airport?"

"What?"

"Well, you know that thing that goes around where you get your suitcases from?"

Some of the girls looked at each other, having never traveled, while others nodded in feigned recognition.

"Yeah."

"Well, one time this lady had a dog. She was traveling with him, and you have to keep dogs in those carriers, ya know? Well, her dog got out and ran all around the airport. It was wild. Then he jumped up on the thing that goes around with your suitcase on it, and the woman started to freak out, and then the dog started to freak out. Everyone was laughing. They had to stop the suitcases from going around so the lady could get her dog off."

Another day, another story.

"I used to ride this horse in camp. His name was Tandar. Anyway, now I'm afraid of horses."

"Why?"

"Well, we'd have to put the saddle on by ourselves. There's this thing called a cinch that goes under the horse and attaches the saddle. One day I was putting the saddle and cinch on my horse. Then we went for a ride, and when we were walking along the trail, my saddle slid and went under the horse. Completely under the horse! I fell, and I was lying underneath him. I was pretty scared. They told me I hadn't made the cinch tight enough, and they had to pull me out from under him, and I've been pretty scared of horses since then."

Another day, another story.

"There was this guy…"

Another day, another story.

"I once saw this really weird…"

Another day.

MY FIRST WISH TO DIE

*A*s time passed I revealed more and more to Meredith. These revelations were slow in coming, to be extracted from my mind as a dentist extracts an unwanted, decayed, dying tooth. It was long. It was painful. It stirred me. It frightened me. As much as I resisted with Meredith, as much as I fought the process, I wanted her to know. I wanted *someone* to know.

"Can you tell me anything about yourself from when you were young?"

"Perhaps."

"What it was like being a kid?"

The large chair in her office devoured me, my slight, petite figure disappearing as I sank into the cushion. A sense of protection came from my scarf, always draped gently over my shoulders. The part of my mind that entered Meredith's office was young, childlike, for that was the part of me that held all my memories. The child would pull the scarf up over her face, leaving no trace of the adult as I slipped into my past.

"You know, I started to think about dying when I was around twelve."

"What do you remember?"

"Well…"

Within the privacy I had created for myself, my face hidden, the corners of my mouth rose to attention. My smile was accompanied by a sense of confusion as my expression didn't match my emotion. The soft fibers of my blue plaid scarf, a gift from a friend during my college years, felt calming between my fingers as I recounted my first wish to die.

"I guess at that point I was already pretty unhappy. I guess I always was. I didn't fit in at home. I felt as though I didn't belong to my family, as if it had been a mistake that I was born to them. I didn't fit in at school either. Friends were easy for me to make, hard for me to keep. I didn't belong to any group for any length of time, and I wished I hadn't been born. That thought went through my mind often back then."

My foot shook at the ankle in an attempt to release the anxiety that was gripping me.

"I remember one day standing in my parents' bedroom. I guess I was around twelve years old, and nobody was home. I was by the window looking out, and I remember wondering, *Should I jump? Could I jump? What would happen if I jumped?* That was the first time I remember realizing life was a choice, and I didn't know what my decision was going to be."

"Tell me some more about when you were a child."

For a moment my blue eyes appeared over my protective gear.

"You know, one of the things that was really hard for me when I was a kid was being alone. I hated to be alone, in my house or outside. I was actually terrified of that."

"What was so scary about it for you?"

"I don't know."

"Can you tell me more?"

"Well, I used to be afraid to walk around outside by myself—I mean, really afraid. This was when I was in, like, sixth or seventh grade. My mother would ask me to go to the store to buy milk or something, and I would give her a hard time about it because I wouldn't want to go. I was just so afraid to walk to the store alone, but I wouldn't tell her because I didn't want her to know. I'm not so sure I even understood it, so to explain it was impossible. Even more important, I didn't want her to see my weaknesses, my vulnerabilities, you know? I was embarrassed."

Meredith's head nodded in agreement, and I continued with my fears—my irrational, developmentally abnormal fears.

"I used to have to arrange for a friend to walk to school with me every day. I was afraid that if I walked outside by myself, a stray dog would attack me. A stray dog never had attacked me. As a matter of fact, a dog never had attacked me at all. I suppose this irrational fear made more sense to me somehow than the fact that I was just so terrified of life. Why would I be so afraid of the world? It just didn't make sense. I didn't know where it came from or why I was like that. It was much easier to explain myself as having a fear of stray dogs. That could be real—I needed real."

The head nodded once again. I continued.

"Well, finally, after a while, my friends got really tired of this. One day this girl Marley came up to me, and she was mad or maybe—I don't know—annoyed. Maybe both."

I played with the tassels of my scarf, braiding and unbraiding.

"She said to me, 'Why do you always have to have someone walk to school with you? Why can't you go alone? Other kids do.'"

Braiding and unbraiding.

"I was so embarrassed when she said that, dripping with shame, you know? I guess they all hated me. They must've. I was needy and clingy, but I hated being needy and clingy. My friends—if that's what you wanna call 'em—eventually started to reject me because of this."

The child pulled the scarf up over her face again, leaving no trace of the adult. A jumble of emotions, intermingled without boundaries, danced wildly inside me. *MyKidsNeededToBePickedUp DinnerDishesGroceryShoppingLaundryDrivingBreathing*

Existing!

Talking with Meredith invited the past into my present, making the pain from back then real to me now. Each word was a bid for more agony. I needed to stop the words to stop the anguish, and so I did, for now.

LADY, WHEN YOU'RE WITH ME I'M SMILING

The lighting was dim, with only a single candle softly illuminating each table. A red-and-white-checked cloth protected the surface from the dripping wax. The shadow from the flame danced happily on the faces of my friends, a group of seventh-grade girls who treated me well at times and poorly at others. I tolerated their teasing because my need for social contact outweighed my need for self-protection. Four of us sat around the table, eating what I remember to be the most delicious pizza ever, each bite having to make its way through the tightness of my throat. Hunger alternated with pulses of anxiety deep within my gut. My father had decided he wanted to relocate his family and had been on interviews in Houston, Boston, upstate New York, and the city where we ultimately moved. This was the day he was coming home from his interviews. "Lady, when you're with me I'm smiling..." came from the jukebox, filling the room with a melody that always will suck me unwillingly to my past, stirring emotions in me that are so old and so powerful. I listened intently, not to the words (I never listen to the words) but to the music, to the sound, to the rhythm. I got up and moved through the dimly lit restaurant—the impression more of a nightclub than a pizza parlor—and made my way to the pay phone, walking with the quickened hesitation that accompanies anticipation and fear. I made my call, the receiver cold and heavy in my hand, the sound of my coin falling down the chute echoing in my ears. The dial tone played side by side with the music.

"Hello."

"Mom, did Dad get home yet?"

"Yes, baby, he did."

Those words rushed through me like a loved one's departure being announced over a loudspeaker, separation imminent.

"And?"

"He liked them. They liked him."

"So we're moving?"

"We're moving."

We're moving; "Lady, when you're with me I'm smiling," background chatter, wax dripping, flames dancing happily, pizza, tablecloths, red-and-white checks, dim lighting. "Lady, when you're with me [I'm crying]." I will never hear that song without pain.

We're moving.

The summer of 1975, between seventh and eighth grade, we left the only home I knew. It was the year we left the house I grew up in, the city I grew up in, the friends I grew up with, the school I grew up in. Though I didn't belong anywhere, my home was familiar and there was comfort in that. Change was never easy for me. My life did not bring me a sense of safety and security so the stability of my home, where I lived, the familiar, was my security, no matter how chaotic it was. If I couldn't make it here, where people knew me and I knew them, how was I going to make it in a new city? The choice was not mine however and I was forced to start over. Would I have new opportunities with kids who didn't know me, with kids who had yet to judge me, to dislike me? I was not yet aware of what was going to be in store for me, of who was going to become a force in my life.

FIGHT

Walking through the parking lot, I left lonely footprints in the dusting of soft white snow as I made my way toward to the two-story brick building. Gripping the icy handle, I pulled lightly, only to find a hopeless resistance. I stood alone, the cold air brushing past my cheeks, and looked around, scanning the property for life, but there was no movement in the building; there were no people outside. I adjusted my school bag on my back and tucked my hands deep into my pockets, searching for warmth. The soft snow crunched under my shoes as I once again left my mark in the clean white perfection that covered the pavement. The city from where we had just moved tolerated weather very differently than they apparently did in my new town, where schools closed at the mere threat of snow. This, however, was not the only threat I had to confront.

Having to cope with the changes and feelings of powerlessness that came with moving frequently brought on a flood of memories in my effort to remain connected to where I had come from. My old bedroom was a place where I safely had toyed with change, rearranging my furniture often. I would move my bed from one position to another, my TV, my dresser. It was a change that I controlled. Longing for my old home, I became obsessed with everything that represented it and endlessly spoke of it to anyone and everyone who would listen. Once I left behind the rejection that had existed among my friends, I quickly forgot that the rejection had existed in the first place. My old friends became the coveted company that made me feel whole. My new peers became the enemy.

The hallways of my large suburban junior high school echoed with footsteps and laughter and chatter. The sounds of shoes clapping against the institutional floors, lockers slamming shut, the sound ricocheting off the cement-block walls; kids rushing from one classroom to another, dashing past one another like a blur; the occasional snicker as one girl leaned into another and whispered into her ear, a hand slap as two boys raced past each other—it all represented life, from which I felt disconnected, an outsider.

In the classroom, as I sat motionless behind my desk, my eyes pivoted from one student to another, watching and interpreting their behavior. Did they act like they may reject me? Did they act like they may accept me? As I sat behind a keyboard, plucking at the letters while being timed for velocity, Rob's blue eyes held on to mine. We smiled.

"You wanna hang out with us after school today?"

"You're Rob, right?"

"Yeah."

"Well, OK. Who do you hang out with?"

"Francis, Theresa, Brian, Ricky, and Lucy."

"OK."

"After school we meet at the front doors, where the buses load."

"OK."

The encounter with Rob left me with hope—hope that I would soon feel a connection to this new school, this new city, my new home. The bell shattered the silence in the typing room, giving us permission to get up and run out, making our way to our next scheduled class. Mine was gym.

I followed along as the other girls readied themselves, changing into the dreaded sports shorts, where the parasitic organ that fed off my bones would be exposed. A few of the lockers on either side of the bench where I was sitting were open, with a piece of each owner revealed—a handbag, lipstick, a pack of Marlboro cigarettes, sneakers, deodorant— while others remained empty. There was a group of girls who had class before us, the steam from their showers adding warmth to the air while the smell of soap and perfume rushed past my nose. I watched some other girls, taking them in, admiring their sense of social prowess – a girl resting her arm on another's shoulder, whispering into her ear, some laughing and talking about the night before or a teacher they didn't like or a rock group they went to see in concert. Meg, who was a chunky, pretty, friendly, popular girl, empathetic beyond her years, turned to me and smiled. I smiled back. The moment was interrupted as Carry walked past me, the pressure of her weight on my foot drawing my attention away from Meg. Like a pump the pressure pushed anger that had been sitting quietly up to the surface. An impulse hit me, fast and furious, and I jumped up and stepped forward, my fist slamming into Carry's back. Cheers from the crowd filled the room.

"Fight! Fight!"

Carry's body spun, and we stood eye to eye. I spat my wrath at her, wetting her face with my fury.

"You stepped on my foot, you bitch. You stepped on my foot on purpose. You've been bugging me since I came to this school. You're gonna stop now!"

From the group of girls gathered around us, a voice again shot out like a bullet.

"Fight!"

My chest strained at containing the pressure that was rising, my abdominal muscles tightening with the purpose of holding in any more of the rage that threatened to emerge. An impulse to lash out and seek my revenge—my revenge on Carry, my revenge on my past, emotions that took the place of rational thought, that consumed my waking hours, hovering around me like a swarm of gnats as I brushed them away frantically in a futile attempt at peace—obscured my ability to see. I wanted to take revenge. My eyes pierced Carry. Her back looked vulnerable as she turned around and walked away, defeated before we had even gotten started. Meg took her spot, standing before me, with soft eyes, a soft smile, and three simple words: "She deserved it."

My heart slowed as the tension I held slowly seeped out of my body, Meg's acceptance the valve for its release. I finished getting changed, and I walked away, not saying anything, just smiling.

A DEALER WHO NEEDED FRIENDS, FRIENDS WHO NEEDED DRUGS

The towne was the neighborhood where my friends lived, just a short drive from my house. Rarely did we get together in my neighborhood, where a group of kids hanging out on the corner, smoking joints, cigarettes, alcohol coating our lips, was not likely to be tolerated. My street was quiet, with spacious houses, large front lawns, and no sidewalks. The towne had quaint homes—duplexes— with small yards and sidewalks that ran throughout the neighborhood, encouraging community and connection. A factory resting on the boundaries of the neighborhood became our hangout, the loading platform the ideal place for shelter, protecting us from the cold winds of the harsh winter and the neighbors' eyes peering through the curtains, curious about our laughter. To the side of the platform, a low brick wall, where we sat when the weather permitted, became our code name, "the wall." Let's meet at "the wall." Let's hang at "the wall." Let's party at "the wall." It was our summer spot, once the snow melted and the winds died down. Day after day we hung out where my friends all lived, a few houses from one another, with me the only outsider.

My mother didn't really like my friends, wishing her daughter had become a part of a group who did not smoke or drink. She did not see me as the initiator of any harm. It had to come from others, so with her hands tied, forced by the gun of guilt aimed stealthily at her head, she drove me to the towne. When our car pulled up, my friends already would be sitting on "the wall" or on the platform, and as I stepped out, as soon as my foot touched the hard concrete, laughter and screams of delight would cut through the air, my group, my friends, my people, running to greet *Me*. The chills of acceptance rippled through my body as I waved to my mother, signaling her departure, and disappeared into my world.

Ryan was a drug dealer who needed friends. We were friends who needed drugs. I met Ryan one evening when my friends and I went to his apartment in the towne. He was an adult, maybe in his thirties, who looked remarkably like an actor from my generation. Ryan lived alone and welcomed the company of Theresa, Brian, Rob, Ricky, Lucy, and me. The wall-to-wall carpeting and large sliding glass door that led to a small terrace, the soft sofa, armchairs, and big television, the toned-down lighting on the end tables, all worked together to create an environment of warmth. He had the music on, Jimi Hendrix, the speakers vibrating with rhythm while the television remained muted with characters mouthing words we could not hear. I sat there watching the silent TV and listening to the chatter from my friends, who were excited by Ryan, who was rolling a joint. I had smoked pot once before, in my old home before we moved, when I was in the seventh grade, but as it had been my first time, it had no effect.

Ryan passed the joint to Theresa, who passed it to Brian, who passed it to Rob, who passed it to Ricky, who passed it to Lucy, who passed it to me. We smoked. Ryan lit a second joint and passed it to Theresa, who passed it to Brian, who passed it to Rob, who passed it to Ricky, who passed it to Lucy, who passed it to me. Sometime later we smoked a third. We sat around listening to music, eyes glazed and fixated on the silent television, the music at times lining up in sync with the moving lips of the actors. At one point someone shook his head side to side, with eyes closed, side to side.

"Hey, you guys, try this. It's so cool."

We all closed our eyes and shook our heads from side to side, the motion of an adamant no, like that of a toddler caught in a tantrum. Colors. Lines. Streaks. Red, yellow, orange. The warmth in the room became intense. Flushed. Colors and lines and streaks emanated from a central source in my head. A voice shot out into the room.

"Oh, my God, you guys, cool."

I could hear everyone talking about the experience, the intensity it was adding to their high. I could hear them, but I could not participate. I just kept shaking my head side to side, experiencing the moment, experiencing the colors, shapes, the warmth, the sensations. I was high for the first time, and I liked it.

As the evening went on, we continued to smoke joints and cigarettes and talk, and shake our heads from side to side, until the moment came. My friends had curfews, but they made their own ways home, and since they lived close, they could stay longer. I had to make arrangements with my parents to be picked up, since I didn't live in the towne, since I was the outsider.

"You guys, shit, I gotta go. I can't believe it."

"Already?"

"Yeah. My dad's coming to pick me up. I gotta wait outside."

"Bummer. OK, we'll see you tomorrow."

"Cool. Catch ya later."

Theresa got up.

"I'll walk you down."

"Thanks."

I turned to Ryan.

"Thanks for the high, Ryan. Hey, has anyone ever told you that you look like..."

"Yes."

I laughed. My joy was a fleeting sensation, passing quickly over the surface of my skin but never quite penetrating any deeper. My chuckle served the purpose of social acceptance, but in my core, I felt alien, as far from my friends in connectedness as the stars from the earth. They got to stay. I had to go.

"Later guys."

In unison: "Later."

Theresa and I made our way to the elevator. I liked her. She was pretty, with blond hair and bright blue eyes. She was my friend—unconditionally my friend.

"You know, I hate that my house is so far from everyone else's. I hate that I can't stay out like you guys because I have to get picked up."

"Yeah, I wish you could stay later."

"Thanks for walking down with me."

I looked across the parking lot, and as I saw my family's car, my stomach tightened, trying to prevent the taste of disgust from escaping and slipping into my mouth. I spat.

"Man, I'm so stoned. I can't believe I gotta get into the car with my dad."

Theresa laughed.

"Good luck."

"Thanks."

Our brown Dodge Dart pulled up alongside us. My adolescent aura remained strong to keep the vulnerable child hidden from Theresa. My friend was thirteen like I was, yet she got to stay out—the adult-child-adolescent, carefree, teenage, rebellious, drug-using kid. I didn't. She got to continue smoking, annihilating brain cells—music, lights, shaking heads side to side, colors, lines, streaks, red, yellow, orange, friends, connection. I had to climb back into the womb, a place that I had outgrown yet one that continued to tightly hem me in, restricting my movement and stifling my sense of independence.

Theresa's arms wrapped around me, softly signaling her desire to escape back into the oblivion of our drug dealer's home while my arms wrapped around her tightly, hanging on to normalcy, to connection. Theresa's back slowly moved away from me as I slowly turned toward the car and got in, greeted by my dad's voice.

"Did you have fun tonight?"

The silhouettes of trees and houses began to rush past the window, first slowly then with greater speed. I was alternately caressed with light and darkness, the streetlamps rushing past like soldiers guarding the night. My focus remained riveted to the outside. I felt safer showing my father the back of my head because I feared my eyes revealed the truth—shame, not of the fact that I was stoned but that I was sitting with him and not with my friends.

"Yeah, I had fun."

"What did you do?"

Got high all night. What the fuck do you think we did?

"We sat around and listened to music, talked, stuff like that."

The rest of the short ride home was void of conversation, the only sound coming from the hum of the motor. I always loved being in the car with the hypnotic rhythm and the soothing movement forward and was always disappointed when we reached our destination. This time I craved escape, wanting to be in the privacy of my bedroom. However, as we arrived home my mother was waiting.

"Come. Sit with me and tell me what you did tonight."

A couch pillow separated my mother from me. The bright lights that were keeping the night out were an insult to my eyes, my mother's voice an insult to my ears. "What did you do tonight? You like these friends?

Are they right for you?" Blah blah blah blah blah blah and on and on and on. Once again my adolescent aura dominated, keeping down the vulnerable child, hiding her from the sad hazel eyes of my mother. I cringed with every breath she took, with every word she spoke—vulnerable, pathetic me.

"We sat around and talked and listened to music."

"Well, Lilli, do you think these kids are a good influence? Do you think they're the right friends for you?"

Were they right for me? These friends who screamed out of delight when they saw my parents' car pull up to the factory, and they knew I was inside. These friends who made me feel good, wanted, needed, like they thought about me even when I wasn't with them.

"What are you talking about?"

"Lilli. I just think these new friends may not be a good influence."

"Maybe *I'm* not the good influence. Maybe it's me. Anyway, they're fine. We have fun. It's not like we're doing anything wrong. Man."

The flame burning inside me was hot, scorching, foaming at the mouth as a devilish thrill pushed past my fury, the laughter of a crazed lunatic rumbling within. *Can I be stoned, so fucking stoned, right in front of you mother, and you don't have a clue?* Oh, the joy of it all. Oh...the pain of it all.

"I'm going to bed."

My lips pressed gently against my mother's soft cheek...and then I walked away. The weight of my stoned body was an effort to pull up the stairs. As I finally passed the threshold into my room, my bed was like the song of the Sirens, seductively luring me in, but I resisted, needing first to strip myself of the filth that coated my body. My feet moved from the soft carpeting to the cold tiles, putting me face-to-face with myself. I stood firmly, my eyes dilated and glassy, staring back as I reflected on my features with discontent, analyzing the mirror image with great scrutiny. I did not like what I saw. Breaking my gaze, I leaned forward, allowing the cool water and the sweet smell of soap to cleanse me. The dirt now stripped from my skin and my teeth polished and unsoiled, I slipped into my pajamas, hiding the perception of immense grossness, and finally succumbed to the Sirens' song.

As I lay searching for sleep, the quiet of the night was interrupted by another siren, not one that was singing passionately to me but one that was blaring through the neighborhood for all to hear. It seemed to last indefinitely. This siren was a call that somewhere someone needed help, that his or her house was on fire, and the constant tone became an irritant as my high became less desirable, less wanted. By the end of forever, the noise stopped. Finally I drifted to sleep, escaping the cruel world of reality and slipping into the safety of unconsciousness.

Getting high became a regular, enjoyable activity my friends and I engaged in. It was liberating. It was pleasurable. It was needed, greatly needed. The drugs I used moved from strictly marijuana to pills, giving me even more undeniable pleasure. The pills pulled me to a very special place, into a world that felt good, that felt right, that felt safe. The idea that I could actually love to be in the moment was exciting and way too delicious to resist.

"You guys wanna get high?"

"Yeah. What do you have?"

"You know Ed?

My friend Brian held out his hand revealing a fistful of little blue pills. On that day it was just Brian, Theresa, and me. We looked into Brian's hand, my cheeks hurting as the muscles held on tightly to the ends of my mouth in a grin that wouldn't let go. The tingling sensation of joy and excitement ran through me like a stampede of thirsty zebras coming upon a cool lake with no predators in sight.

"His mom does Valium. He gave me ten. I figure we can take three each."

A watery celebration exploded in my mouth. Anticipation triggered elation. Theresa and I exchanged glances, reflecting each other's excitement as we eagerly laid our hands out flat, with Brian placing three precious little wonders into each of our palms. We slipped them stealthily into our pockets, protecting them like the gems that they were.

"Let's go get sodas and food and then get high."

The heat on that day embraced me like a thick blanket. Ripples of air danced above the hot tar that coated the street's surface as we walked toward the convenience store, our pace matching our excitement, chatting hungrily as we purchased our snacks. I got a Tab and a coffee-cake junior Tastykake. After our purchases we stepped back into the embrace of the hot air and crossed the blacktop street, making our way back to "the wall." I opened my coffee cake and started to pull off the pellets of sugary dough that coated the top, eating them one at a time. Delicious. When the pellets of sugary dough were gone, I pulled apart the rest of the coffee cake and ate it—precise compulsion. With our snacks gone, the time had arrived. Already high from the anticipation, we began to negotiate with each other regarding how to proceed.

"How many are you gonna take?"

"I'm taking all three."

Brian smiled, resting the three little gems on his soft, slippery tongue. He pushed them down with a wave of fizz, Pepsi or Coke.

"Theresa, you taking all three?"

"I guess. Are you?"

I looked at Brian. I smirked with delight.

"Yeah."

Theresa and I both put three little blue pills in our mouths and drank.

The train that went into the city ran along the back of the factory. There was a little hill that went up to the tracks, where soda cans, bottles, empty bags of chips and other debris hid quietly among the weeds and tall grass. Care was taken as I placed my hand systematically, attempting to avoid contact with other people's litter as I tried to support myself during the short climb up. When we reached the top, we walked along the tracks, listening for an oncoming train as we waited for the three little pills to take effect, to embrace each of us in their warmth and security—the warmth and security of not having to feel anything that was real. We waited. Patience. Anticipation. Pleasure.

"I think I'm starting to feel something. How 'bout you guys?"

"Yeah. Nice."

"I like this."

I was happy. I was high.

TEACHERS

The sound of Meredith's breath was the only thing that reminded me that I was not alone in the room. Feeling isolated on an emotional island, I felt the dark winds whip past me with the harsh reality of my past, sending me on a search for shelter. I crouched for protection, once again covering my face with my blue-and-gray scarf, as my memories emerged. Meredith's voice grabbed me and pulled me out of my head with a sudden jolt.

"What are you thinking about?"

As I pulled myself from the past to the present, my focus shifted to the patterned rug, neglected on a regular basis by the cleaning crew.

"Middle school."

"What about middle school?"

"It sucked."

"How?"

"Well, I kind of had a hard time not only with the other kids but also with my teachers."

"Can you tell me in what way?"

"I always got into some kind of trouble with my teachers. I wanted attention. I needed attention, but I always seemed to want the negative kind."

"What made you want negative attention?"

"Who knows? At home I never had any structure, any discipline. Maybe I was just trying to get it from them. Maybe that's all I thought I deserved. Who knows?"

"Can you tell me what some of your experiences were?"

Her words hit my ears like a tornado that had caught debris in its wild, whirling wake. It forced its way into my mind, where memories were neatly tucked away, undisturbed until now.

"Well, I remember my eighth-grade science teacher, Mr. Gannon. One day he was walking behind me as I made my way to an assembly in the auditorium."

My mind brought up a vivid picture—a long hallway opening up to a large space, the cold institutional feeling reinforced by the light-green tiles that lined the walls. Benches outside the auditorium attempted to make the space inviting. The only natural light that was allowed in came from a set of glass doors that led out. Children moving silently through the space in my mind, bumping shoulders, exchanging glances, were like ghosts with no names haunting me from my past.

"He was gay. We all knew it, but I didn't really care. That kind of thing never bothered me—people's choices. Mr. Gannon was walking behind me, and I turned around, saw him, and stopped dead in my tracks. I looked directly at him..."

A heavy coating of shame slowly dripped over me, thick and greasy, and a flush of heat burst up inside me. I was being bombarded from the inside by feelings that cut through my core, by feelings that revealed the evil that used to lie within, by feelings that were old and long gone, by feelings from my past.

"...and I called out, 'faggot.'"

"How did he react?"

"He was enraged of course. He took me and walked me to a bench outside the auditorium where the assembly was going to be. He sat me down and sat next to me, and with this intent look, like he was looking into my soul, he said, 'If you *ever* say that again, you'll find your teeth in your stomach.' I didn't say anything. I just looked. When he let me go, I went into the auditorium and joined my class. It felt good. It was exhilarating. I feel guilty about it now."

Meredith nudged her head in my direction, silently pushing me for more information. Receiving her wordless message, I sent her one of my own, silence. There were parts of me pleading for silence, my voice being hushed by the need for self-preservation. I struggled against myself; I broke free, and I continued.

"One time I remember getting into trouble with Mr. Daimler, also my science teacher, but the following year, when I was in the ninth grade. I can't remember what I did, but I can see it clearly. He had me in this room that divided the two science classes where the beakers and scales and other stuff were kept for lab. He was standing over me, his presence pushing me up against the wall. I remember his anger. His voice was low and restrained, yet his spit was hitting me intermittently. The blood had all rushed to his face. I can't remember if I was terrified by his momentary insanity or if I was holding back laughter, but whichever, I do remember enjoying it. How fucked up was I?"

As I relayed my stories of Mr. Gannon and Mr. Daimler, my eyes rested comfortably on my scarf. I wanted to lift them to catch Meredith's reaction, but their heaviness made it difficult. I fought against the desire to push out the present, and using all my strength, I made momentary contact. Unable to sustain it, my eyes once again rested on the soft blue and gray.

"Are there other accounts from middle school?"

"Yeah. Well, there was this history teacher I had in the eighth grade I really liked. His name was Mr. Richardson. He was probably in his forties or something. I remember he was starting to bald and had sad eyes."

"In what way were his eyes sad?"

"I don't think he *was* sad, but his eyes were. They were—I don't know—kind of droopy in a way, with dark circles under them. Maybe he didn't get enough sleep. You know who he looked like? The actor Dick Van Patten."

"What was it about Mr. Richardson that you liked?"

"I remember that I bonded with him in the eighth grade. I don't know what it was about him. Maybe he didn't judge me. I used to go to his classroom and sit on one of the desks, and he would do things to prepare for class, and we would talk."

"What kind of things would you talk about?"

"I remember he said something to me once about the way I walked down the hall."

"How did you walk down the hall?"

"I wore this army jacket. It was fatigue green and had big sleeves and pockets that were prefect for shoplifting. I can see myself in that jacket, my head hanging, looking at the ground. That's how I used to walk around because I didn't want to see my world. I didn't want to take it in. I didn't want to be a part of it. Maybe if I couldn't see them, they couldn't see me. He commented on that, if only I would walk with my head up."

The past seemed so real that I could almost smell the classroom. I continued.

"I thought he was the best. I loved Mr. Richardson. He was the only teacher…"

Pausing.

"No, the only *adult* who understood me. I loved him."

I held on to the image of Mr. Richardson. I could see his heavy eyes, dark circles adding to the weight. This was not a handsome man, and frankly I don't even remember his having much of a personality, but he was always available, to me. Me. I don't know why—what he thought I was going through, what he was aware of, why he felt I needed his special attention—but he gave and I took – and then I spat him out.

"They gave me Mr. Richardson again in the ninth grade."

"It seems as though they cared about you. They saw someone in trouble and tried to help."

A surge of heat raced through me—the flashback to junior high school, Mr. Richardson, Meredith's voice: *They saw someone in trouble and tried to help.*

"Well, they didn't help enough! When they gave me Mr. Richardson again, I hated him. I absolutely hated him! I didn't think he understood me at all."

Trying to make sense of the split in my experience, I paused in an effort to consolidate my thoughts, and then I continued.

"It was kind of like being trapped in a box with each experience. When I loved him, that was all I knew of him, but when I hated him *that* was all I knew of him. It was as though each experience occurred separately and was hidden from the others. In the beginning of ninth grade, a new reality presented itself, and I simply could not hold both of them in my mind. You see, there was a new history teacher, Mr. Titus, who was young, a big guy with red hair, and I desperately wanted to be in his class, so I asked them if they would switch me, but they said no. I couldn't be refused the cool history teacher I now wanted *and* hold my bond to the old history teacher, so I never spoke to Mr. Richardson again."

As I thought back to my junior-high years, feelings that were so old and so far away had emerged and spilled out. It was as though dozens of little elves were bickering in a well so deep that no one could hear them, until they climbed out, momentarily, and ran around Meredith's office, wreaking havoc. They emerged to torment, to create chaos that I had to clean up before I left to face the city streets and my life. Meredith's asking about our next appointment and pulling out her book was the distraction I needed to orient myself to the present and my life in the here and now. Even though the session's end was a reality I knew I had to face, it always seemed to leave me feeling angry and rejected. I knew these were old feelings, old reactions that were accompanying my trip into my past. I held these feelings down, silencing them with my strength.

"See you on Friday?"

"Yeah, see you on Friday."

LIFE LINE

The sound of music bounced off the hard concrete floor, and the harsh fluorescent lighting bounced off the white stucco walls, adding a cold impersonal feeling to the house party of some unknown kid. My boyfriend James, one year my senior at fifteen years old, had his arm around me while I sat on his lap.

"Lee, I have something for you."

A ripple-like fluttering ran through my chest, not because of my feelings for James—because I had none—but out of anticipation.

"What?"

"I take this stuff. It's gonna make you feel great. It's gonna make you feel like you can do anything."

"I want it!"

I put my hand toward James as though he were going to read my future. Instead he placed six small pills gently on my life line. Again a ripple moved through my chest. Some hesitation began to surface but was quickly pushed back down, out of my mind, out of my way, as I moved the pills from the palm of my hand to the soft flesh of my tongue using a glass of whatever I was drinking to chase them down. Eye to eye, my weight supported by James, I loved him. For that moment I absolutely loved him.

"How long will it take?"

"Oh, I don't know, maybe half an hour. You'll know when it hits."

"How?"

"You'll see. You'll know."

The music, the bright lights, the other kids, motion, movement, music, party, youth, drugs, alcohol, waiting, patience. I waited to feel good, to feel good. To feel good? I asked, "Has it hit yet? What do you think? Has it hit? Did I take enough?" Talk, talk, talk, talk, talk. I continued on and on and on and on. Talk, talk, talk, talk, talk. James laughed.

"I think it hit."

"How do you know? How can you tell? I don't feel different. Oh, my God, I love this song. How can you tell? Are you sure it hit? I'm thirsty. You know what I want to accomplish in my lifetime?"

I was awash with excitement, draped under a cloak of artificial confidence. Feelings I never knew existed emerged. The chaos in my mind seemed directed, seemed to make sense, seemed to be there for a perfectly good reason. The world could crash. I could cope.

The evening went on, fast. A single moment seemed to bring it to an end. Fluctuations from the excitement of elation to deep lulls, drawing me down into anguish, became shorter and shorter. Eventually the lull seemed to gradually encompass the joy, like a dark smoldering cloud snuffing it out.

My soft, inviting bed teased and mocked me. The comfort I would take in escaping through sleep was replaced with hours—endless hours—of agitated wakefulness. Thoughts raced, scrambling, like atoms bouncing rapidly in a heated petri dish. I was unable to shut the thoughts down—the angry, negative, intrusive thoughts; those with which I was familiar...*amplified.* Eventually the dark sky was replaced with an uninvited blue glow intruding into my bedroom. The silence of the night gave way to the song of birds, sweet birds, reminding me of yet another dreadful day in the life that was mine. Pressing down on me was the weight of the world. Eventually I began to feel light as I slowly disconnected from all that was conscious. The pain in the moment was finally put to rest.

THE ADMISSION

Caged like a prisoner, Theresa on one side of me, Brian on the other, the car my jail cell. Outside, moving slowly past us, were thick trees barren of leaves, cold and rigid, running the length of the driveway. Fear, anguish, anxiety, racing, swirling, pushing, pulling, sweat dripping, desperately trying in panic to escape. I was being driven from the [medical] hospital where I had spent a week recovering from an overdose to an institution that would hold me captive in my sickness and dependency. Directly ahead stood a large, sprawling house with a red door, waiting for me, waiting to take me in, to suck me in, to keep me against my will, to hold me caged, incarcerated.

"I can't believe you're taking me here. I told you I'd be OK. Just take me home!"

My mother responded to my protest.

"If we don't bring you, the police are going to do it. We don't have a choice. You'll be in and out quickly."

In and out quickly. A small detour in my life.

The neurons in my brain were firing as they battled the unknown. The motion of the car pressed me against Theresa. We stopped, and the hum of the motor ceased. As we climbed out of the car we felt the chill in the air until we walked through the red door, where the relief from the cold was intertwined with my entrance into hell, the Devil waiting for me. My friends Theresa and Brian were asked to sit in the waiting area. My parents and I were immediately whisked off into a room, like celebrities being protected from their hysterical fans. The sign on the door read, ADMISSIONS. I walked in wearing my cloak of shame, which I had yet to take off. We were asked to sit down and wait. *Could I have escaped?* A woman came in a few minutes later and introduced herself. My parents introduced themselves and me in return. At this point in my life, I wanted people to call me "Lee." They had introduced me as "Talya." Through my lens of rage, I looked at the woman.

"I like to be called 'Lee.'"

"Lee?"

After acknowledging my nod, she moved her eyes from victim to perpetrators.

"Do you understand why your daughter is here?"

The weight of my mother's guilt and shame and fear pulled her head low and curved her spine. As though in slow motion, she nodded. My father chose to use words.

"Yes. We were told at the [medical] hospital that she was a threat to herself and needed to be in a psychiatric hospital for treatment."

The words *threat to herself, psychiatric hospital, treatment* slapped my ears, leaving them stinging. My cloak of shame became heavier, almost too much to bear, the weight of my pain crushing me, pushing on me, hard and unforgiving. My arms, my neck, my back, my legs, my body— they were all tight. I hated all those in the room with me. I hated them, but I listened, catching all their words. I listened, trying to find an angle to get out of the horrific story in which I had found myself. The woman from admissions continued.

"Yes, exactly. We feel your daughter is still quite a threat to herself. We need to admit her here. We would like Lee to sign some papers. This will amount to a voluntary commitment. You'll then meet with the psychiatrist who will take care of your daughter while she's here, and then we'll go down to the unit and she can get settled in."

Her eyes left my parents and found their way to me.

"Lee, do you understand everything so far? Do you have any questions?"

Rushing through my veins like speeding electrons, fear, vulnerability, loss of control, panic, fury, terror jeopardized my composure. My arms crossed firmly, helping to contain the internal chaos and protect me from the external threat. I sat, not having removed my dark-blue pea coat, expecting to meet the cold temperatures outside once again. *They must be aware that I have no intentions of staying.* Doubt filled my head, pulling it down with its weight. I wanted to cry, but they already saw me as weak. I chose not to cry. I also chose not to answer.

"I know you're scared, but if you have any questions or concerns, I would like you to ask them."

Back and forth, from them to me to them, her eyes shifted, rejoining those of my parents as she continued to talk.

"After the papers are signed and we're on the unit where she'll be staying for now, she'll be able to spend some time with you and the friends who accompanied her here."

This time my father chose not to use his words. Like a bobblehead, he showed his agreement. One of my parents then asked, "What is the unit?"

"There are three units at The Hospital: the adolescent unit, the adult unit, and the geriatric unit."

"How long will Talya be here?"

"That's a question you can address with the psychiatrist who's been assigned to Lee's case."

Eyes shifted again.

"Lee, are you ready to sign the papers?"

My coat on, my arms crossed, my head down, I did not answer.

"Lee, it's important that you sign them. Can you look at me?"

My coat, my arms, my head—I did not answer.

"Lee?"

Coat, arms, head.

"I know how frightening this is. I understand. But you don't have a choice. You have to sign the papers, and then we can take you to the unit, and you can settle in."

A wrecking ball, huge steel words held by an iron chain, bashed me in the head: *Settle in! What the fuck? Settle in! This is not where I want to be! I want to go home! I want to be home! I don't want to be here! I don't want to settle in here! Fuck you! I want to go home. Oh, please, please, I want to go home! Help me! Fuck you! Fuck you! Fuck you!* Terror bled from my wounds. I was unwilling to cooperate in the most frightening moment of my life. I would not voluntarily allow myself to be led to the gallows—my coat on, my arms crossed, my head down.

A little puff of annoyance slipped through the lips of the admissions lady. She was very patient, but she knew she had been defeated. She knew it was time to give up. She knew when to pass the buck. She turned to my parents with a smile filled with frustration, sympathy, reassurance—all at once, all in one smile. Her gaze turning away, she leaned back in her chair and fondled the papers in front of her.

"I'm going to introduce to you the psychiatrist assigned to Lee's case."

Again the bobblehead. The motionless silence that came from my parents spoke loudly. Grasping at a rope with slimy hands, slipping helplessly into an abyss, they were paralyzed by the realization that their lives were about to change drastically. Feelings of guilt suffocated and immobilized them. Finally they would get some questions answered. Finally they would know how long their daughter would be kept locked up like a captive animal. My father spoke, since the turmoil of the moment had caged my mother in her mind, as a moist, salty display of her emotions quietly made itself known.

"Is it really important that she does? That she stay here?"

"I'm going to let him know we are ready for him. You can ask him all your questions."

The admissions woman got up and walked out. My father addressed me.

"Talya, will you sign the papers?"

In that moment an electric surge, unexpectedly, awesomely huge, grotesque, full of anger beat down on my father.

"*Fuck you*, Dad! *Fuck you*! I'm *not* signing *anything*! I'm *not* staying here, and *no one* can make me! I'm *not* staying here, so *fuck you*!

My nails dug relentlessly into my palms, my knuckles white. My anger released tears that irritated my cheeks. My mother's pity—the pity I hated, the pity that made me feel sick and vulnerable—spilled out of her mouth.

"Lilli, baby, don't cry. Please don't cry."

As she spoke, tears flowed from her eyes. Her tears were out of sadness. Mine were out of rage and terror. All was suddenly interrupted as a man walked in and demanded the attention of my parents simply upon entering. This was the first time I saw him. This was the man who was going to change the course of my life, and I looked away. Never turn your back on danger.

He was a small man, his ego inversely proportionate to his stature. He caged me with his presence, instantly frightening me. Smiling, he reached out his hand to my father and then my mother.

"Hello. I'm Dr. Bennett. I'm going to be taking care of your daughter while she's here."

As etiquette demanded, my father stood to shake his hand; my mother remained seated to do the same. After the introductions my father's eyes turned toward me. His eyes, his retinas, took a photograph, upside down, sending it back to his occipital lobe, inverting it so his mind could see me as I was in reality. His gaze guided my mother's. His gaze guided Dr. Bennett's. I felt them coating me—their eyes, their retinas—taking a photograph, upside down, sending it back to their occipital lobes, inverting it so their minds could see me as I was in reality.

"This is our daughter. Her name is Talya."

I pierced the doctor with my anger—anger at my parents for not knowing what I needed: to be valued and given a choice.

"I like to be called 'Lee.'"

Dr. Bennett smiled, his head tilted to one side.

"Hi, Lee. I'm Dr. Bennett."

He stood looking at me for a moment, suspended, and then he sat. His body made its way closer to mine, my reflection in his glasses a mirror to my existence.

"Do you understand why you're here?"

I did not answer. My teeth worked the inside of my bottom lip, a painful distraction, while every muscle constricted, fight or flight; every muscle ready to react, fight or flight. Fleeing deep within myself, I was not going to give those bastards what they wanted: my cooperation. Coat on, arms crossed, head down, I did not speak.

Slowly my image disappeared from Dr. Bennett's glasses, my space becoming more my own. The smile on his face disappeared with my image. His brow and his lips became tight. The room was quiet. The doctor, deliberating. My parents, waiting. Me, not cooperating. As swiftly as the quiet overtook the room, Dr. Bennett's voice broke it.

"Lee, I'm going to need a few minutes alone with your parents. You're going to sit with the woman from admissions."

A brief phone call brought the admissions woman through the door.

"Lee, I'd like you to come with me. Dr. Bennett is going to talk with your parents for a few minutes, and we're going to try to get this worked out."

Worked out? In my mind—my panicked, terrified mind—that meant there was hope. Maybe it meant I would be able to go home. I got up and went with the woman, and my parents stayed and talked with Dr. Bennett. They stayed to "work it out."

I had always wondered what happened once I left the room. It was sitting at my parents' table during one of our Wednesday night dinners that my curiosity was finally appeased.

Dr. Bennett spoke in an even tone, leaning back in his chair, one leg crossed over the other.

"It is very important that your daughter stays here. I hope you are both aware of that. She has just made an attempt on her life, which is a very serious action on her part. She is not safe in your home right now. She is not safe at her school right now. From reviewing her records, I understand that she was about to be expelled from her high school."

My father answered, my mother still mute.

"Yes. According to the school, she's been showing several behavior problems. They don't think they can manage her. They asked us to find help for her, which my wife did. She tried."

Dr. Bennett's gaze left my father's and joined my mother's.

"What happened?"

Sheepishly—which my mother is not—she looked at Dr. Bennett. His words took hold of her like two hands reaching into a pool of water, pulling her to the surface. She answered.

"I brought Talya to three different psychologists. They wouldn't treat her. After the second or third time, they would tell me that she was too angry, too resistant, too difficult and that they wouldn't treat her. None of them would."

"So it was after this that Lee overdosed on pills at her school?"

"Yes."

"Do you see how important it is that she stay here? Her school won't take her back, and no one will treat her. I'm the one who'll be able to help her. This is Lee's only hope."

My parents were speechless by his testimony, beaten and trampled. They were terrified to leave me there. They were terrified to take me home. Knowing their dilemma, having strategically planned it, the doctor spoke.

"Lee is very resistant. We're going to have to convince her that this is what's best. Since reason may not be the best course right now, I think showing her how hard this is for you, how frightened you both are for her safety, may be helpful."

My mother spoke.

"How can we show her that? I've told her how scared I am, how sad I am. I cried. It just makes her angry."

Dr. Bennett gestured toward my father.

"It wouldn't hurt if she saw *you* cry."

My father's brow furrowed, his eyes peering into the doctor's, as though he were trying to see something that may be hiding deep inside, searching for meaning.

"Do you mean I should start to cry?"

"Maybe if she sees you crying, she'll understand how you're feeling, your sadness and fear given the situation. That can be more powerful than words. I'm going to call the admissions woman and have her bring Lee back in. You muster up the tears."

The bobblehead, out of desperation, agreed. In the mind of my helpless parents, this intimidating man who stood before them was knowledgeable and charismatic. This was their daughter's only hope. He was the savior.

As I entered the room, my father's tears greeted me. Stone-faced, I watched him as he cried. The pathetic sight did little to convince me. I saw my parents' pain, but my pain was deeper. My fear was deeper. It lay embedded within my very fiber of life, every breath tearing through my lungs.

Changing of the guards—it was now my turn alone with Dr. Bennett.

"I need some time alone with Lee."

"Should we go out to the waiting area?"

"Yes. I'll call you in when we're done."

Now it was on. Him. Me. Face-to-face. The battle was to begin.

"Do you understand why you need to stay here?"

Coat, arms, head—I did not answer.

"You tried to kill yourself. You're sick, and you need help. I'm the person to do that for you."

He paused, waited, suspended—retina, upside down; occipital lobe, inverted.

"You need to sign the papers. Then we can get you settled in on the unit."

Emerging from my shell, I faced him, eye to eye.

"I just wanna go home."

"I can't let you go home. You would be in too much danger if you went home."

"I promise. No, I won't be."

"That's not an option."

"*Please.* I promise I won't. I won't do it again. I was just trying to get attention. I won't do it again because I don't want to end up here."

I could not imagine how my life was about to change. If I could only convince him, I knew I could get him to let me go home. Before I could continue, he spoke.

"I know you don't want to cooperate. I know you aren't going to make this easy for yourself, for your parents, or for me. We need to get these papers signed. If you don't find it in yourself to cooperate, I'll have to start proceedings to have you committed. You're not going home. If you did you would be Dead in a Month."

DEVIL RED

A glimmer of hope was ignited in me as we were informed that there was not space on the adolescent unit. Sixteen years old, and hardly an adult, I was sure this was going to secure my freedom, creating a lightness in my heart I had feared I'd never feel again. As quickly as my hope for freedom was handed to me, it was ripped away, as their creative solution to incarcerate me was a temporary bed with the adults until one opened up among my peers. Making our way from the admissions office to the unit was a painful process, as we waded through the thick, murky waters of anguish and fear. Catching my eye from every corner were red doors, everywhere, from the main building to the units—fire-engine red, devil red. A gentle push through one of them, and there I was... trapped, imprisoned, incarcerated.

"Hello. I'm the head nurse here on the unit."

Polite smiles quickly crossed my parents' faces, in a similar fashion to those who thank a police officer after being handed a ticket. The head nurse was a tall young man with dark hair and soft eyes. The admissions woman introduced us.

"This is Dr. and Mrs. Wasserman. And this is Talya, though she prefers to be called 'Lee.'"

Turning to me, the admissions woman gave me an understanding smile.

"And these are her friends, Theresa and Brian. We thought they could tour the unit together then have some time to talk before saying good-bye."

The words sunk in, leaving me with a bitter taste of disgust. Pressure welled up in my chest, my diaphragm tightening, my lips stiff. My friends would be allowed to leave. I had to stay. The sick and pathetic had to stay. My heart racing, I wanted to outrun the anxiety that was consuming me, to flee, escape, bolt, break out, and disappear; to scream, cry, howl, screech, and wail. The walls around me came in closer and closer. The doors and windows receded farther and farther. My eyes searched for an escape, frantically scanning. The door to the outside was available only to the admissions woman, as she bid her farewell and disappeared into the cold air of an East Coast February afternoon. The head nurse's soft voice pulled my attention back.

"Let's walk around so I can show you the unit."

We walked as a group touring hell, the head nurse playing the role of our guide. First stop: a set of double doors.

"This is the recreation room. It's a nice place to come during free time. Tonight there'll be a movie in here."

As soon as the double doors opened, the smell of institutionalized cooking wafted through the air, coating my nostrils. As I experienced the olfactory assault, my parents experienced a visual one as they took in the room, memorizing it, their eyes shifting rapidly from the kitchen, where pizza was heating up in the oven, to a Ping-Pong table, to the stereo, to the tables and chairs, where men and women were sitting, smoking, playing cards, talking...laughing. As the head nurse turned, leading us out, my parents had to pull themselves away, as though stuck by a strong adhesive. I, on the other hand, fled from the room as though it were the fiery depths of hell and demons were trying to grasp my soul and lure me in. Again the head nurse's voice begged for attention.

"Now I'll show you the lounge, and then we'll go to Lee's room."

We made our way from the recreation room through the wide hallway with bedrooms on either side. As we walked the head nurse gestured to a phone on the wall.

"That's the phone the patients use to receive calls, and there's a pay phone for them to make calls."

We all acknowledged with our eyes the sources for outside communication—free when others wanted to talk to me but at a cost should I want to talk to them.

"And this is the lounge."

The lounge was a large room furnished with big, comfortable-looking chairs and a television. Sitting motionlessly, several people were glued to the idea of normality that was being portrayed on the TV, while others sat around talking or reading. A few heads turned, the curious ones, to see the "new person" on the unit. I brushed their glances off my skin, and we turned and left the lounge, continuing our tour of my prison. As we walked, the bedrooms on either side were casting soft lights into the hallway, adding an illusion of warmth to the building. We kept walking to the back of the unit, and though there was an equal distance between each room, this area somehow felt separate from the rest of the building. We stopped.

"This is Lee's room."

I stared blankly, numbly into the room. Two beds, one closer to the window and the other to the door, were neatly made. Each one had its own nightstand with a reading lamp softly illuminating the room. Two dressers pushed up against each other were at the wall opposite the beds, a desk next to them with another lamp. I could see through the window from where I was standing. It was large enough to entice escape yet sealed shut, never to be opened. We stepped tentatively into the room and noticed the small suitcase with the few things my mother had packed for me, sealing the reality of my fate. The silence was penetrating and the tension was building. No one dared make eye contact, fearing that all that stood before us would become a reality if we did. Breaking the deafening silence, the head nurse finally spoke.

"I'm going to leave you and your friends to spend some time togeth-er. You can stay in your room or you can go into the lounge or rec room."

He then turned to my parents.

"Can we have a few minutes?"

My parents nodded and silently walked away with the head nurse. I silently walked away with my friends, Brian and Theresa. We made our way through the terrifying, stifling halls toward the sterile rec room, brightly lit with fluorescent lighting that jumped off the white walls and light-colored tile floor. People were playing Ping-Pong, sitting around ta-bles, talking, drinking coffee. We each pulled out a cigarette, my friends and I, though none of us had matches, having had them confiscated upon entering the gates of hell. After finding a table, we sat, trying to look as though we knew what to do, three adolescents, never wanting to be seen as vulnerable. As we sat, unlit cigarettes cradled gently be-tween our fingers, we made awkward conversation in an effort to dis-tract ourselves from our unpleasant surroundings. Two women happily approached us, each making herself comfortable in the orange plastic chairs that circled the table. One of them spoke in an upbeat, chirpy voice.

"Hi. You're new here."

Her eyes shifted from me to Theresa to Brian, waiting for a reaction from one of us, unsure which of the three was the incarcerated victim. Desperately wanting to make a human connection in this inhumane circumstance, I responded.

"Yeah."

Her smile turned toward me, and she introduced herself and the other woman. My need for defensive action put at ease, I asked her, "Do you have matches so my friends and I can light our cigarettes? They took ours."

"Yeah, they take everyone's. You can't have matches in here."

"So how do we light our cigarettes?"

"Over there, on the wall. There's one of those in here and one in the lounge."

She gestured to an apparatus on the wall.

"Otherwise you have to ask staff for a light."

I got up, and she walked with me over to the wall—mentor and mentee, learning how to survive institutional living. She showed me how to put my cigarette into a shallow hole that had a grid inside. Next to the hole was a button you pushed, and—voilà—the grid inside turned red, hot, ignited. With cigarette against it, you drew in and exhaled, drew in and exhaled, drew in and exhaled. Cigarette lit, the nicotine gently slid down my throat and into my lungs, covering my noisy addiction like a warm, soothing blanket. I drew in hard, and with it came relief. I turned to the woman.

"Thanks."

"No problem."

We walked back to the table, where my friends, who were free, and her friend, who was incarcerated, sat waiting. I handed my cigarette to Theresa and Brian to light theirs, and then I sat down, the five of us talking. I liked these women. They weren't scary. They weren't mean. They didn't appear to be sick or different. They were nice to me and made me feel safe in a very unsafe moment. The woman then asked me, "You're really young. What are you doing on the adult unit?"

"They didn't have a bed with the kids my age, so they said I had to come here. Do you think they'll let me stay here? On this unit, I mean?"

"They should. I can't see why not. You could be our mascot. We need someone young around here."

"Yeah. I'd like that."

Distracted by my mother's voice, I turned to my parents, who had just entered the rec room. Her words carried a tone of pity that reached deep down inside me and pulled out the wrath that had been lying quietly, uncorking the anticipation of the inevitable that was about to greet me with ruthless abandon.

"Baby…"

Pity.

"…we have to go."

Pity.

Hearing her words, her pity, pathetic rejecting letch, the rage spewed out of my mouth and onto my parents.

"You guys are actually going to leave me here? I can't believe it! I can't believe you're making me stay here! I can't believe you're going to leave me! Why the fuck would you leave me here? I don't belong in this place! I don't want to stay here! I'm not going to stay here. Don't fucking leave me here!"

The head nurse, responding to the flurry of temper that now coated the walls of the rec room, made his entrance. His eyes spoke louder than any words could have, but to ensure he was being heard, he addressed my parents.

"You need to leave now, please."

As he turned toward me, his eyes changed from stern to soft.

"Walk with me, Lee. Let's see your family and friends out, and then we can go into your room and talk."

His voice carried a tone of confident concern, pulling me into his sphere and delivering a sense of protection, a shield from the emotional storm that was raging within me. Stiff and anguished, I walked with him to the front door and watched Theresa, Brian, and my parents as they disappeared into freedom. Side by side, as if in a death march, the head nurse and I made our way to the back of the unit, to the section that felt disconnected from the rest, somehow separate. What appeared to be a gallant gesture—the head nurse stepping aside to allow me to pass before him—became a gesture of confinement as he reached to either side of the hall and pulled at two big brown doors, slowly closing them behind us. My mind scrambled to make sense of what was happening, and with a sudden realization, the word *incarcerated* slammed across my consciousness. I was being locked in. My watery pools, bluer than usual as the redness intensified the color, begged for mercy, an emotional torrent welling inside me.

The head nurse spoke softy.

"You can hang out in your room."

He took my arm gently, reassuringly and walked me into my room then slowly made his exit. The bed my only comfort, I lay down and spiraled into a nightmarish place in my mind. The soft light gently caressing me offered little comfort as I lay motionless, sequestered in my head, my face gently cradled by my hands. Suddenly a noise coming from the door, a heavy step, made its way closer to me. Letting out my rage and fear, I screamed.

"Get out! Leave me alone!"

Calmly the voice answered.

"No, I'm not going to leave you alone right now."

"I wanna be alone! Get the fuck out of my room!"

Again, with a steady tone, the voice repeated itself.

"No. I'm not going to leave you alone."

"I wanna be alone, so get the fuck out. Get the fuck out. Get the fuck out!"

Soft and consistent, with hardly an edge of frustration, the voice responded.

"I don't feel you're safe in here alone. I'll just sit here. We don't have to talk."

Sobbing until my body was exhausted and empty, I finally was able to acknowledge the man who sat silently next to the bed—the head nurse. In that moment I bonded with Joe, finding in him the safety I desperately needed, a human who understood what I was not saying.

After a few minutes he spoke.

"There's a movie being shown in the rec room. Would you like to go?"

Not wanting to show any enthusiasm, which would give my captors satisfaction that there was hope for cooperation, I answered glibly.

"Yeah, I suppose."

"OK. Why don't you put away the things from your suitcase and I'll come back to get you in a little while? If you need anything, there will be a staff member back here at all times with you."

He smiled, a little antiseptic for my pain.

"They'll be in the back lounge if you need anything."

A gesture from his head showed me the direction of the room ordinarily used for groups, and, when necessary, for staff and the locked-up person to hang out in. It was equipped for the purpose, with a television, a table and chairs, and a phone to call for help.

"OK, then. I'll be back in a little while to get you."

A shrug of my shoulders was the only communication that would not stir up a fiery rage as I watched Joe walk out of the room. Turning to my suitcase, which had been waiting patiently for my attention, I reached down and opened it. The few clothes my mother had packed for my short stay in a private psychiatric hospital took me only minutes to shove into a drawer, and then I lay waiting for my escort to the movies.

Once Joe and I arrived in the rec room, people already had gathered and put their chairs in suitable places for an optimal view of the screen. I looked around and saw the two women from earlier. They had saved a seat for me right next to them. Feeling touched by the human connection in the inhumane circumstance in which I had been placed, I started to walk over to them until Joe blocked my path. A sudden rush of fear moved through my body. His soft, brown eyes had hardened, penetrating mine with a look of authority. I felt his grip apply pressure to my skin, his fingers tightly embracing my arm. The formerly soft voice became as hard as his gaze.

"I'm going to be here the whole time, and I'm going to be watching you. If you try to run, I *will* catch you. I'll then put you back in the locked unit, and you won't come out again. Do you understand?"

His hard eyes were a mirror for my own.

"Yes."

With the pressure released, I walked slowly toward the two women and sat in the chair they had saved for me.

"Keep it up, bitch, and I'll put you in seclusion. Seclusion is a cold room where we lock you inside with nothing more than a bed."

As I looked out into the dark February night through the large bedroom window, the words from the female staff member, my prison guard for my first evening in the locked unit, jolted me. I have no memory of what I did to provoke such a response, nor do I remember being aware of it at the time. The next day the same staff member came to me and apologized. Little comfort considering what was yet to come.

THE TRANSFER

s I sat alone on my bed, four men marched in like the military
police coming to take their prisoner into custody. My only escape
was to throw myself facedown on the bed, shutting out my captors in the
hopes that they would go away. Instead they commanded my attention,
my cooperation for the transfer. I pleaded with them to let me stay on
the adult unit.

"Dr. Bennett promised he would think about it."

Believing the good doctor had understood, I thought he would have
allowed me to escape the inevitable, the adolescent unit, where my fears
of rejection awaited me. The four staff members—two from the adult
unit, two from the adolescent unit—stood stone-faced over my bed.
Throwing out my words, not sure where they might land, I pleaded yet
again, thinking perhaps they had not understood.

"I don't want to go. Why can't I stay here? Dr. Bennett said he would
think about it."

I don't know which one spoke, male voices intermingling in the
room, indistinguishable from one another, yet the words echoed clearly.

"It's not an option for you to stay on this unit."

Emotions were triggered, a violent storm brewing with memories of
rejection and submission. Trying to avoid abandonment at all costs, I
convulsed with fear.

"I'm not fucking going! *I'm not fucking going!* Dr. Bennett said he would fucking think about it!"

Again the indistinguishable male.

"He may have thought about it, but his decision is based on what's best for you, and that decision is that you need to be on the adolescent unit, so here are your choices: You can walk over cooperatively, or we can put you in restraints and carry you there."

In the face of two terrifying choices, neither one offering comfort or safety, I battled in my mind regarding which one would bring about less shame. To walk was a cooperative behavior that signified compliance to a program I was so vitally against, so fundamentally fearful of. To be restrained—a concept I could only partially grasp at that point—meant seeing myself hanging like a slaughtered animal, front and back legs tied together, a stick running through them with men on either end carrying their kill. Angrily I responded.

"Fine, I'll walk."

Now, as I sat up and faced the four men exerting their dominance and control, a slight man with medium-length, straight brown hair and glasses similar to Clark Kent's leaned in toward me and took my arm, while another took my other arm. Between these two men, I was led out of the building to the vehicle that was waiting to take me the very short distance from one unit to the next. My head hung heavily in submission, weighed down with such force that my eyes dragged along the floor. We walked out to a big, sixteen-seat van normally used to take patients on trips. One staff member slid into the driver's seat, while the slight man with medium-length straight brown hair and glasses similar to Clark Kent's slid in next to me. I ignored his presence and turned my head toward the window, my eyes taking in the grass, the trees, the birds, the freedom, knowing that none of it was mine.

The Hospital sat on several acres of land in the far suburbs, mostly open space with some wooded areas. The buildings that stood on the property were three long, one-story units, an old two-story cottage, and the Main House, big and impressive, my first exposure to my new world. As with all the other buildings, the red door of the adolescent unit was my separation between incarceration and freedom. As I sat in the hovering van, waiting for instruction, a saturated feeling of fear overtook me, an otherworldly entity rushing through my body and taking possession. The slight man spoke.

"Lee, come on."

Terror stealing my voice, I quietly slid out of the van and stood next to him. I felt his hand, his fingers interlacing between mine, making us one, with him in control and escape impossible. Slowly, breathlessly, we moved forward, pressure from the slight man pulling me forward as I resisted, pulling back. As we made our approach, my body felt detached, as though it may float away. I wanted it to float away, I wanted to leave where I was and find a safe retreat, out of my body, out of my mind. Slowly his fingers loosened as he reached for the red door. The institutional smell hit me instantly, the aroma as thick as a wall, sanitary and distinct. We passed through the waiting area and swiftly, still controlled by intertwined fingers, walked through the last door of my incarceration. Within seconds I was a prisoner. The man released me, leaving me alone to feel the anguish I was now ready to verbalize. Sequestered in the corner, my head resting on the door, the fear pushing up from my belly, I emoted, the voiceless quality to my terror now lifted.

"I don't wanna be here. Please, I don't wanna be here. I don't wanna be *here*! Please let me go home. *I don't wanna fucking be here!*"

My cries tore through the halls, chasing after anyone who would listen, but each person seemed successful in outrunning them.

IN THE PURSUIT OF FREEDOM

*D*esperate pleading, begging, and imploring, over and over, each time and every time.

"Please, Mom. Please take me home."

"Lilli, I can't. They won't let me."

I begged my mother on each of her daily visits—the same desperate request, the desperate same desire.

"But it's up to you. I'm your daughter. They can't say no. I'm your daughter. Please. I promise I'll be OK at home. I don't want to stay here. I don't belong here. Please, just give me a chance. If you give me a chance, and it doesn't work out, I'll come back."

"I want to bring you home, but I can't. You know, the police called us. They asked us if we put you in a hospital. They said if we didn't, they would have to. We really can't bring you home."

The pressure of my blood increased exponentially with each rejection, with each word that came from my mother. The wall of abandonment was being raised higher and higher as I worked with hopeless vigilance at tearing it down. I prodded with delusional optimism in search of salvation on the other side of the invisible brick structure that stood solidly between us. A sense of utter aloneness swept over me like a tidal wave crashing over the wall as I realized that my mother was not going to run in and rescue her daughter from this most frightening and outrageous experience, that she was not tucking me under her arm and running—running as fast as she could—with her free arm stretched out in front of her as she made her way for the touchdown, pushing over with savage mama-bear force anyone who got in the way of her saving her youngest child. Instead I sat before her and continued to plead.

"But you can do whatever you want. You're my mother. No one can tell you what to do with me. Please, let's just try."

My pleas had come to permeate her daily visits, and she was unable to dodge my desperation as the bullets of pain shot out of my mouth. We sat in the lounge of the adolescent unit on two big orange chairs that offered a physical comfort that was a stark contrast to our anguish. The lounge was empty of other patients, the lights softly illuminating the only scene and the only players, focusing on the tears streaming down my cheeks, the saltiness slipping into my mouth, the taste of sadness, fear, angst, misery. My mother, in her exhaustion and frustration, spoke.

"Lilli, I'm sad. I'm sad you have to stay here, but I can't take you home."

Pushing my face close to my mother's so my words could hit her with my breath, I yelled.

"Then I want you to *leave now!*"

As no response was wanted, I jumped up and fled, leaving the lounge and my mother sitting as alone as I felt. Once her mind caught up with what had happened, she made her way out of the lounge as well and walked toward the door that led to freedom, until one of the staff members intercepted her.

"Mrs. Wasserman."

"Yes?"

"I need to speak with you for a few minutes."

"OK."

"Dr. Bennett and the staff have been discussing the visits you and Lee have been having."

My mother, grief stricken and exhausted, looked with sadness and despair into the eyes of the staff member who was confronting her.

"What is it?"

"Lee becomes very upset during these visits and remains upset for a significant period after you leave. We feel her adjustment here is compromised by these visits, and until she has adjusted to being here and can grasp the notion that she is not going home and can come to terms with that, we feel it's best that you don't come."

My mother's eyes grew wide and the look of astonishment, of disbelief, could be easily read on the canvas of her face.

"What are you telling me? Are you saying I can't visit my daughter?"

"For now, yes, that's what I'm saying. It really isn't good for Lee. She gets very upset and remains that way. If we allow you to keep coming, she'll continue to think there's a chance you'll take her home. If you stop coming until she has adjusted, your visits will be more productive. At that point she'll be able to visit without asking to come home, since that's not an option. You do understand that her going home is not an option?"

"Yes, I know. Dr. Bennett explained."

"I'm glad you do. Dr. Bennett thought two weeks would be sufficient, and then we can reassess."

"I can't come see her for two weeks?"

"At least. At the two-week point, we'll reassess."

"Can I call her?"

"We would like to cut off all contact for that period. Then we'll reassess."

"Can I go and let her know?"

"We'll take care of that."

Dejected, aware of her subordinate status in the face of this new authority, my mother acquiesced without a fight.

In the depths of the ocean, the water was heavy and weighted, pushing down on all sides. There was a suffocating feeling as I tried to swim to the surface, frantically kicking my legs, my eyes attempting to focus on the water's edge—kicking and kicking and kicking but not moving, stagnant in the pursuit of freedom. A dream had me trapped in its grip as I tried to reach the top, the point of escape so I could breathe again. The air sucked from my lungs, freedom sucked from my existence, I tried in vain to reach the surface, where I could escape and breathe again.

THE CONNECTION

*D*igging up so much of my past while sitting with Meredith or with my parents or alone in my head, I felt it was time to connect, not just with whatever memories and emotions were swirling within me from that dark time of my life but with the people. As my past haunted my present, I stood alone in the emotions, as images of the buildings at The Hospital—the trees, the grass, the sky, pictures clear yet stagnant—etched in my brain, taunted me, and twisted me. The sounds and smells as I lived my life pulled me, hands reaching into my present and gripping, yanking me to the past, out of my control, and each time I arrived in the image—so real, so vivid—I arrived there alone. The people... gone. The life...gone. No longer having the strength to withstand the loneliness, I decided it was time for me to find someone from back then, someone who could keep me company today with my memories from yesterday, so I started to search.

I can still see his face. Thirty years have passed since I first met Todd Carson, a soft-spoken guy with a great deal of compassion, new to the field of mental health. I had developed a bond with him early in my stay at The Hospital. He offered me a sense of safety and protection. I spent much time talking to him, Todd Carson, the man who never raised his voice, never yelled at me, never frightened me. So I decided this was the person I wanted to find.

I didn't know how I would track him down, how I would find someone from so long ago. I didn't know where he worked or what he did. Somewhere, however, in the back of my mind, I had a memory. I had heard he was in some way involved with a "special"* department. I don't know how, when, or where I'd heard this, but I had. I began to search on the Internet. I put his name in, linked it with "special" department, and this is what I got – a deposition posted on the Internet.

ABC Court Reporters
TODD W. CARSON

A: Todd M. Carson. My home address?

Q: Yes.

A: [It is here where he provided his home address.]

Q: And what is your business address?

A: [It is here where he provided his business address.]

Q: And what is your current profession, sir?

A: I am the director of "special" services in [it is here where he provided his township].

Q: And for how long have you been the director of "special" services?

A: My title was changed from [his former title] to director of "special" services in 19XX.
Prior to that, from 19XX to 19XX, I was the [his title prior to that].

Q: Since we're on your work history, why don't you just give me a brief summary of your work history leading up to becoming the [his former position] and your current job as director of "special" services?

---

* The word *special* appears in place of the name of any identifying professional department to protect anonymity.

A: In 19XX I was hired by [the township name], [the county
name], as [his title].
Prior to that, following college, I was in the psychology
department of a private hospital with adolescents as an
adolescent counseling specialist.

The words smacked me hard, stinging without relief: *the psychology
department of a private hospital with adolescents.* My heart raced and my
eyes became wet with moisture, the dew of emotion. A tingling sensation traveled from my head to my feet, threatening to cut me off from
all feelings, numb and cold. I fought it. I wanted to feel. I wanted to
experience the moment. I knew I had found him. The words on the
screen, Todd Carson's words...*a private hospital with adolescents,* that was
the boom boom retreat, the name I had given The Hospital at sixteen
years old to camouflage my shame. I sat at my desk, my eyes glued to the
computer screen glaring at me, mocking me, gripping me, my reflection cast in the background. I saw myself, and I saw Todd Carson. All
sound—from the computer, from outside—stood silent, allowing me to
hear the blood coursing through my veins, a swooshing in my ear. Time
stood still, suspended endlessly, gripped by the moment, captured by
the knowledge...I had found him.

I now had more information—his work, his township, his title—so
I entered it, and several links came up. Accessing the first one gave me
a phone number. My heart tried desperately to push through my chest
cavity. My blood rushed to my face. The room spun. I drew in a deep
breath, the blanket of oxygen soothing the writhing beast inside me.
Collected and in control, I dialed.

"Hello. [The name of an office.] How can I help you?"

I worked hard to seem professional, so as to not raise suspicion as to
my intentions, the recovered mental patient searching for her keepers
to validate her reality.

"Hello. I'm trying to reach Todd Carson."

"Mr. Carson isn't with the [name of the department] anymore."

"Can you tell me where I may be able to reach him?"

At this point I was certain my exploration would be put to an end. I could not imagine that this man on the other end of the phone would be forthcoming with information to a complete stranger. Disappointment already began to surge within me. I was not, however, going to give up. I would persevere. The need, the desire, the urgency to make human contact with my past was overwhelming. I was by myself in a cavernous dwelling in my mind, and I did not want to stay there alone.

"He's with the [name of the department]."

Listening intently, I was stunned that this man was giving me information, and I hoped the sigh that escaped me—and the release of all the anticipation that had built up—would go unnoticed. I felt myself getting closer to a goal—a goal I was afraid would be unattainable, with the fear of success standing by its side. There stood a chance that I would be able to reconnect with someone from my adolescence, with someone who had experienced and borne witness to the most terrifying period of my life. What I wanted so desperately I also did not want. I wanted it and needed it, yet I feared it. Opposing emotions battling within, I wrote down the phone number the man gave me, hung up, and sat transfixed to the screen.

I saw Todd coming toward me. Frightened by his approach, I backed away.

"Please. No. I don't wanna go. Please, I don't want to."

A second figure, intimidating, approached. The two figures came nearer and nearer until contact was made. A touch, a grip, hard—not hurting but hard—firm, holding.

"Please. I don't wanna go."

"You don't have a choice. Walk with us, and it'll be OK. Just walk quietly."

Struggling, resisting, pulling, Terror.

"I don't want to. Please, I don't want to!"

With the firmness of their grip pulling me forward, I had no choice.

"Why do I have to go? Why are you putting me in there? Why? I Don't Want To Go!"

My pleading was ignored. My words were heard but not acknowledged. Invisible, I was talking to people who did not see me. For the first time during my incarceration, I was being put into the room with white walls, a bed, an unbreakable window looking to the outside, a door with a window looking to the inside, and a cold, unforgiving fluorescent light looking down from above.

"Lee, you don't have a choice. You have to sleep in seclusion tonight. If it goes well, we'll let you out in the morning."

"What did I do? Why do I have to sleep in there? What did I do? What Did I Do?"

"You've been cutting yourself, and we have to keep you safe."

"I don't wanna go in there. I promise I won't cut myself anymore. Please."

As I was guided with force down the long hallway—pleading for my very sanity, resisting out of instinct—Todd and another staff member led me toward seclusion, the room intended for safety, the room that provided punishment. The gentle push from them and pull from me finally ended as we reached the door, the mouth of the demon waiting to swallow me up. Once we arrived three other staff members were waiting patiently by the bed, the only piece of furniture in the otherwise barren room.

"Lee, we need you to lie down."

Like a statue made of cold, hard marble, I stood silently, still held firmly by Todd and the other staff member. My fear stole my words. I searched the depth of my soul for strength, for reason, for understanding but found none. I found none of these things to give me the courage to endure the confusion, the isolation, the abandonment, the loss of control. I stood with a tension that could—*would*—break me, like a frozen twig, inelastic, stiff by cold, easily snapped in a moment of pressure.

"Lee, we need you to lie down."

Like a statue made of cold, hard marble, I did not move.

"Lee, lie down."

Like a statue, I did not move, so Todd and the other staff member did it for me. I did not struggle, but I resisted, refusing to cooperate with something I strongly opposed. They moved me forward. I had reached the side of the bed the same way I had reached the mouth of the demon, through gentle, firm guidance. Gentle, firm guidance, forcing me forward. Todd and the other staff members, five in all, spoke with one another in organized chaos.

"Let's get her on the bed."

"We'll put her in two-point restraints."

"Lay her down."

"It's OK, Lee."

"You're going to be OK."

"We're going to keep you safe tonight."

"Lay her down."

"Hold her head down."

"Get her arms and legs."

"Hold her still."

"Let's get these on her quickly."

"Lee, we're going to put you in two-point restraints."

"We're going to restrain one arm and one leg."

"Hold her head. She's struggling."

I lay tethered to the bed like a rabid animal, control been stripped away from me, leaving me vulnerable and exposed. Todd pulled up a chair and sat with me. His soft smile felt like a security blanket, until it was yanked off me.

"I'm here tonight if you need me, but Bess is going to come in now. You have to be searched."

Searched. The word brought a painful flush of redness to my face, fire beneath my skin.

"No fucking way! I don't have anything!"

The point didn't seem to be whether I was harboring any contraband but whether I could be made any more exposed, vulnerable, powerless:

Strip the girl of any protective defense, and then we can replace it with sporad-ic acts of compassion…build the dependency, build the identification with her captors.

Todd met my pleas with another reassuring smile.

"I'll come back and see how you're doing a little later."

He sat for another minute until Bess walked in—the changing of the guards. Bess was an older nurse, slightly heavy, with a long braid run-ning down her back and a ready smile. Behind that sweet exterior was a stern psychiatric nurse who demanded respect. As I lay tied to a bed, powerless to protect myself, my cooperation was the only weapon I had to ensure my safety from the shameful attack on my body and psyche.

The deed now done—the search complete and no contraband found—Bess's cheerful voice sang out.

"OK, Lee. We're done."

Sleep being the next order of business, I made what would appear to be a natural request for a naïve psychiatric patient spending her first night in seclusion.

"Will you turn off the light?"

Fluorescent beams assaulted my eyes—harsh, intense, merciless.

"No. We have to leave it on so we can see you. We'll be checking on you every fifteen minutes. Now I need you to sleep."

Bess turned to leave, shutting the door behind her. Keys inserted—the sound bold and harsh, key to metal, metal to metal—the mouth of the demon shut. The room became a metal strongbox with me trapped inside.

I lay on the bed, fighting the blanket of exhaustion that weighed on me, fighting sleep, and fighting the restraints. I started to work my left hand, twisting and turning, slowly and methodically, until it began to make its way out. Suddenly, the silence was broken, pulling my concen-tration away from the task at hand. Keys inserted—the sound bold and harsh, key to metal, metal to metal—the mouth of the demon opened. Todd made his way to my side and took my hand.

"Lee, don't do this."

He gently slid the restraint back up my wrist.

"Don't do this. I don't want to make it tighter."

The hum from the computer, my reflection in the screen, the knowledge that I had found his phone number, that there was hope that I could reconnect with Todd brought me back, brought me to the here and now, brought me home. I picked up the phone and dialed. A tingling sensation ran up and down my body, my heart imploding.

"Hello. Department of [special] services. How can I help you?"

"Yes. May I speak with Todd Carson, please?"

"May I ask who's calling?"

"Yes. Well, my name is Talya Lewis, but he'll know me as Lee Wasserman."

"Are you a friend of Mr. Carson?"

The question posed a dilemma, but with a reminder to myself to breathe and an overwhelming drive to get the job done, I answered.

"Yes."

"OK. Could you hold, please?"

"Yes."

The phone was silent on the other end, with only a soft humming noise keeping me aware that we were still connected. Time slowed. I anticipated the woman on the other end coming back on and informing me of the meeting Mr. Carson was in. *Can he call you back? What is your number?* Barely perceptible was the passage of time. One minute? One hour? It was hard to tell. I waited with whatever patience I could muster to contain the emotional bedlam brewing within...and then I heard a voice.

"Oh, my God, Lee!"

That voice.

"Todd?"

"I can't believe it's you. I think about you a lot. Oh, my God, how are you?"

It's him; it really is.

"Todd!"

The sunny warmth of his voice cleared the internal storm. With barely a breath, I prattled on, trying to convince myself that what I was hearing was real.

"Todd, I can't believe I found you. Is it really you? Are you the Todd from The Hospital? I can't believe I actually found you."

With almost the same sense of disbelief, Todd threw some breathless questions my way as well.

"What are you doing? What have you been up to? How are you?"

"I'm great. I'm married, and I have three kids. I'm doing well. I just can't believe I found you."

Flooded by a swollen river of vague memories and powerful emotions, I was barely able to contain myself, so I continued to talk to link myself to the present.

"This is amazing. Your voice sounds exactly like it did back when I knew you."

"Yours does too."

"Are you married?"

"I am. I'm married, and I have two kids."

"Boys, girls, or one and one?"

"Two girls. How about you? What are your three kids?"

"Girls. I have three girls."

A sudden drop in Todd's pitch signaled an awareness I presume hit him in the moment: I was not the kid he remembered, sixteen years old and institutionalized.

"You sound really good, Lee."

The sound of Todd using my old name, Lee, reverberated in my mind, as I heard it over and over, the same voice, the same name, thirty years later. I was happy that I'd found him and overwhelmed that I'd found him, but a chat on the phone wasn't going to satisfy the deep hunger I had developed, so now I had to take another risk.

"Todd?"

"Yes."

"I was wondering if there would be any way you would meet with me. I would love to see you."

Again time halted, as I perceived a long lull that most likely did not exist.

"Yeah, I would like that. I would like to see you too."

My cheeks were becoming sore from the tension of my muscles holding a grin I felt would never cease. I was overcome that this man, after experiencing me during the darkest time of my life, seeing what he saw, knowing what he knew, would want to—would be willing to—reconnect and see me in person. As though a piece of me still lived in the anguish, familiar feelings from my past began to encroach on me, tear me down. *Do I deserve a meeting with this kind, compassionate man?* I pushed them hard, pushed them away. I wanted this; I needed this—this connection from the past with this important presence in my life—from a terrifying place where feelings still unresolved kept me cocooned in the trauma. I was going to have it. Todd had agreed, and I was going to have it. Reassuring him that this could be on his terms, I asked about our next step.

"How would it work best for you? I'll be flexible for you."

"How about we meet for coffee? Where are you living?"

I told him where I lived, and he suggested our meeting place.

"How about we meet at the mall? That's halfway for each of us."

"Sounds good."

I didn't know what it would be like to meet with him. Anticipation about what we may talk about already was clouding the experience. To save us from embarrassing, wordless moments when we met, I realized it was time to hang up, before he told all, and I told all over the phone.

"Todd, I'm really looking forward to meeting with you. I think we should save some of our questions for then."

"OK, Lee. See you in a couple of weeks."

"Looking forward to it, Todd."

"Bye."

"Bye."

With the disconnection of the phone came a disconnection from the joy. Swirling memories, potent images like vivid photographs, passed rapidly through my mind. Darkness settled as I continued to stare at my computer screen. Todd W. Carson.

THAT NIGHT

*H*ands, reaching down, searching, then finding. They gently grab hold, and pull. They do not have to pull hard. Yanking me out of the safety of sleep, I find myself alone next to my husband, the sound of his breathing spreading through the space. Darkness fills the room then fills my heart. I was pulled from sleep; now I'm being pulled to the past. The same hands that reached into my mind and wrenched me out of my dreams are now leading me back, back to that night, a night that has me caught, transfixed. I play it over and over in my mind, reliving it, remembering details, listening to the voices, smelling the smells, seeing the lights, the bright lights, feeling the tugs, the pulls, the voices, the pain—a detailed, stagnant image. Trapped, unable to escape the grip of the hands, I fight, pulling myself back into reality. I remember the present, the scars—the physical scars I have to endure. As I remember I weep. My tears are quiet, silently flowing, so as not to awaken my husband. My tears are quiet, flowing until I once again fall asleep.

REMOVING THE LID

I parked at the mall, walked in, and headed to the large area in the middle, where pianos were on display from a local music store. I distracted myself by watching the people mill about and carry bags from the surplus of stores that dotted the hallways. My heart raced with excitement and anticipation. Every few minutes my watch called for attention as I counted down the minutes. I knew it might take Todd a while to find me, since it had been a little confusing on the phone where our meeting point was, but I couldn't help think that he was standing me up, or that he had forgotten entirely that we were getting together. As sitting became intolerable, I got up and was pacing when my cell phone rang.

"Hello."

"Hey, Talya. It's Todd."

"Hi."

With my mind gathering its thoughts, still not sure where he was or why he wasn't where I was, I tried to locate him.

"Where are you?"

"I'm by Nordstrom. Is that where we're supposed to meet?"

"Close enough. Stay there, and I'll come find you. I hope I still recognize you."

"Yeah, I think you will. I look pretty much the same, just less hair."

We shared our first laugh of the day, and I hung up, making my way toward him, wanting to and not wanting to. This was a man who had made me feel safe, cared about, secure, and valuable during a wretched part of my life, but this was also a man who was part of the system that had made me stuck, dependent, traumatized, and terrified. He had played a part in my terror. Hanging on to the desire, I walked the halls of the mall, almost ghostlike as I passed people with their agendas, so different from mine, and then I saw him, unchanged but with less hair.

"Talya?"

I was impressed with how skillful he was with my name, since "Lee" was the only way he knew me.

"Wow. Hi, Todd!"

We shared a courteous embrace.

"You look great."

"Thanks Todd, so do you. I can't believe I'm here with you. I can't believe I found you."

"Yeah, pretty weird. Where do you want to go?"

"I don't know. You?"

"How 'bout coffee? There's a Starbucks."

"OK."

Fortunately the Starbucks was only a few feet away, as I found it difficult to connect, to talk with him, before sitting down. I was uncomfortable and felt a shyness sneak up on me. We walked in and got our coffee, found a table, sat down, and finally I could breathe, sort of.

"So you look good, Talya. You've really come a long way."

"Yeah, I guess. It's funny, though. I'm still so stuck back then. I can't get The Hospital out of my head. Sometimes it's all so vivid—certain events that I remember—that it's like I'm still there."

"It was a crazy time. I can see how it could still haunt you."

"It does, too much. That's kind of why I wanted to meet with you. It was so traumatic for me that I have little memory of that time. There're some things I do remember, but I don't have a lot of memories."

"What kinds of things do you remember?"

"I remember some of the times I was put in restraints. I remember things that shamed me. I remember how long I was in The Hospital."

"You held the record."

I laughed, not sure to which of my three remembrances he was referring. My guess was all of them, so I responded with a protective, sarcastic undertone.

"Great."

I looked down and gently stroked the plastic lid of my coffee cup, gathering my thoughts for this precious visit. I continued to form my connection with this human link to my painful past.

"I remember some of the people—not all but some. I remember what the place looked like."

Todd was looking at me, but it seemed as though what he was seeing was the past.

"They tried to make it look nice, like home. Dr. Irvine hired people there to take on the roles of parents. The men were kind of hard, some of them. The women softer, like a mother role. He tried to make it resemble home."

After removing the lid, I looked down into my coffee, as though if I looked hard enough I would get a glimpse of The Hospital hiding in the creamy liquid. I held the cup between my hands, its warmth caressing me and keeping me grounded as emotions swirled helplessly and chaotically inside me, hidden from Todd. I was in awe that I was sitting with this man who had been there with me then. He knew what I looked like. He knew what I acted like. He knew the people I knew. He had been there with me then, and he was here with me now.

"Todd, I have to ask you a question. It's really hard for me, but I have to know what happened."

"OK, take your time."

"It's just really embarrassing, but I have to know, and you were there, so you might."

I paused, again looking into my coffee, but this time looking for strength hiding in the creamy liquid. Slowly my eyes made their way back to Todd's and locked in place.

"Here goes. I know I ended up in seclusion and restraints a lot."

"Yes, you did."

"Well, there was one time that was different from the others, and I was hoping you would remember it."

"What happened?"

"It was the night I lost it so badly that they called staff from all the other units to help. I was sitting on the table at the nurses' station with Meg. Do you remember Meg?"

"Yeah, I do."

"OK. Well, I was sitting on the table with her. I don't remember what happened. It's like I blacked out or something. The next thing I remember is that I was on the floor being…"

Eye contact was lost again, and the shame began to swell inside me. A sip of coffee tamed the flames.

"…tied up. It's scary because I realize now that quite a few minutes must have passed from my sitting with Meg to being on the floor with a bunch of people on top of me. I mean, you guys were all talking about me in the nurses' office because I was having a bad time of it. It would have taken time for the staff to notice what was happening outside the closed office, even though you could see through the big window that looked out onto the unit. Everyone would have had to react, come out, tackle me…"

Shame, coffee, taming the flames.

"…open the locked room where the restraints were kept, come back out, and well, you know. It means I blacked out for several minutes."

I tried to repel the feeling of disgust that coated my skin, like a horse whose muscles twitch to rid itself of flies. Twitching my muscles to rid myself of the shame, I continued, spitting out the words as fast as I could, keeping them as separate from my reality as I could.

"Once you guys dragged me down to seclusion, Jeff, the nurse, gave me two shots of Thorazine, and then I was put on the bed, tied up, and left. You came in and I told you that I was uncomfortable, that I had so much anxiety I felt like I was going to go crazy. I actually said I felt like I was going to start screaming, and in my mind, I thought you knew what that meant...insanity. I need you to remember that night, Todd. Do you?"

Emotionally out of breath, I saw the look in Todd's eyes, wanting to remember for me.

"Talya, I'm sorry. No, I don't remember that night specifically. I remember your being put in restraints quite a bit, but I don't remember that night specifically."

Our eyes now taking in opposite sides of the room, a moment of silence grabbed me as though a gag order had been put in place. Disappointment accompanied my silence. Thoughtfulness appeared to accompany Todd's.

THE USELESS INTERVENTION

*E*very time I was in Meredith's office, I felt a resurgence of old, painful emotions that had been reserved for the middle of the night
when I was awakened from deep sleep, fighting the grip of nightmarish
dreams, or emotions that surfaced momentarily in the summer when
clothing revealed visible scars that I tried so hard to hide. Now, the intensity of my past permeated my present, always, and it was becoming
almost too much to bear. Feeling vulnerable, feeling exposed, I would
make my way slowly to Meredith's office, knowing already what would be
stirred, which internal struggles I would have to contend with. When I
reached her floor, the elevator door would open, and I would get off, my
nostrils assaulted by the smell of the newly installed carpeting. Walking
down the short hallway to Meredith's office, I hoped I would not pass another living being. I wanted to avoid the shame I carried regarding the
therapeutic relationship. Slowly I would open the door, again hoping to
go unnoticed by anyone who may be in her waiting room, as though others, should they get a glimpse of me, would get a glimpse into my past.

Once in her office, I sat in the big chair and waited for her to settle
her dog, which seemed to demand and receive more attention than I.
With little Fido finally quieted, she asked the question that was intended
to send the session into motion.

"How are you today?"

Thinking back to the last session I had with her, I answered.

"OK, I guess. I've been kind of thinking about last time. It was hard for me to share that with you, about the day they brought me to the adolescent unit. It brought up a lot of old feelings."

"I understand that it's very painful."

"I'm getting extremely frustrated. I feel like I'm not getting anywhere. I'm sharing this painful stuff, but what am I getting out of it? Where is it taking me?"

"Let's talk about that."

"Well, I'm coming here to work through things from my past, to try to figure out why certain things happened. I want to get past it so it doesn't permeate my life. I want to get past the feelings, the negative ones, which seem to invade my sleep, and now my wakefulness. I just don't know how. It doesn't seem to be making any difference, coming here."

Perhaps I was too blunt. My expression of hopelessness was not intended to knock her down a notch but rather to focus my own attention on the emotions that were welling inside me. I began to distract myself, taking in the details—of which there were many—of her small office. My eyes went to her bookshelves, filled to the rim with therapeutic texts, to her plants, whose green leaves were muted by a layer of dust, to the pictures on her walls, to the pile of papers that littered her desk, and poured onto the floor. My eyes shifted, an attempt to keep out what I was remembering.

Life in a mental institution. That's what it was. A mental institution. At sixteen years old, when other kids were in high school, hanging out with friends, going to dances, football games, school events, family events—living—I was being raised within the confines of an institution.

Within the walls of this locked adolescent unit, in one of the most reputable boom boom retreats in our region at the time, twenty-four adolescents spent their days going to therapy—art therapy and group therapy and individual therapy and sports therapy and psychodrama—and "school." We tried, in this unreal world, to act like normal teenagers. We made bonds with one another, and like our normal counterparts, we hung out, though for us it was around a big table outside of the nurses' station. We would listen to music in the rec room, where the large floor-to-ceiling windows were made of unbreakable glass, and the only way to open them was with our imaginations, or with a key provided by staff. We watched TV in the lounge, where twenty-four patients had to compromise over how to share, and we smoked cigarettes, lighting them from a grill in the wall, since no matches were allowed on the unit. We represented kids from all the different groups: We were cool; we were nerds; we were jocks; we were outcasts; we were a subculture of the society in which we were unable to cope. We were sick. With this sickness that we carried like a ball and chain, tightly and securely strapped to our ankles, we lived in a sheltered, controlled world. To us it felt as normal as the outside world felt to teenagers who were free to live within the population at large.

"Did you ever have fun in The Hospital?"

"Yes. It was life after a while, after I got used to being there."

"How did you have fun?"

"I wish I could remember more of the good times, but it's hard. I know I was able to manage my friendships better in The Hospital than on the outside. They were safer in there. Things would get talked about if you had an issue with someone, and staff was there to protect you. There was also a feeling of being stuck, though. We were trapped there together, all the time, with no way out. I remember two friendships, one of which I wanted and one of which I didn't. Patty and Nicole. With Nicole I felt stress. With Patty I was comfortable. She was funny, and I wasn't intimidated by any spontaneous expression of temper, because there didn't appear to be any. She was predictable, and in that I took comfort. Otherwise friendships were very scary for me."

My mind shifted from one set of friends to another, and my monologue continued.

"My friends from home scared me. Whether it was reality or paranoia, I found myself having to cope with chatter that would rattle behind my back. My feelings were stifled, so I could protect against abandonment, until they would swell so large that I couldn't contain them, and they would rush out in a flurry of rage. Sensitivity was the portal to my pain. I guess I allowed anything, real or perceived, to enter my soul and haunt me. Abandonment was the Devil, always looming near. The expectations of rejection followed me wherever I went, so I expected this from Nicole and Patty too. The closer I got to them, the more scared I got. One night I told a staff member that I didn't know what it meant to care about someone and that I didn't care about Nicole and Patty. In true psychiatric hospital fashion, he decided this needed to be discussed… with Nicole and Patty. So one evening the four of us filed into one of the group therapy rooms: the all-knowing staff member, the psychopath, and her two victims. He told me to talk. I did. I told my two best friends that I didn't care about them. I explained to them that I didn't know what caring meant, that I wasn't in touch with the basic components of humanity: respect, caring, love. Naturally hurt by my words, they got angry. I don't know what good that did me. I don't know what good it did them. But that was institutional living."

As I wrapped up my monologue, proud of the poetic energy I felt had accompanied it, I reflected on the dastardly deed by the psychiatric staff member who had engineered the useless intervention. What had it accomplished, to have me stun my friends with an admission as hateful as that? I never really understood.

"How did it end?"

"Well, eventually they forgave me. I don't remember how long after, but they did. It was safe in The Hospital—safe to have friends and hurt friends. It was all a learning process there. We were learning how to be human by showing our inhumanity."

Still wanting to get a glimpse into the fun side of psychiatric life, Meredith pulled me from my reflection with her original question.

"How did you have fun?"

OVERDOSE

As I sat on my bed, legs curled up, my excitement mounted as I planned a way to self-destruct behind institutional walls.

"I have an idea."

"What?"

"Hoard them."

"What?"

"Hoard them. It's perfect. You hoard them—I don't know...for about a week—and then we take them."

"OK. I guess that would work. I can do that."

"Good. It'll be fun. What're you on anyway?"

"Sinequan."

I don't remember her name, but she was my roommate at one point. I had a knack, a skill, a will, a desire to hurt myself in any way—utilizing anyone—in my effort to calm the anguish. Internally my pain was intense and extreme, and I was unwilling, unable, and ill equipped to cope with it. I couldn't just sit and experience the intensity of what felt like a hurricane of emotions. Like walking across the beach, barefoot, the sand scorching the soles of your feet, you run as quickly as you can to the water, not noticing whether you are inadvertently kicking sand into the faces of innocent sunbathers—anything to relieve the pain. My internal experience was so painful that self-destruction was a salve for my soul as I tried desperately to escape the torment I had to endure, day after day, week after week, month after month, year after year. I struggled and thrashed to survive the intolerable, and I lost every time. I chose distractions that caused me harm, regardless of the potential for death. They gave me a vent for my anxiety, allowing the exhaust to escape. My roommate, ready and willing to self-destruct with me, hoarded her medication for a week, or maybe it was two.

She laid the pills out on the counter in our bathroom. Excitement raced up my back like little snakes racing to the finish line. My stomach swirled with anticipation. Slowly we counted our treasure, the waiting almost more exciting than the doing. I divided them evenly, and together, in a united act of destruction, we took them, lukewarm tap water our chaser.

As I lay on my bed, the light, excited feeling that had been so present in what appeared to be moments earlier, was now a heavy weight pulling me into sleep, one I could not fight with whatever strength I had left. The iron weight of the Sinequan pulled me down, deeper, deeper, deeper.

"Oh, my God, Lee. Get up. You have to get up."

Like a crane, the urgency of tone, rather than the words attached to it, pulled me from the depths of sleep. I barely could climb out of the Sinequan-induced haze as Bathsheba and Bruce, staff members at The Hospital, barreled into my room and stood looming over me. They seemed bigger, distorted. My eyes locked onto them, but my head remained motionless, glued to my pillow with the rest of my body, heavy as though I had been infused with liquid lead.

"Lee, you need to get up and come with us."

My roommate, whose body was accustomed to the Sinequan, was better able to tolerate the quantity she had taken. Mine was not so ready, willing, or able to metabolize the drug, and succumbed to its effects. In a panicked realization of what we had done, my roommate had gone for help.

"Come on, Lee. We need you to get up and come to the nurses' station with us."

The fog of confusion and the weight of intoxication held me firmly on the bed. I uttered the only word I could muster.

"What?"

"Can you get up? Can you walk?"

"What?"

Bathsheba and Bruce each became a support and navigated the way to the nurses' station, where all the staff converged to the spot where I was now sitting—or attempting to sit—my body heavy with sleep. Voices shot at me like bullets, but none of them penetrated.

"Lee, you have to stay awake. An ambulance is coming, but you have to stay awake."

My head slowly dropped as sleep called out to me, the temptation to great to resist.

"Lee, pick your head up. You need to stay awake."

"Come on, Lee. Stand up."

"Lee, you need to walk around. Stand up. You have to keep walking."

Supported by two staff members, I was paraded around the big table at the nurses' station in an effort to keep me conscious, my feet dragging, my eyes begging to close. The discomfort was supreme, exhaustion gripping me.

"Keep walking, Lee."

Like a zombie, I forcibly shuffled around the table outside the nurses' station.

"Keep walking, Lee."

Around and around, unending and cruel.

"Keep walking."

Around and around, around and around, around and around.

After I finally was able to sit—when the staff had determined that I was sufficiently awake—a rush of exhaustion once again swept over me, and I agreed to succumb. With all my muscles relaxed, my head dropped as I greeted my slumber, only to be rudely interrupted by a splash of water. With an affect flattened by an overdose of Sinequan, I sluggishly revealed my opinion.

"I can't believe you just did that."

The water Bathsheba threw at my face from a small paper cup was intended to shock me awake, keep me awake, essentially to keep me alive. The fog around me muffled my emotions, making action difficult. An angry flame lit up inside me yet remained encapsulated by my weary body mercilessly begging to sleep.

Finally there appeared to be an end to my torment as the ambulance arrived. Told to lie on the stretcher, I was caught between the shame of my vulnerable state and the strong desire to lie down. As the illusion of control always held great appeal, I refused the yearning that tugged at my core and shuffled out with my weighed-down feet to my awaiting chariot. My roommate, the guilty culprit for hoarding and ingesting with me, and Becky, a staff member, made their way out to the ambulance as well. Sitting on the bench, I positioned myself next to Becky, and in what I believed to be a darling gesture, I laid my tired head on her lap. I wanted to be mothered by her, to be loved by her, to be thought of as adorable and in need of special tenderness. In the warmth of the love I felt from Becky and the accepting physical reassurance I was getting from resting my head in her lap, with an oxygen mask placed over my nose and mouth by the EMT, I finally was allowed to succumb to the exhaustion.

In the [medical] hospital I was put in a room, and a repeat of my first overdose played out once again. The bright lights overhead shone on my tired, weak body, and as before, I was handed a cup containing the liquid medicine that would create so much nausea that the pills would be forced out. As instinct took over, I fought the sensation as it swelled within me. What I fought so hard against became inevitable, however, as a tongue depressor was plunged into my throat, repeatedly, tickling the sensitive reflex that was a means to an end. Over and over. Heaving and retching. Powerless. Vulnerable. Lost soul. The evil from within hurled its way out, again.

The torment ended, and a quiet calm took over the room. I lay there semiconscious while a nurse hit my hand in an attempt to get a vein. The calm shifted as irritation pushed through my body.

"Stop fucking doing that."

My irritation was hard; my words were soft, as I slurred my speech in an attempt to be heard. Despite my request, the nurse continued relentlessly, quietly tapping, *hitting*, tapping, *hitting*. Finally an IV was inserted, and it didn't take long before my body was shaking uncontrollably. In a surreal experience, the nurse floated quietly around to the side of the line that fed my body with clear saline and adjusted a control, my last memory as the gift of unconsciousness was finally mine.

The next morning we were returned to the boom boom retreat: my roommate, Becky the staff member, and me. My roommate seems to have vanished from my memory, yet I, still exhausted, remember being sent into the lounge and plopping myself down on three of the comfy orange chairs, pushed together to form a couch, waiting to hold me and cradle me. The unit was still. With all the other kids at their groups and activities, the "house" was mine. Lulled by the silence, I once again drifted into a comforting sleep with positive thoughts moving through my mind. I felt ready to work. I felt as though something had been lifted, as though an opening for the pressure that had been building within had been created, allowing an escape. A vent was creating relief, the drastic measure of an overdose releasing the emotions that had been raging within me. I lay in the lounge and drifted as I waited for instructions regarding what I was to do next. I knew I probably would be put down to level zero. I was aware that many privileges would be taken from me, but I was ready to work and earn them back. For the first time during my incarceration, I felt ready to make some progress. As I drifted with this positive feeling, sleep was safe.

"Lee. Wake up, Lee. You need to come with us."

The tone awakened me harshly, and I opened my eyes to find two staff members standing over me.

"What? Where are we going?"

"Just walk with us."

After pushing myself off the comfy orange chairs as though I had been glued to them, I walked with the two staff members, out of the lounge, down the hall. Savvy to institutional ways, I already knew their plan.

"No, please. I don't need this. I really don't. I'm good. Please don't do this."

With a quick, smooth gesture, a hand reached around my shoulders, firmly guiding me as my pace slowed with resistance.

"We need to put you in the locked unit. You and your roommate need to be separated from the community right now." (Aha, there's my roommate.)

"But I'm ready to work. Please don't do this."

"You don't have a choice now. You made that when you overdosed. Now you're going in the locked unit."

Like a bolt of lightning, a rage struck hot inside me. My words, my pleas, were being unheard, screaming out to deaf ears, futile. I was invisible. They misunderstood the quieting effect of my dangerous behavior. They failed to see the opportunity that my overdose was offering: permission to engage my cooperative self, even if only temporary.

Escorted down the hall to the locked unit, I continued with great effort to enlighten my captors.

"Why can't you all leave me alone? Just leave me alone! You don't understand me! *Nobody understands me!*"

I ran into my room, which by mere coincidence was already on the "right" side of the big brown doors. Rummaging quickly through my drawers before a staff member thwarted my efforts, I found my stash of glass. The hope and motivation that had been there just minutes earlier was leaving my body through drops of blood, leaking softly from my flesh—red, bright, real, warm. As the blood poured from me, the hope, the anger, the despair poured out with it. Each flesh-destroying action I took upon myself bought me more time in the locked unit, created solely for my roommate (aha, she appears again) and me.

FREUDIAN-LIKE CLINICIANS

The day was cold and dismal, not unusual for April. Only the rain beating down on the roof interrupted the silence as I sat alone in my house. As I ruminated on intrusive thoughts, an ache clenched my heart, holding it in a viselike grip as the cruelty of those painful memories washed over me like a flood of water escaping a broken dam—a dam made to contain the many memories that now clouded the fine line between what was then and what was now.

"Lee, come on. We're going."

"I'm coming."

I turned to face Dave.

"You're coming too, right?

"You bet."

"Thanks, Dave."

"Are you nervous?"

"I don't know. I guess. What if I say something wrong? What if I don't answer the way I'm supposed to? What if I don't understand the questions? I'm glad you're coming."

"There's no wrong or right answer. My guess is they're just going to talk to you about your experience. You just have to answer what's true for you."

Dave, a staff member on the adolescent unit, and I made our way out the locked door, his keys dangling from his belt loop, reminding me of the limited reality of my freedom.

The dark brown of Dave's hair and the light gray of Dr. Bennett's held the sharp contrast of their age. Barely able to see past their heads as I slid down in the backseat, hidden from view from the outside world, I felt my gut swirl. I could taste illness on my tongue, my breath smelling of it, my pores bleeding it. I was being brought from The Hospital to a special meeting because I was a sick, institutionalized adolescent with so much to teach about the baffling illness that afflicted me. I was being brought to this special meeting because this baffling illness of mine held so much interest for others, who vainly tried to make sense of why people like me acted the way I acted, felt the way I felt, saw the world in the skewed fashion in which I saw the world. I was going to be emotionally poked and prodded, fondled and jabbed, cut open and dissected.

As we drove, I heard the noise of words as the sound floated softly to the backseat, small vibrations in the air caressing my ears. I could not quite grasp Dave and Dr. Bennett's words enough to put them together, the anticipation of the task at hand grabbing most of my attention. I was absorbed by the image of several middle-aged men with pipes dangling from their lower lips, bow ties putting forth the illusion of intellectual curiosity. They would be ready to judge, their eyes peering over reading glasses balanced delicately on their noses. The car began to slow and made the final turn into the driveway that led up to a large Tudor-style house. After I pulled myself from the backseat, my head immediately dropped as I trudged behind my leaders to the front door. Dave's arm dangled by his side, grasping a paperback book between his fingers.

"Why do you have a book?"

"So I can occupy myself while you and Dr. Bennett are in the session."

"Aren't you coming in too?"

"I'm coming into the house, but I'm going to hang out in the waiting room."

"Why?"

"You'll be fine. You're going to be with Dr. Bennett."

Though offering little comfort, Dr. Bennett allowed the dialogue between Dave and me to continue uninterrupted. My heart knocked at my chest with heavy fists, pounding to get out. Every emotion that took up residence displaced the next, each of an enormity that no words could describe. A tingling sensation ran across my forehead, a thousand little needles pricking me. Fear was more my companion than Dave or Dr. Bennett, who smiled as I looked his way—little comfort to be taken...or given. As we entered the large Tudor-style house, the chairs in the waiting area summoned Dave and me. Dr. Bennett disappeared with an air of confidence, but returned within minutes.

"Come on, Lee. Are you ready?"

"I guess."

"All right then. Let's go."

Dr. Bennett and I, the powerful and the powerless, walked down the hall to a door, opened just enough so he didn't have to knock before entering. Glancing back for a moment, I looked at Dave, held him there, and then let him go. Dr. Bennett pushed gently, and the door swung open, revealing five men sitting in the kind of chairs you would find in a gentlemen's club. Flushed with fear, I stood motionless so as not to allow the flood of emotions to escape onto the pristine oriental rug that adorned the floor. They acknowledged me with the head tilt, the "Thank you for coming," and the "Please sit" that would come in any social setting where superiors wanted to hold their ground. The only way for me to respond was with the redness that overtook my face.

Directed by one of the men to take a seat, I made my way past the semicircle of big pretentious chairs to the one lone ottoman in the middle. The lighting was delicate and warm and gave off a safe calming illusion. But it was indeed just that, an illusion, untouchable by the human hand, a vision for only the human eye, based in the moment and taken away with the flip of a switch. The men sat around in the chairs, and I was asked to sit in the middle at the mouth of the semicircle with no one behind me.

I sat and waited for the first question to be shot out at me. I wanted to please Dr. Bennett by answering to the best of my ability. What made that so uncannily arduous was the perplexing nature of identifying my experiences and myself. Was I real? Were my thoughts really mine? Would they see through the facade? Would I be established as a fake, caught in the act of impersonating a human by several white-haired, bearded, Freudian-like clinicians peering over their reading glasses so as not see me as a blur? With numbing as my shield, I was ready for the first bullet…and they came flying.

"What is your experience with borderline personality disorder?"

"How do you see your self-image?"

"Can you describe yourself?"

"What's your biggest fear?"

"What does it mean when someone important to you leaves?"

"How do you deal with rejection?"

"How do you deal with criticism?"

"What does self-mutilation accomplish for you?"

"Is it difficult for you to control your anger?"

"How do you manage when alone?"

"How does your manipulative behavior serve you?"

"Are you prepared to deal with the chronicity of your condition?"

In my mind I rolled the questions around and around, fearing to disappoint anyone and everyone. I endlessly answered those that made sense and those that were as far from my understanding of myself as earth is from Mars. I answered and squirmed and fidgeted and writhed inside until they were finished. Finally, their chambers empty, the firing stopped.

Climbing into the backseat of the car I felt drained from the storm that had torn me up inside. The anticlimactic shock numbed me. I sat motionlessly gazing out the window, the lit lampposts saluting one by one as we passed. Again Dr. Bennett and Dave talked, their words cutting into the space we all shared, though on different levels and different plains. Theirs was an emotionally attached, communicative world made of understanding and mutuality, whereas mine was a numb, detached world devoid of skills to communicate or understand the intentions of those around me. I was guided by the internal experiences that I had no words to name or give reason to a world based on perceptions, real or imagined, of rejection and anger and criticism, engulfing and terrifying. I was a capsule filled with poison.

A crash of thunder startled me. The rain steadily clapped on the roof of my home, and the daytime hour mimicked early evening, the sun hidden behind a blanket of gray clouds. I sat motionless, relieved to have escaped yet another memory.

THORAZINE

taff was there for many reasons: to protect us, to reparent us, to keep
order, to babysit, to listen to us unfold the inner workings of our
minds, to use as a tool to get to know ourselves better, gain insight into
our behavior, probe our past, and explore our feelings. Nightly we were
expected to find whichever staff member made us feel most comfortable,
the one with whom we most connected and felt an element of relative
safety, and spend time talking. We would make an appointment to meet
at some point during the evening. We could talk about our parents: "Oh,
the awful things they did." We could talk about our relationships: "Oh,
nobody likes me." We could talk about our feelings: "Oh, I'm feeling so
depressed today." We could talk about our intentions: "Oh, I feel like I
may cut myself." Though the latter was likely to have repercussions, we
were expected to talk, so I did, but mostly about nothing.

I did not know how to talk, how to search, how to verbalize the pain
that held me captive in the world of mental illness, the pain that had
embedded itself within me like a parasite, sucking the life out of me.
Pulling the pain from my belly, packaging it neatly into words, and delivering it to open ears to be kicked around and analyzed then tossed
back my way to be fiddled with and processed wasn't something I did
well, but it was an expectation at The Hospital. We had to learn how
to put a name to our intense pain so we could learn how to manage it,

which ultimately would help us control our behavior, so we could keep privileges that allowed us some freedom within our highly structured lives. My need for human contact was so great that cooperating with the impossible became tolerable, even desired.

Ethan and I walked the short distance from where I had tracked him down at the nurses' station to my sanctuary, where he took up residence on an orange cloth chair my roommate and I used when we sat at our desk, and I, on guard and ready to flee, sat on the foot of my bed. Our conversation was lengthy as he cast the line, hook and bait, and with a struggle and ample resistance, pulled out my intense despair. I try now to capture whatever flickering memory of that conversation I can, but it escapes me. It lies deep down in my mind, so far away that as I reach out to touch it, I feel myself slipping, unable to grab it without losing my balance. It's too far, too deep, for me to grasp. I stretch my mind; I stretch my reach; I wiggle my fingers to shorten the distance between the unconscious and the conscious, getting closer to the dark hole in my mind that holds the memories I have lost. I struggle against a force so strong that I cannot win. The conversation may be gone, but what happened next lives vividly in my mind, repeated over and over, a moment in time, stagnant, displaying an image, then moving to the next stagnant scene, experienced as real to me now as it was then, though all sound is muted.

I hurled my addiction at my conversation partner, a pack of Marlboro cigarettes flew through the air, heading toward Ethan. Though he made a rule of crushing the pack anytime my impulses grew too strong to resist, for some reason, this time, he picked them up and handed them back.

"Lee, I'm concerned about you. I need you to come with me and sit at the nurses' station while I talk with staff."

My fight stifled by the enormous weight of depression, I complied.

"I'm going to have Meg sit with you."

We walked out of my room, my gait similar to what many would call the "Thorazine shuffle"—motionless movement.

Meg, with her short blond hair, freckles, and ready smile, approached me as I stood outside the nurses' station.

"OK, Lee. Let's sit here, and we can talk while we wait."

We sat together on the big table, side by side.

"Lee, why are you breathing so heavily?"

"How do you know I'm breathing heavily?"

"I can see your chest going up and down."

Those were the last words I heard.

I was stunned by the chaos around me, as staff shifted rapidly between loud commanding tones to one another and soft, reassuring directives to me—rapid movement, pressured grips on my arms and legs, the industrial carpeting offering little comfort beneath me. Suddenly an intense pain targeting one spot on my calf grabbed my attention.

"You're hurting me! Get the fuck off my leg! You're hurting me!"

Instantly my words seemed to erase the pain.

"It's OK, Lee. We've got you."

"Get off me! Get the fuck off me!"

My cries and screams raced through the empty halls of the adolescent unit, a ghost town compared to how they were when the usual parade of kids coursed through them. I attempted, though in vain, to fend off the invasion that had made its way into my reality. My awareness had shifted so abruptly from one moment (sitting on the table with Meg), to the next (being on the floor mounted by staff). The horror—which was so great and my temper so extreme that they called staff from the other units to assist—was one of darkness, a black hole with no light to see what was inside, no memory to link the two moments in time: the quiet conversation one minute, the chaos following a tragic impulse lost in darkness the next.

"Get the fuck off me!"

I fought and struggled, twisting my arms and legs in an effort to release myself from their grip so I could jump up and run, flee as fast as I could, so fast that I could not catch up with myself, outrun myself, hide, disappear, vanish.

"Get off me! Get off me! Now!"

"Lee, you're going to be OK. We've got you."

The power of my emotions strengthened my body, and I fought hard though futilely. In the end they had my arms restrained behind my back and my legs restrained tightly together. My only fight left was through my words, as I pleaded and cursed, begged and shrieked.

"Get the fuck off me!"

Like prehistoric men bringing a large kill back to their compound, each holding on to the tethered beast, four men brought their "kill" to seclusion.

"Get the fuck off me!"

The fluorescent lighting overhead cast a harsh, inescapable illumination that took up every corner of the room. My nostrils instantly were filled with the smell of vomit and institutional disinfectant, a patient from the night before having left his mark in the carpeting of the seclusion room floor. I lay there, stunned and humiliated, surrounded by staff, some sitting by my side, others making the bed to which I would be bound. So frightened were they by my primitive display of emotions that they hustled to prepare the most binding restraints that their imaginations allowed, taping pillows to the headboard and strategically placing a sheet under the mattress then pulling it up on either side to use as a harness, ensuring my "safety" in every possible way, with hard leather arm and leg restraints as the final touches. As they prepared the bed, the binding on my legs felt tighter and tighter, restricting my blood flow.

"Ethan?"

"Yes?"

"It hurts around my legs."

"The restraints are too tight?"

"Yes."

"OK, I'll fix them. But if you struggle, I'll stop."

Ethan moved slowly down to my ankles and started to loosen the restraints, triggering an unrealistic hope that he may be releasing me.

As the external restraints were prepared, a chemical one also was being drawn up, along with a threat from Ethan to gain my cooperation.

"You don't have a choice. If you cooperate and don't struggle, we'll do it in your arm. Otherwise we'll have to pull your pants down, and you don't want that."

Bound and helpless, I succumbed to my conquerors. Sitting by my side, Ethan was the staff member in charge of this project. He took his role seriously, getting the job done in as compassionate a manner as he could. Accepting my powerless position, and the strong desire to keep my pants pulled up, I obliged, motionless, cooperating. Towering over me from my prone perspective, though not a tall man by most standards, Jeff, the male nurse, approached me carrying a syringe with a needle as long as the ocean is wide. Quickly he plunged the needle through my skin, pushing the chemical into my muscle. Prone on the floor to prone on the bed. Fear and helplessness welled larger in my system than the Thorazine used to calm it. Noticing the ineffectiveness of the drug, Ethan rested his hand heavily on my back and spoke to me softly.

"Just try to relax and let the medicine work."

His voice was soothing. I listened to his words and focused on the warm, weighted pressure of his hand. I tried to lose myself in the connection, but my attempt was futile.

Prone on the bed to supine. The crowd of people who had gathered in the cold, isolating holding cell became clear. Frantically working, allowing moments of freedom as they tethered me to the bed—arms above my shoulders and legs spread-eagle—then strategically placing the sheet behind my head, pulling it through, under my arms, and securing it tightly. I was completely immobile, tethered like a rabid animal, like Hannibal Lecter.

As I lay helplessly, with not a limb for defense, a white sheet was draped gently from my waist down. Again the nurse approached, holding another syringe like the Olympic torch.

"No, not again. Please. Not again!"

With the sheet put in place to protect my dignity, the syringe was plunged deep into my bare thigh, penetrating the muscle with a searing pain, the wail traveling throughout the unit.

"*Aaaaaaaaaahhhhh!*"

Heavy breaths replaced my cries. Ethan, taking advantage of the silence, spoke to me.

"Lee, you need to sleep now. Relax and let the medicine do its job. We're going to leave the door open, and someone will be watching you."

My eyes begged Ethan for release, as he and the others filed out of the room, mission accomplished. With each person who walked out, any sense of security left with them, and my stress level rose to psychotic levels. My physical discomfort—being unable to move or adjust, being tethered so tightly—ripped away any illusion of control or autonomy. An unyielding pressure grew rapidly inside me, pressing against me unrelentingly. My mind scrambled, trying to outrun every overwhelming sensation that was tackling me. The pressure of immobility sent electrified pellets of panic rushing through my arms. The rising insanity had a hope for resolution as Todd walked back into the room.

"Todd, please, can you move my arms down to my side? I'm too uncomfortable. I feel like I'm going to start screaming."

Screaming in that moment would have severed the thread of reality I was hanging on to. The vocal release of the pressure that was intolerably permeating my being would have sent me into a spiral that I feared never would end. I would be lost in the scream forever. In that moment control was crucial to my very survival, but the discomfort I was in was so great, exacerbating the tension within me. I begged Todd to be my savior, begged for salvation, begged for release.

CEDAR LODGE

*M*eredith's question—"Did you ever have fun?"—had remained unanswered, so I finally decided to appease her curiosity.

Steve Brady was a big fellow with curly hair and a perfect smile. He was fun, and he wanted us to have fun. As with a small minority of the staff at The Hospital, Steve's career goal wasn't in mental health. He understood our pain, cared about our pain, wanted to help abolish our pain but didn't clinically treat our pain. Steve was the recreational therapist. He had us play sports, or what I might call mandatory "fun," which I detested. I detested the competition, the pressure, the lack of skill I was sure I would bring to the field, disappointing and angering my teammates, rejection hiding behind every missed ball. I detested the use of my body that was a necessary part of sports. I detested mandatory "fun," but I did not detest Steve.

Cedar Lodge was a historic property, open only for tours, which had belonged to an old, wealthy family from bygone days. Cedar Lodge was haunted.

"Come on, guys. Trip. Into the van. Who's going?"

Excitedly those of us with trip privileges (yes, that meant me this time) would gather at the door, waiting for our keepers to unlock it so we could scurry out to our awaiting chariot. We would climb in, and Steve would sit behind the wheel and start the engine. We were excited when we went with Steve because we knew he would take us somewhere where our anxiety and fear could rise to exhilaratingly high levels for a socially acceptable reason: ghosts.

The drive to Cedar Lodge wasn't too long, maybe twenty minutes. On the way Steve always regaled us with scary stories, ensuring the predictably heightened response from the van full of mentally ill adolescents giddy with excitement. The route he took was off the main thoroughfare, a small, winding, country road with a forest of trees blocking the sunset and hiding eerie fantasies among its branches, complementing the stories with which he was fueling us. A creepy sensation filled the van as we drove toward the horror of the dead revisiting the living. The twists and turns of the road suddenly opened up to a long driveway, a two-hundred-year-old mansion visible in the distance, sitting alone and rigid, holding the dread of otherworldly phenomena, holding the dread of the unknown. The van made its way up the driveway as Steve gave us his usual warning.

"If anyone comes, run for the van, jump in, and we'll make a speedy getaway. Even though nobody lives here anymore, the property is private."

That was Steve's final touch to enhance the exhilarating fear we were already experiencing. Slowly he would make his way closer and closer to the house. Once we were in front of the mansion, he would turn the van around so it faced the street to ensure an easy escape, should it be necessary. He would turn off the engine. Nobody daring to move, we sat motionless with only our eyes and ears surveying the property. As the last of the sun slowly made its way behind the mansion, our bright companion was now out of sight. Hearts racing, we stepped out of the van, one by one, maintaining our vow of silence. Once we stood in the open air, with the breeze gently caressing us, we stared wide-eyed at the third-floor window, where the ghost supposedly resided. Softly we broke the silence with a whispered, "Do you see anything?"

"No, do you?"

"Not yet."

"Shh."

"Why? Do you see something?"

"No, but I'm getting a chill. Just shh for a minute. Look."

"What? Do you see something? What? Where?"

"Shh. Oh, my God. Look!"

"What did you see?"

"Didn't you guys see that? A shadow. A big one. It just ran across the I of the house. Didn't you guys see that?"

"Oh, shit. Yeah, I saw it. I think I saw it."

"Shit, I'm getting the chills. This place is fucking creepy."

"It's getting dark. This is so freaky."

"Look!"

"The window—was that light on before?"

"Oh, God, no. It wasn't. Look!"

"I saw that too. Something just moved past that window. God, tell me you guys saw that too."

"Fuckin' creepy. I saw it."

"The shadow. There it is again, running across the house!"

"OK, guys. Let's get out of here. In the van! Hurry!"

In our contagious, excited panic, the flurry of activity surrounding us was exhilarating. We stampeded into the van with rapid caution, hurrying to make our escape but not wanting to step too fast so as not to alarm the specters that were hovering around us. Steve advised us to close the door quietly. He turned the key in the ignition, sparking the engine with the same electric excitement his charges carried within them. Quickly, to make it appear as though our very lives depended on it, he made his escape and drove us off to safety. I never will forget the rapture that embodied our trips to Cedar Lodge.

Thank you Steve for the fun amidst the anguish.

I've got a friend ^who is special to me
I talk to him about feelings so he
can see
What my head is all about
so he can know me with less doubt.
He's a big fellow with curly hair
And to mess with him I wouldn't
dare.
QUST KIDDING 88
He'd be there to help most anyone.
And teach you, too, how to have fun.
He's a good friend and I'm glad he's one
of mine.
So when I'm alone and I feel like
cryin.
I can think of him and try to smile.
Because, as ~~the~~ we know, ~~fot~~ real friendships
are all worth while.
                    ~~Lee~~ Wasserman "79"

HAGGARD AND WORN

R eaching out to the only person who came in to see me, the person who was put in charge of watching me, the person I trusted, I pleaded with Todd on that night, as I lay bound so firmly to the bed that movement was an impossibility, except for my nose, my fingers, and my toes, which I wiggled to ensure that blood was still running through my body. Begging Todd to be my savior, begging for salvation, begging for release, I pleaded.

"Please help me, or I'll start screaming."

"You can scream. Screaming can be good."

"Todd, please. I can't. I can't. Please help me."

In that moment my connection to reality was so nebulous that I was unaware of the fact that he could not see through me and read my thoughts, that he was unable to grasp what I was experiencing deep in my head, that he could not see insanity standing beside me, mocking me, waiting to step in as soon as I opened the door. He could not see my fear that if I started screaming, craziness would wrap around me and bind me tighter than any restraints could. He could not see this, and I did not tell him.

"Please, Todd. Can't they just move my arms down to my side? This is too uncomfortable. Please."

"I'll go find out if I can move your arms and make you more comfortable. Hang in there for a minute."

Todd left the room, and I summoned all my patience, waiting for and anticipating some relief. A few minutes later he returned.

"They said no. You need to stay like that for tonight. I'm here, Lee. I'll be right out in the hall, talking to someone. Just call me if you need me."

Todd walked out, leaving me alone, my determination to remain sane cradling me, eventually pulling me toward unconsciousness as the Thorazine slowly washed over me, my mind, my body. Slowly I drifted into a chemical-induced sleep that hung on to me until the next morning.

I awoke to Karen—"Sarge," as we kids liked to call her behind her back, accurately depicting her demeanor – standing rigidly by the bed.

"Lee, I'm going to take the restraints off. Once they're off I want you to stay on the bed. When I tell you, I want you to get up very slowly. Do you understand?"

I was saturated with shame, disgust oozing from my skin like venomous pus. The weight of my emotions made me a willing participant to her request.

"Yes."

We were like an officer and her prisoner as Sarge made her way from one corner of the bed to the next, cautiously releasing me. Compliance was my safety and my only hope for liberation from the confines of my prison.

"OK, Lee. Now I want you to get up very slowly. Then I'll bring you to the nurses' station, where we can keep an eye on you."

Doing as much as I could to avoid eye contact with the militant nurse, who may have been hiding a very soft heart, I followed her instructions and slowly got up from the bed. I don't know whether the request was due to her fearing that any quick movement from me might pose a threat to her or because getting up too fast could have caused me to collapse after being chemically and physically restrained all night. I didn't know whether her self-interest or mine lay at the core of her request, but whatever the reason, I complied.

Standing brought some relief from the tension of being shackled, but it also brought a keen awareness of the tenderness at each point of injection. My arm was in pain. My leg was in pain. My muscles pulsated with a throbbing ache deep beneath my flesh. Walking to the nurses' station, where I was to spend my day under the watchful eyes of the staff, was laborious as I limped down the hallway, looking haggard and worn, much older than my sixteen or seventeen years.

I spent the day sitting at the big table. Friends sat and talked with me. Staff sat and talked with me. My meals were brought to me. My cigarettes were lit for me. I watched the other kids come and go, in and out of the lounge, in and out of the rec room, on and off the unit. Everything around me moved, changed, with me a stagnant image confined to one place. If it weren't for the changing pattern of the sun, time would have stood still, with the chaos around invisible to my presence. Three in the afternoon was shift change. Day staff would leave, and evening staff would come. They would huddle in the nurses' office and exchange their game plan, talking about all the players' weaknesses and strengths, which patient did what, who needed this or that, who was on which precaution, and of course, "What did Lee do today?" After high fives all around, the huddle broke, and the shifts officially changed. Jeff was working again and approached me.

"Lee, can we go to the end of the hall and talk?"

"Yeah. Why?"

"I just need to talk with you. Come on."

Freed from the nurses' station, I followed Jeff down the hall like a curious puppy. As we approached the little table and two chairs that were used for private conversations, Jeff suddenly took my hand and made a sharp turn to the left.

"Not again! Why? What're you doing?"

"It's OK, Lee. Don't struggle. We don't want to put you in restraints again."

I resisted slightly, pulling back against Jeff's directed movement into the bright, terrifying room, into the mouth of the demon.

"Not again! I haven't done anything wrong!"

"This isn't a punishment. You won't be alone. Someone is going to stay in here with you at all times."

Beaten and confused, I curled up on the bed in a fetal position. Within minutes John Hazelton walked in and stood looking over a pathetic, drenched wretch barely hanging on to the reality before her. He sat on a chair next to the bed.

"Do you want a cigarette?"

"Yeah."

After opening the red box that brought me so much comfort—that soothed the crying addiction that would wage a battle if too much time went by—he passed me a cigarette and lit it. The first drag, the pull of the nicotine deep into my lungs, brought immense relief, the cravings leaving my body as the puff of smoke left my mouth. It was comforting and quiet: John, me, and my three-inch pack of leaves wrapped in white paper, smoldering at the end. It was comforting until Jeff walked back into the room. In one hand was a little white paper cup filled with pills, in the other a plastic cup filled with water. In an affirmative tone, Jeff made his command.

"Here, Lee. Take these."

"I don't want them."

"I need you to take them. If you don't I'll have to inject it. Take them."

He handed me the cups. I put the pills—two or three of them, if I recall correctly—in my mouth and pushed them gently down my throat with the lukewarm water. Once I had taken them, Jeff spoke.

"Open your mouth."

Becoming accustomed to the lack of trust that influenced our relationships—those of patients to staff—I opened my mouth and flung my tongue in his direction, up, down, side to side. The ruminating thoughts in my head were hardly as compliant, as little voices called out big words: *Fuck you, Jeff!*

I waited, smoking what was left of my cigarette then lighting another, as John sat loyally by my side to make sure the little pills took their big effect. Barely aware of the passage one moment to the next, I awoke from the chemical restraint, and true to their word, I was not alone. It was no longer John but another staff member.

"Are you hungry?"

"Yeah."

"Your dinner's here."

"OK."

I was given my meal.

I was given a cigarette.

I was given another cup of pills.

And again I slept.

SPEEDO
(NOT TO BE CONFUSED WITH THE BATHING SUIT)

*I*n the crux of an illness, consumed and tormented, I was still able to reach out to some of my peers. There was a safety at The Hospital in making these connections, a learning process for each of us suffering from personality disorders, rejection fears, and exquisite sensitivities to our environment. An "us against them" mentality kept us feeling independent from those on whom we so heavily relied but so desperately wanted autonomy from—the staff. One of these girls who normalized my existence, as I normalized hers, was Marsha Perloski. We hung out and talked, listened to music, went on trips from The Hospital when our levels permitted, and explored the idea of normalcy. December 1978, for reasons that I no longer recall, though she was eligible for a pass, Marsha was staying at The Hospital on Christmas. So I invited her to come with me.

"You wanna go to my house?"

"Sure."

And so she did. This particular Christmas was made up of my sister, her friend, her friend's twin brothers, my mother and father, and of course, two institutionalized girls out for the day, though our secret was well kept. We were not living in a locked unit for the emotionally unstable, suicidal borderline type; rather we were at boarding school, an aristocratic lie to cover up the shameful truth. It was easy during the winter, the cold forcing us into long sleeves, which hid any physical evidence of the secret we were keeping.

The Christmas tree was the center of attention, with colorful ornaments, shiny tinsel, and bright little bulbs reflecting the joy of the season. It was framed by a bay window that looked out into the cold December evening. Sitting around the living room, this motley crew talked uncomfortably, ate, and drank. Though drinking was forbidden for Marsha and me—hospital rules—we did what we had to so as not to call attention to ourselves and joined in the festivities, indulging in just one small glass of wine each. Our stomachs already satisfied by the hors d'oeuvres and wine, eventually we went to the table in the dining room to eat the Christmas dinner put together by my mother and my sister. As we sat my discomfort grew, the small amount of alcohol doing little to tame my fears. I was certain that these boys, who were close in age to Marsha and me, knew something was different about the two "boarding school" girls. I was certain each glance carried with it a smirk of knowledge as to where we really lived, our situation, our insanity. Throughout the meal tension surrounded us, thicker than the air we were breathing. We sat and ate, Marsha and me, occasionally whispering to each other then glaring toward my sister's friend Ruth, or my parents or the boys or my sister. A giggle escaped us on other occasions. We felt large and obvious, vulnerable and weak. Finally, when the meal was over, Marsha and I fled. The safe haven of my bedroom embraced us in comfort, hiding us from the expectations we could not meet.

Eventually the evening came to an end, and we were driven back to The Hospital. With my parents' departure, our good-byes all in place, a staff member poked her head out of the window from the nurses' office, which looked directly into the waiting room where Marsha and I sat.

"OK, who's going first?"

Marsha and I shrugged, out of helplessness not cooperation. We shrugged because volunteering to go first felt like condoning the shameful action that we were made to endure each time we returned to The Hospital from a pass, the ritual each patient was exposed to – a punishment for the privilege. Like a leprechaun suddenly appearing on the scene, a small female staff member stood before us with a taller one beside her. Divide and Conquer.

"All right, Lee. Why don't you come with me? Marsha, you go with her."

The leprechaun took my small travel suitcase filled with some belongings from home.

"I'll search it afterward. Let's go into the bathroom."

Humiliation reddening my skin, I followed the staff member into the bathroom as Marsha followed the other, compliance in our best interest.

"OK, off with your shoes and socks."

Leaning against the wall for support, I hesitantly took off my shoes and socks, leaving them on the floor for her to pick up. Holding them diligently and running her fingers along the inside of each shoe, she performed a thorough search for any contraband. My socks, regardless of whatever odor may have been coming from them, were turned inside out and studied as well. The process seemed slowed by the anticipation surging inside me, grounded only by the cold floor underneath my bare feet.

"Take your shirt off, please."

My eyes dropped like heavy weights. Looking at her at this point would blind me, bleach my cornea, and take my vision away.

"Your bra."

Half naked, I stood vulnerable and motionless.

As she had done with my shoes and socks, she inspected my bra for anything that may have been hidden in the seams that I could use to cut, smoke, or snort. Only half satisfied she continued.

"OK, your pants."

Slowly I slipped out of my pants, one leg at a time, releasing my clothing and exposing myself to the staff member put in charge of securing my reentry to the unit. Clothed only in my underwear, I heard, "You need to slip your underwear down a little."

The Shame.

"Good. You can get dressed now."

After standing and watching as I dressed myself for the second time that day, she walked me to the unit. Her next task was to search the little suitcase I'd used to bring some necessities back to The Hospital and disappeared into the nurses' office. Waiting for my bag, I sat at the big table and talked with friends when another staff member approached me.

"Lee, you're looking a bit hyper tonight."

"Oh? What do you mean?"

"What did you take when you were home?"

"Nothing."

"Well, you seem like you're racing. Did you do a little speed while you were home?"

"No!"

Peter Summers, a staff member with a tough exterior, approached me, flashlight in hand. A few others gathered around to help manage whatever situation they thought he had found.

"Look at me."

Sure of my innocence, I complied with Peter's request.

"Your pupils are dilated, even with the light. Yeah, I think you did speed."

My drug of choice not having been made available to me during my Christmas trip home, I pleaded my innocence.

"I didn't. I swear."

"Let me feel your pulse."

With his fingers he gently took my wrist. My heart racing from the fear of accusation, he announced his verdict.

"Fast."

"I didn't take anything."

"I do think you took something. Tell me why your pupils are responding the way they are, why your pulse is fast."

"I don't know why, but I didn't take anything. I can't believe you don't believe me."

"Right, Speedo. I think you'll be sleeping in seclusion tonight. Tomorrow we'll draw some blood, and then we'll see."

"Yeah, *you'll* see. And I'm not sleeping in seclusion. I didn't do anything!"

A powerful, self-righteous burst of laughter pushed out from Peter's belly.

"You're sleeping in seclusion, Speedo."

Peter stood his ground, his thin lips curved into a mocking smile, his piercing green eyes peering through his rectangular black-rimmed glasses. He was one of the Vietnam vets on the unit—the Napoleon complex guiding his behavior—and was intimidating yet beloved by me. He appeared powerful with the knowledge he thought he held. He pointed and shot his threatening glare through me, piercing me with excitement. I was not going to back down. He was strong, but I was stronger. I had my love of negative attention on my side.

It was true, my mind was racing that night, my energy bounding, climbing, electric, the after effect from an evening filled with parents, friends, secrets, and lies. My body and mind frequently took me to places without my consent, without my control. On this night I was swept out of my emotions by an energy that mimicked my drug of choice. As I buzzed about, I was removed from the dirtiness of my life, from the emotional cavity that was damaging the structure of my being. I was numbed by the manic impulses that coursed through me and severed my pain from my awareness. As I had developed strategic ways to cope with my internal environment—an automatic response of my nervous system to survive through the night—my self-protection and self-preservation were being punished. I was going to be made to sleep in seclusion for a crime I had not committed. (At this point you may be thinking, *But you had a glass of wine,* and you would be right. However, it wasn't drinking that I had been accused of.)

Faith in me and in my word carried little weight in the minds of those there to help, as my reputation was more on the side of passive-aggressiveness, manipulation, and dishonesty. I was not to be trusted. The empirical evidence—my overly energetic behavior, which was normally more subdued—took precedence over my word. I was asked to remain at the nurses' station until staff was ready to escort me to seclusion for the night.

Normally the anger I felt at those secluding me, and the anger I felt at myself for allowing it, would take control and push me into resistance. This evening, though willing I was not, I walked down and let staff close me into the bright and terrifying room. I surrendered to the mouth of the demon. Once I had been searched yet again, humiliated by my nakedness, my ego's strength challenged in the face of abandonment, I was left alone, utterly alone—door locked, metal to metal, the sound of the keys grating my nerves. My cooperation was being tested; my spirit was being tested; my will was being tested; and I lost.

Thoughts raced frantically through my mind, dashing here and there, chaotic and frenzied, the anxiety in my body rising with a feverish velocity. *I can't fucking take this* played over and over in my head. My arms and legs tingled with agitation, begging for relief.

With each punch I gave the wall, excitement rushed through me. The pain from the impact radiated through my hand, over and over, providing liberation from the internal torment, pushing its way through and replacing it with an unexplainable sense of relief. Eventually I was able to purge the hysteria that writhed inside of me. My hand pulsated and swelled in response to the savage beating it had received. I sat on the bed. I held my hand in my lap, palm side down, and admired my work, knuckles red hot with trauma. I smiled with gratification. I laid my head down. I slept.

Night passed, and the fluorescent light that shone down was gradually replaced by sunlight piercing through the large window, invading my rest. I lay still, waiting for sound, and within minutes I heard keys making their way toward the door.

"OK, Lee. Time to get up. You're going to have your blood drawn so we can see what you took last night."

I asked if I could first remove the filth and slime that coated my body every morning.

"Can I shower?"

"The lab woman is here. We'll take care of that first. Then you can shower, and your breakfast will be down."

"What do you mean? Can't I go up to the dining room?"

"Your level has been dropped. You're on level zero now."

"But I haven't done anything!"

"Well, that's what you claim, but we'll see once the lab results come back."

Rage wrapped around me instantaneously and left me motionless, fearing any movement would bring on a storm. In that moment of stillness, the staff member cocked his head to one side, his jugular vein protruding, and spoke.

"Can I see your hand?"

An infraction that I did not commit had led to an incarceration within my incarceration that I did not deserve, which had led to the physical pain that I craved in order to cope. And so the cycle had begun.

"Why do you wanna see my hand?"

"You've been hurting yourself. Let me see your hand."

In a momentary regression to the mind of a toddler, I hid my hand behind my back, hiding my guilt. Proving some kindness did exist behind institutional walls, he gently took my arm, my wrist, my hand.

"You were punching the wall last night."

"So?"

"You need to stay at the nurses' station after your blood's drawn."

The cycle.

I trudged down the hall toward the nurses' station, where I saw the "blood lady," our endearing name for the vampire that visited the unit with her portable supplies. Cooperating but resenting it, I allowed them to stick a needle into my arm to confirm or clear me of their accusation. The blood lady put a rubber band around my arm and tied it tightly, the intensity of the strain making my veins ripe and ready. She wiped the area clean with a sterile pad to rid any bacteria from my skin. Slowly she inserted the needle into the narrow passage where blood flowed, carrying oxygen through my body, the essence of life being invaded. The task complete, the needle was removed, and a Band-Aid was applied to camouflage the invasion. She packed up her belongings into the plastic box in which she carried her bloodletting supplies and quietly left. I'm not sure I remember the blood lady ever talking. She was more like a shadow that passed through the unit when needed. But the staff member standing guard readily barked out his orders.

"You need to sit here until we decide what happens next."

Sitting in one of the orange plastic chairs with metal armrests that curved their way around to form the legs, I curled my body up, folded in on myself, and tried to wrap my head around the events as they had unfolded. Yesterday: level four, a pass home with a friend, back at The Hospital, accusations, seclusion, physical pain to release unbearable emotional torment. Today: level zero, restriction at the nurses' station, no privileges. My downward spiral had been that fast.

Towering over my huddled body, a staff member spoke.

"Can I sit with you?"

My upward glance was the only answer he required.

"We're putting you on self-injury precautions."

"*Why?*"

"Well, first, because you spent time in seclusion last night punching the wall. Second, because last night, when Katie searched the suitcase you brought back from your pass, she cut up her fingers."

"What're you talking about?"

"When Katie searched your suitcase, she ran her hand along the inside of the lining and got cut. You brought glass back."

"I didn't put it there."

"Well, it's your suitcase, so I think we'll hold you responsible. SIP one and a twenty-four-hour restriction for bringing glass in, which you'll serve here at the nurses' station."

Usually twenty-four hour restrictions were spent in one's room, except when self-harm was a threat. Sitting at the big table, friends tried to sit and talk with me but were quickly redirected by watchful eyes.

"Lee is on restriction. She can't talk."

A mocking voice took up residence in my head, repeating the words over and over.

Lee is on restriction. She can't talk.

Lee is on restriction. She can't talk.

The warmth of the morning sun streaming through the skylights that were positioned directly over the table at the nurses' station changed and shifted and moved and cooled as the morning turned to afternoon then turned to night. The staff changed along with the motion of the earth—day, evening, and night. Each shift would come in and huddle with the one that was already there, exchanging information and ideas. Staff meeting over, the huddle broken, I was approached with the news of their plan.

"You're going to sleep in seclusion."

"Why? Not again!"

"You can't be trusted in your room."

"I can. Please."

The orders hardly seemed fair as I reflected on what I thought had been impeccable behavior. I had sat at the nurses' station, compliant to the demands that had been placed on me. Helpless in my ability to argue my case, as their authority was more a source of pride for staff than any reasonable request, at least from my perspective, I acquiesced. Once I was in the room, the search of my dignity completed, the staff member spoke to me.

"I'm going to check your hand in the morning and see if you've been hurting yourself."

I laughed at the ludicrous statement, the ludicrous expectation that I would reveal to him any self-inflicted damages that may increase my penalty.

"How're you gonna know? Do you think I'm gonna tell you?"

"I'm going to compare. Give me your hand."

His extraordinary degree of perception, superhuman comic-hero level, was not to be believed, so I complied, placing my hand into his. His touch was gentle and caring, sympathetic and warm as he ran his finger across the back of my hand, leaving me feeling unsettled. Satisfied with the visual image he was able to ingrain into his memory to use the next day, he looked at me, nodded, and left, securing the door on his way out, the mouth of the demon shut.

Allow images of a dimly lit room with soft padding on the walls, as television may portray a room intended for one's safety, to be replaced by the reality of a harsh fluorescent light and white stucco walls, rough in texture, hard on the knuckles. The chill of isolation, creating an aura of frigid solitude, seeped into my skin through every pore. The segregation I had been made to tolerate, with little skills to do so, ripped through my body, anxiety surging like bubbling lava in an active volcano, a repeat of the night before.

That night I slept a troubled sleep.

The seclusion-room door opened slowly. He approached quietly, his footsteps softened by the industrial carpeting that covered the floor. I lay motionless, trapped in a sleep state, restrained by my own mind, unable to move and unable to communicate. Frantically I clawed to reach the surface of consciousness, panicked to escape the grip of paralysis, but my efforts were futile. I could hear and sense my surroundings but remained helpless in my paralyzed body. He leaned over and searched for a pulse. Without a word, and obviously satisfied with the results, he left the room, locking the door behind him. Before I could make any more efforts to dig my way out of the surreal prison within my own body, the hypnopompic state released me.

The next morning repeated itself much like the day before. My restriction continued at the nurses' station, with the hustle of institutional life passing me by while friends tried to sit and talk with me, only to be met with same refrain.

"Lee is on restriction. She can't talk."

Evening brought the staff member who had committed to memory the evidence of my self-induced relief.

"OK, Lee. Let's have a look."

I knew I had no choice and hoped one swollen hand looked like the next. He repeated the intense investigation that he had performed the night before with the same softness and care, eliciting feelings that belonged more in a romance novel than a memoir of a young woman's fight for survival, of her battling a savage beast that threatened to consume her in a gruesome attack on her life.

"You did it again last night."

"No."

"Yes, you did."

My restriction continued as I sat obediently in one of the orange plastic chairs. As I had no other outlets, my leg released the anxiety that was building violently inside me with rhythmic shaking, like a jackhammer on overdrive. After a few minutes had passed, the staff member returned with the plan of action.

"Tonight you'll sleep outside the nurses' station. After dinner and community meeting, once the unit has quieted, we'll bring your mattress out."

My mattress was brought out by staff and set on the floor in front of the nurses' station, against the base of the big table. The lights from the office shone sweetly in the darkness of the hallway, casting over me, warm and cozy, with the soft murmuring of the night staff to keep me company. Why they occasionally had me sleep there, close to them, as opposed to the isolating experience they usually exposed me to, I don't know. I never will know, but I never will forget. This, however, did not happen the following night.

THE ALTERNATIVE SCHOOL

The smell of early-September mornings has become a vivid reminder of my youth. Wet dew soaked through my sneakers as I cut across the grass to make the school bus, my backpack weighing me down as I ran. The corner had three or four neighborhood teens waiting. We stood together, gossiping and laughing. The big yellow school bus pulled up, and we filed in. As I looked out the window, my daydream was interrupted as I saw the white van hovering in front of my house, "Intermediate Unit" plastered on both sides. When I wasn't in The Hospital, I was placed in a special school for special adolescents with special issues, a structured environment to complement my outpatient needs. The driver of the van always reserved the front seat for me, the last one to be picked up and the last to be dropped off. We would make our way to deliver all the kids to their appropriate schools: The School for the Deaf, The Developmental Center, The Alternative School.

The buildings were large, sinister structures built in the latter part of the 1870s, their presence as beautiful as they were ominous. Its history long, accepting its first patient July 12, 1880, the state hospital was a throwback to a bygone era. The intermediate unit of my local district rented space in the basement of building X for the Alternative School. Though we were not part of the state hospital—of its asylum past or its institutional present—we were there, day after day.

The grounds were large, with acres of land. The layout was what was referred to as the "cottage" model: separate buildings dedicated to patients of different degrees of functioning, with a web of tunnels interconnecting the entire institution. When I think of my school, a heaviness weighs on me as I revisit in my mind the pathetic warehousing that embodied my experience. The school was small, managed by four teachers specially trained in the management of the twelve young people in their care who were struggling with mental illness and deemed hopeless in their ultimate quest for survival...we were warehoused. I had friends at school, but as I have no clear intact memories of them, they remain shadows lurking behind a fog.

The tunnels—long and dark, forbidding yet enticing—always intrigued these friends and me. On occasion I coaxed one of them to escape through these sinister passages on an exhilarating attempt to cause an external barrage of activity to quiet my internal barrage of activity. We would look to make sure the teachers were distracted, and once the opportunity arose, we bolted. Running and laughing in a hushed frenzy, we'd escape down the halls, our footsteps echoing as the sound bounced from concrete floors to concrete walls. A cold chill in the air held the ghosts of the past, anguished people who had been institutionalized and led through these very tunnels during the years and years of the asylum's history. An eerie feeling coursing through our veins spurred us into a hysterical giddiness, like two children during a sleepover sharing the scariest of stories. As we ran, footsteps quickly echoed behind. Our pace quickened, spurred by the adrenaline of the chase, as the two male teachers who became aware of our escape yelled, "Girls! Stop! Now!"

The command grabbing her and holding her, my friend stopped dead in her tracks. Within seconds there was significant distance between her and me.

"Lee! Stop!"

As the distance between my friend and me greatened, the one between the two male teachers and me lessened.

"Lee!"

My forward movement was halted suddenly and harshly. Gripping my arms, they walked me back toward the classrooms.

"Get off me. You don't have to hold me" was my normal retort.

"Yes we do" was theirs.

All the students had been shuffled to the far room of my two-room high school. The empty one now became the pen to hold the incorrigible. I sat alone, locked in by one of my teachers. The moment the sound of the key securing the door brushed past my ears, my anger rose, rushing up my body like mercury in a thermometer thrust into piping-hot oil. My leg began its attempt to release the anxiety. Pulsating sensations of loneliness, anger, and anxiety overwhelmed my system, consuming me from the inside. *Where is everyone?* A feeling in the back of my neck, like an electric spark ignited by the push of a button, forced an explosion that emanated from my core. *Destroy.* Desks and chairs became weightless props in my rage. A glass sitting on the teacher's desk shattered into a million little pieces. My emotions spilled out of the red liquid dripping down my arms. The sound reached the far room. Teachers rushed in like bounty hunters coming to claim their prize. I stood frozen. One of the teachers, a stocky man with short brown hair, took the initiative.

"Let's get you cleaned up."

The school day was over. Kids had left, and the far room was empty. We stood in the bathroom, his soft warm touch supportive and nurturing as the cool water ran over the gaping wound. The water was then replaced by a piece of gauze, secured with white tape. The caretaking complete, I was put on the bus and sent home. Just another day at my high school.

THE APOLOGY

Sleeping in the warmth and safety of the protective light of the nurses' station provided the feeling of loving, soothing parents protecting their child in the fits of a nightmare. Twenty-four hours later, and night was upon us again, carrying an indescribable sense of despair. I sat in the nurses' office, still not allowed to venture away from the watchful eyes of staff, my privileges reduced to none. I sat talking with two staff members, one of them Meg. She hid behind a lot of makeup, the mask of the 1970s. She had a way about her that at times intimidated me, and I was never really sure whether Meg liked me. As a matter of fact, I was sure she did not. Despite this we sat and talked.

"I'm depressed."

"Why are you feeling like that?"

"I don't know. I just feel bad, really bad. I don't have anything to look forward to."

"What would make you feel more hopeful? What would you like to look forward to?"

"I don't know."

"Think of something. Is there anything?"

The nurses' office had three chairs upholstered in orange fabric, a favorite color of the institution in which I resided. For comfort they had backrests and for convenience wheels. The built-in desk wrapped

around the wall, giving staff ample space in which to work as they diligently took notes on all the youth in their charge, tracking behavior
– regressions and progress. I sat on one of the orange chairs in front of
the window that looked out onto the waiting room and thought about
what Meg had asked me. *What would I like to look forward to?* My life held
no hope, no future, no short-term goals, no long-term goals, no happiness, no health. I was in despair, consumed totally by a darkness and
an emptiness that sucked me in like a vacuum, strong and powerful—a
battle between the inner forces of good and evil.

"I don't have anything to look forward to. I can't think of anything. I
can't find anything. I just hate myself—that's all. Just hate."

Meg said something that in the moment had no impact, no effect,
but thirty years later gives me pangs of regret and the realization that
she had cared.

"How would you like it if I gave you a back rub each night?"

My answer was simple.

"No."

I think back to that moment today—one of the joys that costs me
one dollar per minute, that my body craves as I hunch over my computer
for endless hours copy and pasting my past from inside my head to the
screen. Her sincerity, her desperation to reach the kids in her charge,
to save them, to give them a moment of happiness, of comfort through
a gesture so authentic grabs me by the throat. I wish I had said yes. I'm
sorry, Meg, that I could not.

Once again I sat at the big table outside the nurses' office. That
night Peter Summers was on the evening shift. He approached me with
a gait that could only mean trouble.

"We've decided you're going to sleep in seclusion in restraints."

Silence.

How do I convey the lull that hung suspended as I tried to make
sense of what he had just said? Can I say the air was suddenly thick,
breathing a challenge, fiery heat rising inside my body, a fog instantly
covering me, protecting me from reality? Yes.

"*Again?* Why? I haven't done anything!"

"We've decided to have you sleep in restraints anyway. We're going to bind you to the bed so you can't move."

"I can't fucking believe you! I don't want to sleep that way. Why the fuck would you do that? What did I do?"

To prevent my head from spinning around and spewing green vomit on the messenger, and most likely a coconspirator, I froze, sitting rigidly and ready to crack. My glare, blue and sharp, was like a knife cutting into Peter, wanting to rip him open and pour my wrath into the wound that I had created. To keep the volcano from erupting, I muttered one more word.

"Why?"

I was not sure he heard it. I was not sure I really said it, because he never responded.

"We're going to lie you facedown, restrain your legs, then restrain your arms behind your back. That way you can't move. You seem to get out of restraints often. Not this time."

This was true. I was adept at the art of escape, and not being equipped with cooperative tendencies, I frequently attempted to relieve myself of the leather binds that restricted my movement, invaded my comfort, and stole my autonomy. As I always was skillful at freeing my hands, frustration guided the staff, eventually using leather gloves instead of wrist restraints to keep me bound, yet never succeeding in their attempts. Peter's words had the tone of absolute. Negotiation would lead my rigid core to sever, robbing me of the little sanity I felt I was barely hanging on to. Peter and I walked together, another staff member on my other side, like a prisoner and her guards marching to the gallows. As always there were at least four staff members during every restraining, prepared for the inevitable...a fight.

"Get off me!" became my mantra. The altercation with staff came from my need to show my rebellion, my disagreement with the treatment being imposed, and an impulsive response to a powerless position.

The fight came from the hyperaroused, primitive portion of my brain—a struggle for survival.

"Get off me!"

My fury was tantamount to a volcano on the verge of eruption, making the struggle cathartic though terrifying, controlling though powerless, taking hold of me and spurring me into a whirlwind of frenzied explosions. With every pull and push and scream for deliverance from their hold came an evil, foul alter ego that dwelled within my core—my empty, spacious, vacuous core, my evil, rebellious, pathetic core, the true me, the real me. The shell that presented for all to see—my skin, my appearance, my good days, my kind words—was a facade put in place to protect, shield, safeguard, to screen the alter ego that would scare away the most nurturing of humans, running from the ugliness that spewed from its very pores. It was the alter ego that fought. It was me that fought. It was my anger, my perverseness, my anxiety, my need for a release, my fear, my desperation, my suffocating, overwhelming pain that fought. It was me.

"Get the fuck off me!"

I was strong through my illness. Taking a team to get the job done, they were stronger through the power of their numbers. As I lay ultimately defeated, with sweat caked on my face and body, Peter sat next to me. In a last ditch effort, I pleaded with him.

"I don't want to sleep like this all night. I'm uncomfortable."

"Well, you need to tonight. You're not going to be able to get out of the restraints like this."

My desire to swing with clenched fists was thwarted by the leather tethers. As luck would have it, I needed my hands for another reason, an irritating sensation that I was helpless to remove.

"Peter, I have a hair in my mouth."

He got up and returned within minutes with a wet, white washcloth from the bathroom.

"Open your mouth. I'll try to get it."

I opened wide for him to access the stray hair that had made its way from what I hoped was *my* head into my mouth. The sensation of the little fragment tore through my tongue up to my brain and irritated every fiber. Unsuccessfully I had tried to lick the bed in an effort to transfer it from tongue to sheet. Once the hair was transplanted to the washcloth, Peter wiped my face, the coolness of the washcloth soothing as it sucked the heat of the struggle from my skin. The gesture was warm and caring, devoid of any seduction but rather an act of fatherly guilt.

The next morning—now two days since the pass home that had culminated in the accusations that had sent me spiraling from level four to SIP one—brought the results from the blood test. The verdict was in. That afternoon Peter approached me.

"Lee, the results came back."

"Yeah?"

A nervous twang bellowed inside me. Though I was innocent of what I'd been accused of, I *was* guilty of consuming alcohol. Ready for the charge to change from speed to wine, I braced myself.

"It came back negative. I guess you were telling the truth. I apologize for accusing you."

I'm not sure whether I felt more relief for the verdict, shock at the apology, or anger at what a waste all this had been. My progress had been reduced to an accusation, an acquittal, and a rise back up in the levels that was sure to take me months. The punishment held even though the crime did not.

VAGUE MEMORIES

*O*wnstairs my parents were cleaning up from a night of entertaining. Upstairs I was overdosing.

I was on medications—many medications—which I kept in my bathroom when home, responsible for my own psychopharmacological care even though I was a seventeen-year-old with a mental illness and a high rate of suicidal thoughts and gestures. The pills I ingested, morning and night, were supposed to help soften the neuronal firing—like that of machine gun, its bullets ricocheting wildly within me—by cushioning me internally through their action, in an effort to control the emotional cataclysm that resulted in behavioral upheavals, the internal becoming the external, my actions a window to my pain. On this night a war was on. With my feelings so vastly out of control, toleration inaccessible, the only solution to reign in my visceral terror was an overdose.

I lay on my bed beneath a shelf covered with stuffed animals, inanimate objects that had no feelings except those I projected on to them. My bed kept the theme of a teenager gripping on to her childhood, or a mother not wanting her baby to grow up, with yellow sheets donning images of cartoon characters lulling me to sleep at night and greeting me again in the morning. A bright-orange blanket rounded out the illusion of hope and joy. As I sat among these comforting objects and bright colors, I fondled two pill bottles, which sent a surge of excitement rushing up through my body. My mind raced with thoughts of the relief I would feel once I swallowed the pills, one by one, anticipating their effect taking hold. I imagined my limbs tingling as sleep slowly overtook me, emotional pain being washed away like dirty hands under warm soapy water. Once I had ingested a good portion of their contents, the bottles' near empty, I lay down on the bed and eagerly awaited the feeling of peace that death was sure to bring.

Time slowed. The flipping of the numbers on the digital clock that sat on my nightstand seemed to take hours instead of minutes. My mind began to focus suddenly and intently on the doubt that rapidly replaced the excitement. As was common with each suicide attempt I made, once the act was complete, the awareness would invade; I was just as terrified of death as I was of life, maybe even more so. Neatly compartmentalized within each individual episode, the fear never showed itself until after the act. It did not protect me from attempting to end my life by revealing the memory of these panicked thoughts, barring me from the action in the first place. Instead it waited until the impulse overtook me and I acted upon it, as though my emotions took up so much space within me that there was virtually no physical room within my being for rational thought. Once the pills had been ingested, a temporary quiet developed where there was once emotion. The quiet created the peace necessary for thought. This thought brought on panic. This panic pushed me to reach out for help.

"How can I direct your call?"

"Can I have the adolescent unit?"

"Hold on, please."

The silence as I waited for the adolescent unit to respond encouraged the quiet that allowed me to panic in the first place. Shame began grow like a tumor inside my chest. A pathetic sense of humiliation left me feeling vulnerable and hating my existence. *I'm such a fucking idiot* played over and over in my head, a mantra that fed the feelings I had been trying to extinguish in the first place. The mantra played like a tape until a voice came on the other end of the line.

"Hello, adolescent unit. This is Todd."

Relief. My favorite connection on the adolescent unit, my protector, nonjudgmental, understanding, compassionate.

"Todd?"

"Yes?"

"It's Lee."

"Hey. What's going on, Lee?"

"I did something stupid. I was just feeling kind of bad, you know, and I did something stupid."

"What did you do?"

"I overdosed."

There was that quiet again. I really could not seem to escape it, so I filled it.

"I'm fucking stupid."

"How long ago?"

"Maybe ten minutes. I don't know."

"What did you overdose on?"

"My meds."

"How much did you take?"

"I don't know—a lot, I guess. Who cares anyway?"

"OK, Lee. I need you to stay on the phone with me."

I felt his connection with me break away for a moment, replaced by murmuring, shuffling, hushed talking. I waited.

"Lee. I'm here. You need to stay on the phone with me and keep talking. Where are you?"

"On my bed."

"Can you stand up and walk around?"

"I don't want to."

"It'll keep you awake."

"I don't care."

"Can you tell me what was going on today?"

"I don't know."

Our conversation continued, not based on friendship, not based on mutual responsibility, but based on crisis intervention. Only Todd, right then and in the moment, had the ability to reach in through the phone, his voice soft and supportive, caring and reassuring, and hold on to me. The all-important connection. At the moment I had ingested the pills, I had no concrete link to myself, to my family, to any human who could understand and contain the emotional turbulence that spun me out of control. My initial response, immediate in its gratification, was my first defense in conquering the battle being fought inside me. Calling Todd, the connection, was my second line of defense. The order had to be as it was. Only my first response spurred thoughts for the second.

As Todd continued to talk with me, trying to keep me from slipping into unconsciousness, my parents milled about downstairs, cleaning up from their guests. The sounds of plates being cleared, water running, the soft murmurs of my parents' voices as they recounted the evening of friends, food, drink crept up the stairs and into my bedroom, where I lay dying, sort of. They had no knowledge of the crisis that was unfolding. They had no idea that their daughter had been riddled with internal bullets or that the police were about to ring their doorbell. I can only imagine the reaction that took hold of them when they did.

Heavy footsteps, softened by the carpeting that covered our floors, made their way up the stairs and toward my bedroom. Suddenly the door opened, and there stood my parents, accompanied by two of my city's finest. Todd's voice tugged my attention back to him.

"Is help there?"

Quiet.

"Lee, put them on the phone."

Quiet.

"Please, Lee. Put them on the phone."

Making no eye contact, I held the phone out.

"Here. He wants to talk to you."

They talked, one of the policemen and Todd, planning, warning, guiding, updating. When the officer was through, he hung up the phone. My connection with Todd had been terminated. I was left with my parents, whose presence ignited so much anger as my mother's pity seeped out of her wet, brown eyes, and two policemen, whose presence intimidated me as they were not likely to understand my intent, my pain, or my suffering. Supported on either side by two silent authorities, I made my way down the stairs. In a sloppy, slurring attempt at autonomy, I informed the police of my ability to walk.

"You don't have to hold me."

Silence.

"I said you don't have to hold me. I can walk."

My words were unconvincing as I staggered down the stairs, barely balancing despite the support. Quietly we made our way out of the brightly lit house into the dark of the night, where my chariot awaited. Trapped in the ambulance, I was a prisoner of my mother's pity, her hand on my face, her words grinding in my ears.

"Oh, baby. Why?"

The feeling against my skin was repulsive, provoking an intense anger that could not escape my highly drugged body, her pitiful touch speaking to me in ways that I did not want to hear. I could envision her brown eyes—soft and warm with fear and sadness, guilt and blame—boring into me like a laser burning through a metal sheath. I did not want her pity. I did not want her closeness. I did not want her.

In the [medical] hospital I was alone in a room with doctors and nurses whose only obligation was to save my life. My parents weren't allowed in, so I was free of the feelings they elicited. Except for the memory of my body, naked from the waist up with wires attaching me to monitors and bags providing life stats and saline, I have no other memory until they put me in a wheelchair, and sent me home.

Vague memories danced around in my head, followed by panic—memories of my legs being useless in supporting my weight, of being undressed by two women and put to bed, of being shed of my dignity in the process. I could not recall what I had done, what had taken my strength and reduced me to such a level of helplessness that I required aid for my basic needs. I tried to orient myself to the unfamiliar room. Light from the morning sun draped over me like a blanket, pouring in from the window next to the bed. The room was not mine. It was not familiar. I did not know where I was, how I got there, or who was there with me.

"Where am I? Is someone there? Where am I?"

A woman entered. She was dressed in plain clothes and had a soft voice. She walked through the room and stood next to the bed.

"Do you remember coming in last night?"

"Where am I?"

"You're in another institution. I want you to stay in bed for now. In a little while, I'll come back in and help you get up."

A black fog swirled in my head, replacing most of my memories of the night before. What I could recall was consuming most of my medications, talking to Todd, going to the hospital, and being sent home. I remembered being taken care of by the two women. I remembered being put in bed. I remembered I could not walk. I did *not* remember why.

As the soft-spoken, plainly dressed woman left the room, a man took her place. His dress was more formal—a suit and tie. He pulled up a chair and sat next to the bed, looking at me thoughtfully. The lull this man controlled was unnerving. I sat and waited until he spoke.

"I'm your doctor while you're here."

"I don't care."

"Why did you overdose a second time last night?"

"What?"

"Why did you overdose again after they sent you home from the [medical] hospital last night?"

"What're you talking about? I overdosed once. They took me to the [medical] hospital, and then they sent me home. I didn't overdose a second time."

"I would prefer not to play games."

"I don't know what you're talking about. What do you mean, a second time? I didn't overdose a second time."

The accusation this man was firing at me didn't sync with my perception of reality. A fury accompanied the confusion as I tried to grasp his impression of events. I had no idea to what he was referring, if he was trying to trick me, what games *he* was playing. Adding to the caldron of emotions was a feeling of disrespect. It was obvious this man did not believe me. He could not come to terms with the idea of amnesia. Manipulation and deception were more what he was looking for. I had no course of action and could respond only with defensiveness, so I did.

"I don't know what you're talking about! Leave me alone!"

In his stone-cold demeanor, with a cruel undertone, he responded.

"We'll talk later."

His abrupt absence brought on a sense of abandonment, feelings of rejection emerging from the strangest of places. I was alone in the room, uncared for, misunderstood, with no human contact to prevent my bombarding emotions from rupturing my internal core, my organs, my membranes, my being. There was no distraction for my pain, leaving me alone to piece together the accusations he had hurled at me. Either I had never made it home the night before, as I thought I had, or I had made it home only to respond to more impulsive suggestions from my masochistic core.

I lay in bed, frozen by paralysis, by weakness, by fear until the woman came back in, the soft-spoken, plainly dressed woman. She brought with her a sense of safety to a frightening series of events. She came up to my bed and spoke to me.

"I'm going to help you stand up. We're going to do this very slowly. If you feel dizzy or like you can't do it, tell me and we'll stop."

Being riddled with fear that I had caused some kind of permanent damage—a weakening of the connection from the motor portion of my brain to my legs—and would never walk again left me mute. I looked at her as my only acknowledgment of her plan.

"OK. Here we go."

With a gentle hand, I leaned on her for support and sat on the edge of the bed. My legs barely touching the floor, I used her as a crutch and stood. My paralysis was gone! My medically induced inability to hold my own weight had passed through my system, and I could walk. Relief washed over me.

"Are you all right to stand?"

"Yeah. I can do it. I'm OK."

"I'm going to let you get washed and dressed. I'll be right out in the nurses' office, which is directly across from your room. Call me if you need me."

Relief. Absolute, unadulterated relief—but only for me to see. I kept my cool, protecting whatever emotions were trying to rise to the surface. I still had little idea of who these people were and what had happened the night before.

"Yeah, all right."

Alone again, I got into a hot shower and washed my body and my hair, cleansing myself of the greasy disgust that coated my skin each and every morning. The steaming heat from the water caressed my scarred, wretched soul, the warmth brushing away the feelings of shame and isolation. I didn't know exactly where I was, but I did know I was incarcerated yet again, this time, however, in an old building that lacked the comfort, warmth, and familiarity The Hospital now held for me.

Soon I learned that this institution ran very differently than The Hospital. Whereas The Hospital encouraged communication in order to move up the levels as part of my treatment, this institution found that to be a foreign concept. One night, in an effort to do what I had been trained so well to do, I went up to one of the staff and asked if we could talk. A bewildered look washed over his face. Feeling trapped by social etiquette, he agreed, and to my relief, once I realized my gaffe, never followed through.

As time passed at this little unstructured institution I slowly began to build a connection with one of the staff members. He was young—twenty-eight years old—and cute, and he liked me. We would talk, not for therapeutic purposes but rather for the alleviation of loneliness, mine as well as his. Once I had proven myself a trustworthy patient and had been moved to the first floor, where strictly monitored doors were unlocked, at least during the day, and outdoor privileges granted, he took me on the grounds, where we sat under the cool shade of a large tree. The conversation quickly took a turn, crossing over the boundaries that were expected between staff and patient.

"I really like you, Lee."

"Really?"

"Yeah."

My anxiety rose as my respect for this man dropped. I saw him as a protector, a staff member in a psychiatric hospital entrusted with the care of others. His betrayal of the boundaries I so desperately wanted him to adhere to made me withdraw into an intellectual sanctuary that muffled any emotions that sought to find a crack through which to escape. I wanted to cower; I wanted to shiver; I wanted to run in fear. I wanted to feel safe, and he was taking that away.

"Well, what do you like? I mean, I'm in a boom boom retreat."

"Yeah, I know. That's OK."

"I have shit, issues."

"I know. So do I."

My curiosity was piqued, and I had to ask.

"What issues do you have?"

"I have a son."

"Really?"

To me he seemed an appropriate age to have a baby. When one is twenty-eight years old, daddy-hood isn't so uncommon.

"Yeah. I'm raising him alone."

"Oh. Sorry to hear that."

"He'd really like you."

"Why?"

"Because you're spirited."

Though not quite sure what he meant, I accepted it unquestionably.

"I hope you can meet him. We could hang out together when you're discharged."

The one thing I did enjoy when it came to children was holding babies—little babies not yet able to walk on their own, with round fat cheeks, and layers of fat rolls dominating their legs. I imagined this baby, holding him on my hip.

"How old is he?"

A pause.

"Fourteen."

Another pause.

"Fourteen? Wow. How old were you when he was born?"

Silly question, as the math was pretty easy, but as I was caught off guard, it spurred the conversation, staving off a lull.

"Fourteen."

I remember the grass, green and warm, softly cushioning our seat. Trees hovered over us, protecting us from the sun that draped down, casting its warmth. We sat and talked about his son. His son's mother.

How much he liked me. As he expressed his feelings for me, my heart took on my anxiety, racing quickly, as though to escape this man and his efforts. It raced, fast and furiously, until I followed it.

"I want to go inside now."

"OK."

He was gentle and honest, and he liked me. For reasons that I no longer remember but certainly can imagine—such as fearing a boundary violation and wanting to keep the roles of caretaker and person to be cared for separate—the feelings were not mutual.

I served my time at the institution, the small psychiatric facility that was old, locked, sad, and dark. I served my time, and then learned why I had been there in the first place.

ANSWERS

*B*ack at home, the transition, as with each time I left The Hospital, was difficult. Adjusting to the environment that made me feel different, the sense of belonging that one craves in her family replaced with a sense of alienation, was a transition that provoked my anger and threw me into behaviors that mirrored my pain. My family all had dark hair; mine was blond. My family members were all intellectuals; I hated to read. My family loved art; I loathed it. My family was all good. I was evil, the rebel, the outcast, in my home, in school, with friends, everywhere.

This feeling of not belonging spurred my anger and pushed me into tantrums with ease, sliding on a slick surface, plummeting into a dark and scary place, vibrating with emotions so negative that only a violent display could rid me of them. What angered me on this night is not important, and frankly I have no idea. It could have been a small misperception, a comment taken out of context, a look I interpreted as a strike against me, real or imagined, intended or unintended. Whatever it was, it made me angry. I lay in my bedroom, on the floor, on my side, eighteen years old, crying, screaming, purging my absolutely unmanageable fury.

"I hate you guys. I hate you. You're assholes, all of you."

Unendurable pain ricocheted, slapping me with its harshness, my neurons firing a bombardment of electrical activity. It took over hard, fast, furious; it twisted and turned, robbing my reason, my maturity, my reality. The anger swelled and spewed from my pores, from my mouth, from my feet, from my hands. I cried out over and over, my angry tirades pushing the words out of my belly and hurling them at anyone who could hear me.

"*I hate you!*"

The rage that spewed from my mouth coursed through my entire body, sending my legs into epileptic fits that destroyed my closet door, kicking it until it came off its hinges. With my parents downstairs cowering in fear, unwilling or unable to support their enraged daughter, I heaved myself off the floor and stood at the window, looking at the frightening world through the darkest of nights, and *slam!* My fist, in an impulse that lurched it forward out of my own control, slid through the glass, shattering it into as many pieces as my fragmented soul. Glass spraying, blood dripping, a soothing sense of relief washed over me. The impulsive action held my attention, containing me in its protective sheath, until a voice penetrated the lining and grabbed me.

"Talya, what happened?"

I did not attend long enough or closely enough or hard enough to make out who the voice belonged to, my mother or my father. I heard the words, and like a slap in the face, they pulled me back into the moment, a time and place I had to escape, so I ran. I ran out of my room, down the stairs, and out the door.

The brisk winter air hit me as soon as I stepped outside, waking me up with its snap of cold against my cheeks. The fresh, bright snow reflected light into the darkness that surrounded me. Without my coat my body felt the chill, heated only by my anger and fiery inner core. At first running, then walking as fatigue took over, head down, hands slid deep into my pants pockets, my shoulders pulled forward, my step hard with rage, I made my way to a Howard Johnson's restaurant several blocks from my home. I had no money, so I stood in the vestibule, where a concentration of hot air greeted each customer, boxed between two sets of doors.

My mother had a friend who had two children. On this night my mother's friend's son had come to visit. Miles was several years older than me and spoke with a soft, calm maturity that nature had endowed him with. Miles followed me on this night, one step behind me the whole time as I made my way, at first running then walking, to the Howard Johnson's. He entered the box, greeted by the waft of warmth, and smiled.

"Hi, Talya."

For a moment I connected with him, eye to eye, then dropped the connection to the floor with the heavy weight of shame.

"Let's get something warm to drink. You go clean off your hand in the bathroom, and I'll get us a seat."

My posture was protective, shielding my inner core, shielding my organs, shielding my pain. For a moment I lifted my shoulders close to my ears. Then, letting them drop again into their protective pose, I followed Miles into the restaurant.

The warm water that rushed over my freezing hands almost hurt as I stood alone in the pink-tiled bathroom, which was clean enough for being public. I held my hands under the flow as the water pouring over my wounds turned from red to pink to clear. When I came out, I joined Miles at the counter, where we sat on stools that pivoted from side to side but never took us full circle. We sat, both of us hunched over our hot chocolates. Each sip left a sweet taste on my tongue and a warmth in my body as it moved down my throat and soothed me.

Miles talked to me, and I have no doubt I responded, but I no longer have any memory of what we discussed. Yet where my mind lets go, my emotions hang on. With each syllable he spoke, there was a sense of calm and understanding, judgment-free connection. His words wrapped themselves around me like a soft blanket that provided security and warmth from the cold, calculating world. The emotional embrace he provided softened my anger, which burned inside me like a virus, parasitically taking up residence in my soul.

With the last sips of hot chocolate lying cold in the bottoms of our mugs, Miles paid. We slipped off the red stools, reentered the vestibule, and took in the blast of hot air to fuel our bodies before once again being greeted by the slap of winter cold.

When we arrived home, I dodged my parents by scurrying upstairs and slipping into bed, ready for sleep to take me away from the reality of my life.

The next day I met with Dr. Bennett, a man I feared. His power and control overtook my life, squelched my will, robbed me of my reason, and destroyed my reality. I settled back into the routine of appointments, medications, and threats of incarceration. Questions remained regarding what had happened the night I had called Todd, the night I had been brought to the dreary rundown institution that had held me for a month, getting me past the point of being committable then releasing me back into the well of destruction that was my existence. I met with Dr. Bennett and got answers.

"I hated that place."

"The Institution?"

"Yeah."

"What did you hate about it?"

"I just hated it."

Whenever I sat with Dr. Bennett, I had an air of defensiveness, a protective armor that shielded me from his analyzing gaze, which judged me and mocked me. He would poke and pry and pull, analyzing, quantifying, and amplifying all my obsessive ruminations.

"They said I did stuff I didn't do. They said I tried to kill myself twice."

"Do you remember doing that?"

"No."

"Do you remember anything from that night?"

"Maybe."

Cooperating with Dr. Bennett was a threatening experience for reasons that were out of my conscious grasp. Brief answers to big questions were my shortest road to safety.

"You don't remember what you did once you got home from the [medical] hospital the night you overdosed?"

"No."

"You overdosed again."

"No, I didn't."

Frustrated by my constant contradiction of whatever he laid out before me, Dr. Bennett rolled his eyes and shook his head and let a small burst of breath push through pursed lips.

"You did. Then you went to bed, and the next morning, your parents came to get you up. They told me you got out of your bed and were unable to support yourself at all. You crawled out of your room to your sister's room. You don't recall any of that?"

"No."

"Your father picked you up, and they brought you to me here at The Hospital."

"Why?"

"Frankly, at this point, they didn't know what else to do. They were feeling helpless. They brought you here to me, and I put you in my car with your mother."

A flash of an image brushed past my awareness like a slide in a projector.

"I was in the backseat with her, wasn't I?"

"That's right."

An auditory memory was next.

"And you told her to keep me awake."

"That's right."

"Why?"

"Why did I tell her to keep you awake?"

"Yeah."

"I believed you were in danger of going into cardiac arrest. If we had gotten you to the [medical] hospital any later, you may have. If you had lost consciousness, I would have had to step in to keep you alive."

"Why didn't they just call a fucking ambulance or something? Why would they have brought me to you? That's fucked up."

"I think your parents have reached a limit. There's a part of them that wants this to be over...that wants you dead."

"Fuck you!"

Though I portrayed myself as immune to such comments—my shell hard and steely to the inexperienced eye—in actuality I was endlessly yielding to a sensitivity that threw me into despair as fears of abandonment, rejection, alienation, and separation consumed me.

"Don't you think they've had enough? Isn't it time for some responsibility on your part? Maybe there was a part of *me* that also wanted you dead. I could have called an ambulance, but I chose not to."

"Fuck all of you then!"

"Your manipulations push people away. They get tired. They want to give up on you."

"So let them. I don't care. They probably always have wanted to give up on me. You probably always have wanted to give up on me."

The reality was that Dr. Bennett never really gave up on me...until the end.

A BUDDING YOUNG ADULT

The day came when I moved out of the adolescent period of my development, a chapter of my life closed tightly and sealed. I graduated from high school—the Alternative sSchool, the warehouse, the protective environment that held a group of mentally ill adolescents during their academic venture toward normalcy or death, whichever came first. Taking pity on those of us unsuccessful in life's normal routines, the school district allowed me to attend the graduation ceremony at the school I would have graduated from with my would-have-been-had-I-been-normal class. I didn't know what to expect from the ceremony, or if I even should be a part of it, but in those days, I grasped at normalcy wherever and whenever I could. To stand with my class, as awkward as my reasoning today recalls it, provided me with an opportunity to conform—a camouflage for my chaotic existence—hiding it under my cap and gown.

Graduation rehearsals, if they existed, were not offered to me. The day of the ceremony, I watched those around me, sitting when they sat, standing when they stood, smiling in response to theirs, and nodding to the inspirational speeches intended for those with a future. As names were called, including mine, we marched up to the stage to receive our diplomas one at a time. I studied each student who alphabetically came before me—greeting with their right hand, receiving with their left—and committed this to memory so my movements, gestures, actions would conform to those who had preceded me. Greeting with my right hand, receiving with my left. In my fervent attempt to receive the honor of graduation with my peers, I missed one important movement, the culminating end to the years for which I had been deprived. Each classmate, upon receiving a diploma and heading back to his or her seat, with a motion that was so smooth and unrehearsed that it bypassed my extreme scrutiny, moved the tassel on his or her cap from one side to the other. All the five hundred, six hundred, seven hundred students put their tassel to the other side, a sign of their success and accomplishment. I never knew until after I had made my way back up the aisle to my seat and the person to my left told me, just a little too late. Then, with a sudden gesture in a well-timed rush of excitement, a flock of caps were hurled into the air, with screams and whistles, delight emanating and shooting out from every direction. As my peers' caps rose into the air, a flush of shame rose in my body as my cap remained firmly on my head. The moment passed with a speed that afforded me little opportunity to do the same. I quietly removed my cap with as little noticeable motion as possible, keeping ripples in the air to a minimum, keeping the attention away from my ignorance, from my game, pretending to be normal, graduating with a class that was not truly mine, graduating with a class that I was not truly a part of, graduating with a class with which I had no sense of belonging. At least my family wasn't there to witness my shame.

After my graduation from high school, my mother and sister went through my family's usual summer routine: a trip to Europe. It was strongly suggested that I not leave the country, as if I were a criminal awaiting trial or arrest or persecution. Since the beginning of the seeping out of my illness into the world of those around me, at the age of sixteen, I was not permitted, either because of incarceration or fear of those in charge of my care, to travel abroad, thus disrupting the established system in which my family had been entrenched since before my birth. On this trip necessity prevailed. My parents were buying property abroad, so someone had to go. For reasons that became clear as the summer progressed, my father, whose love of Europe enveloped him and held him, offered to stay home with his daughter—his mentally ill, borderline daughter, with unpredictable and dangerous behaviors, always pivoting between the living and the living dead.

A budding young adult, I had no structure during that summer. My father felt safe in pursuing his interests, leaving me to attend to mine. His interests kept him out until three or four in the morning, while mine kept me in bed until the early afternoon. Awakening once again to an empty house, I would shower, brush my teeth, and have chocolate and beer for breakfast. I spent my days with Patty, my friend from the adolescent unit, in a steady decline toward self-destruction. Her house became our haven for whatever drugs we could get our hands on, the community pool our retreat to bask in our high. Patty's mom was divorced and heavy, so the culinary choice was the easy-to-come-by snack food relished by the average teen. My life during this summer was about indulgences, in food, in drink, in drugs. I was eliminating my emotional pain any way I knew how.

Patty's house was safe for me. It was a place where I could be sick in the company of someone who was sick like me. I loved her for her perverseness in understanding my perverseness. We fed off each other, gobbling up and devouring each other's insanity. One night, with little to do but wallow in our overwhelming and consuming feelings, I plotted an effective way to erase my anxiety. After rummaging through my overnight bag, I produced a stash of pills, medications that were intended to be healing, my psychotropics. I ingested them in a rushed desperation until the bottle was empty.

"Patty, I took the whole bottle."

"Oh, shit. Get out, you crazy bitch."

"I know. You know what, though? Life sucks, so I don't care."

"We should probably go to the [medical] hospital."

"I don't know."

"Maybe we should."

As with most of my suicide attempts, the desire to kill myself was not necessarily a desire to die. It was a desperate act to mirror my desperate emotions, delivering a dose of adrenaline and triggering a rush of excitement.

"OK. Who should drive?"

With a chuckle for the obvious, Patty responded.

"How about me?"

There was an ease between us, an understanding of the behavior, of the craziness, of the need for relief.

Once we arrived at the emergency room and approached the desk, Patty told the woman that her friend had overdosed. The smell of antiseptic, the bright fluorescent lights, the rapid movement of people with places to go and lives to save began to overwhelm me. This was another attempt in a repetition of so many failed attempts at bringing on the numbing unconsciousness that I secretly wanted to last only until I awoke. Death was a desire but not a lasting one. It was my answer in the moment to combat the brutal tyranny of my emotions. I looked at the woman, her head down, her pencil ready to fill out a form, as the question, "What's your name?" began to form on her lips. I turned my attention from authority to coconspirator.

"Patty, I'm outta here."

"What?"

"Run, 'cause they'll make me stay."

In a giddy display of adolescent mayhem, we bolted for the door and made our clean escape. I don't remember succumbing to the effects of the overdose, so perhaps the bottle was not so full after all.

DEPRESSION

Theresa and I had our legs tucked up under us as we sat chatting on her living-room couch, a beam of sunlight reaching us from a large window by the front door. The colors her parents had chosen to decorate with were creamy and soft, adding to the atmosphere a warmth that I found inviting, a sharp contrast to my internal experience. I watched the clock that stood in her dining room, easily visible in the small interior of the duplex where she lived. Still heavily ensconced in outpatient treatment, I had an appointment that day with Dr. Bennett.

For many people depression is an experience felt within the body, heavily weighing on the individual. A dulling of the will causes the individual to shut down as desire fades and darkness encases. Depression for me was loneliness, sheer and utter loneliness. The impact the people around me had on me during my bouts of depression was dramatic. They could push me in; they could pull me out; they could turn me around, spin me, topple me, trample me, crush me. The power of people—the power I released into their hands so they could toy with my emotions—drove a wedge between them and me. A sharp-pointed wedge of anger severed any feelings of well-being within me, toward them, about my life, or pertaining to my sanity.

My friends treated me in a way that I perceived as cruel and hateful; my friends treated me in a way that I perceived as caring and affectionate—a split perception in my mind that I could not integrate. If one day my perceptions were paranoid in ideation, as I accused them of talking about me behind my back, which perhaps they were, or excluding me from an activity, which perhaps they were, or annoyed by my presence, which perhaps they were, it would spiral me into a lonely depression of a magnitude difficult for me to control. On this day I was depressed, which spurred another incarceration. My life was reduced to a dependency on the psychiatric treatment that kept me safe, secure, structured.

"You need to come back to The Hospital."

"I don't want to."

I shook my head…no, no, no.

"I don't want to come back."

"You need to. You're feeling very depressed, and that's not safe for you."

I shook my head…no, no, no.

"I don't care. I don't want to."

As I sat in Dr. Bennett's office, on the couch, with the fireplace to the right, and he at his desk directly across from me, leaning back in his chair with one leg elegantly draped over the other, I could see in his expression that frustration was beginning to brew. This was a common expression that Dr. Bennett wore when dealing with me. My stubbornness was my friend. My stubbornness was his enemy. It fueled his anger, year after year, as he tried to dodge, confront, and remedy my stubbornness. A mocking tone frequently accompanied his anger.

Mocking: "I don't care." Mocking: "I don't want to go."

Dr. Bennett paused, his eyes fixed on me, though not really looking at me. He was formulating the question I'd expected him to ask.

"Are you cutting?"

"I don't know."

Hit again by frustration, he once again took the tone that filled me with rage. Mocking: "I don't know."

The room quieted, his gaze fixed on me once again, as he planned out a course of action. Finally the silence was replaced with his plan.

"Why don't you go downstairs and get yourself a candy bar while I get things ready for your admission?"

I knew that cutting was a committable offense and that if I were found guilty, the choice would not be mine. I think that's what I wanted. I think I wanted that protection, that security, that structure I would not get at home but would get in The Hospital. I think that's what I wanted—to know I was cared about and would not be abandoned, no matter how repulsive my actions were, no matter how hard I pushed in my dance of approach and avoidance.

"I won't go today. If you let me go home, I'll come back tomorrow. I can't go today."

Whether it was out of defeat or a master plan to ensure my cooperation, Dr. Bennett agreed.

"OK. We'll admit you tomorrow. Go home. Pack up some things. Be back here tomorrow morning at nine."

Dr. Bennett threw a look at me, one I did not dodge. It was a look of trust.

At nine the next morning, my mother brought me for what had become a routine for us: admissions. Once the papers were signed and it was time to head to the unit, the admitting doctor let me go with my mother, in our family car. He spoke as if his words would prevent me from fleeing.

"I'll meet you on the unit."

My mother nodded in agreement, and she and I headed to the car. Despite years of institutional living, I was able to obtain my driver's license at sixteen years old, before my first admission. With this privilege I informed my mother of my intent.

"I'll drive, Mom."

Sitting behind the wheel, I headed in the direction of the unit. With a sense of humor that always sought attention, I swerved the car toward the driveway, toward freedom. This maneuver did not go unnoticed by the watchful eye of the admitting doctor.

No longer an adolescent, I was now on the adult unit in the young adult program. Though the intensity was not quite as extreme, as I'd been fully immersed in institutional life for more than two years at this point, the unit was new to me so I was scared. The patients were new to me. The staff was new to me. The rules were new to me. To help me feel at ease, Todd had come over from the adolescent unit to talk with me. I asked him a question, hoping he would understand.

"Can't I be on the adolescent unit?"

"If you were on the adolescent unit and had turned eighteen, you would stay there. But coming in already at eighteen, you have to be on this unit. I know it's scary, but you'll adjust."

Adjust. Such a small word with such a big meaning. Once I adjusted to a unit—first the adolescent, now the adult—I would adjust to the point of suffocating, gripping dependency. I would come to rely on the people, the staff, to protect me, nurture me, and define me. This reliance was the definition of my existence, of my character, of my being. Having people in caretaking positions of authority, accessible around the clock, meant I was never alone. My identity, so fragile, was determined by their presence. Like a glass shattered into thousands of pieces, helplessly lying scattered, then pulled together and secured by tape, wrapped around and around and around, protecting and binding, the shattered and fragmented elements of my being, so unattainable to my consciousness, were kept protected and bound by the staff. The two facets of myself—the one that wanted to be normal and the one that wanted to be sick—fought for the foremost place in my life. The needs for dependency and security—the needs that kept me sick—overpowered any movement toward normalcy and recovery. The terror that went along with progress, the abandonment that was sure to follow from these important people who created my internal existence, was overwhelming and all consuming. For years to come, I would remain sick. I would remain within the web of incarceration, treatment, illness, self-injury, suicidal gestures—immersed, drowning, drowning, drowning.

I looked around. The colors on the unit were the same. The table at the nurses' station, maybe five feet by ten feet, was the same big orange table they had on the adolescent unit. The wall-to-wall industrial carpeting was the same. The walls were white, as they were on the other unit. The bedrooms were set up in an identical fashion, two to a room with soft lamps on the nightstands that sat next to each bed. Another soft lamp sat on the desk. Two dressers, one for each of us, as well as two closets and a private bathroom, made up each room—identical to the other unit. The atmosphere on the unit was the same. Sick people, dealing with for the most part severe mental illnesses without accompanying psychosis, roamed freely around the unit. I think I knew, deep down where it was safe for me to let my desires fester—my dreadful, sick desires—that I would eventually acquire the same security and dependency on the adult unit that I had over my two-year period of incarceration on the adolescent unit. And so it went.

I began on this unit as I had begun on the adolescent unit. My beginning on the adolescent unit had been elopement precautions, The Hospital's odd term for runaway precautions. My beginning on the adult unit was elopement precautions, The Hospital's odd term for runaway precautions.

In time my bonds developed, strong and hard, to the staff that suited my personality, my wants, my needs. Steve and Ryan.

STRIP SEARCH

*M*ornings were difficult, as dreams of my past played like unwanted movies. I woke up still holding the emotions from all that was being remembered. Standing in my bathroom, wrapped in a plush white towel and smelling of fresh soap and floral shampoo, I rubbed my hand along the towel, sending a chill down my back. I wiped away the steam that had developed on the mirror and became lost in my image. My hand was remembering something my mind was not. I stood, deep in thought, searching.

The bedspread had a similar affect as I rubbed my palm across its surface, the ribbing irritating my nerve endings. I sat on my bed in the restricted locked unit, punished for some infraction, a response to whatever emotional storm had been stirred up on that day. Two staff members entered my room and spat out their command. Once the words hit my ears, they were weighted with such shame that the desire for a catatonic state to save me was wished for but never received.

"We're going to strip-search you."

Though being stripped to my core, literally and emotionally, was not uncommon, it never ceased to fill me with a shame that left an indescribable mark on my soul.

"Why?"

"We need to make sure you're not cutting."

The plea.

"I'm not. Who said I was? You don't have to search me."

"We do have to. Are you going to cooperate?"

Aware that any control I had in this was an illusion, I made my attempt at taking a stand just the same.

"No. Get out of my room."

Like well-coordinated soldiers, the two women turned on their heels and left. My jaw touching the floor, I stood amid a paradox of emotions: relief and abandonment, confusion and serenity, anger and calm. I sat paralyzed on my bed as thoughts of my body being stripped down, alongside thoughts that they did not care, played over and over like a surrealistic nightmare. Both baffled and relieved by their exit, I sat very still, waiting for the moment to pass.

Within minutes the voices I heard outside my door made their entrance. The two female staff were now accompanied by two male staff, their intimidation far greater than any threat the women could possibly hold.

"Lee, here are your choices. You can go into the bathroom with them and cooperate with what they're asking…"

He looked toward his comrade to ensure the power in numbers was not being missed.

"…or *we* can take you into the bathroom and undress you."

My inner core shrunk, recoiling in horror. The power these two men held over me at that moment felt suffocating. The hands of that power gripped me tightly, restricting my breath like a blow to the gut.

"No. Don't" were the only words I could summon as a plea for redemption.

They stood, all four of them, in their position of power, projecting intimidation, eliciting resignation and cooperation. The thought of being stripped down to my naked core by two men was a rape of my spirit. The women would produce only a severe sense of shame—something, when comparing the evils, I would be better equipped to tolerate.

"Fine."

I stood slowly from my bed, my arms crossed over my chest in an effort to protect my dignity for as long as possible. My footsteps toward the bathroom were labored and heavy. The sun shone through the large window, sending heat radiating across my back, a caress, as if to say, "Good luck." I entered the chamber of torture. The two men stood guard, sentries outside the bathroom. The only element of control I had left was rage-laden cooperation, an agreement for them to humiliate me.

"Do whatever the fuck you want! I don't care!"

Once we had crossed the threshold, the bathroom door was closed behind the two female staff members and me. The bright lights on, I couldn't avoid my image in the mirror. I didn't see me but rather a tortured, brutalized girl standing in a room that no longer was my refuge for taking hot showers, getting high undetected, or inflicting self-injury. In this moment the bathroom became my enemy. It was betraying me, allowing a torment of my body and soul that would not be soon forgotten.

"OK, Lee. Take off your clothes."

"Fuck."

"Take off your clothes."

"Everything?"

"Yes."

"Can I leave my bra and underwear on? Please?"

"You need to take off *everything*, bra and underwear too."

"I can't believe this. I can't believe you're doing this to me."

"We're doing this because of your cutting. You're doing this to yourself. If you keep testing our limits, we'll keep doing strip searches."

The explanation missed the motivation behind the behavior and the intense need to manage dysregulated emotions that threatened to conquer and annihilate me. Self-injury was my tool to survive my tormented mind, a way to live with the unmanageable. The crime for which I was being punished was my ill attempt at self-preservation.

Slowly I began to remove my protection, one piece of clothing at a time. Shame swept through me like a wildfire, jumping the gaps I laid out to stop it, like holding my breath, or moving into my head to distract myself, or resting my eyes heavily on the floor, avoiding any contact with the two women. As I was hopeless in my efforts to contain it, the fire spread and overtook me. It was only the knowledge of the sentries on guard outside the door that allowed me any sense of containment, as the alternative would have meant inner death.

"OK, Lee, good. Now put your arms out and turn around."

I complied, not breathing, not looking, not present. I felt their eyes run up and down, searching for clues as to recent self-injury. I felt the soft, vulgar caresses from their scrutiny.

"Turn around and face us now."

The unimaginable.

"OK, Lee. You can get dressed."

Without words I grabbed up my clothing and covered my ravaged self-esteem. The two women opened the door, and we exited, greeted by the two male staff. With a smile that I wanted to wipe off his face with my fist, one of them spoke.

"Any cuts?"

"No, she's good."

The irony was that before this episode, I had been relatively contained. To reach that same state I was in before they had started, I needed assistance. In the bathroom, once again my refuge, I reached into my pocket and produced the sharp metal tab from a Lipton iced tea can, something we had ready access to in the Main House vending machines. It took only a moment to release the pressure.

As I sat in the little lounge of the locked unit, there was another girl back there with me on this day. She was angry—always angry, angry with the staff, angry with her peers, angry with herself—and on this day, she was angry with me. Minding my own business, easily sucked into the mindless television show that hummed in the background—a "privilege" during the day offered to those of us locked up with little else to do—I puffed away on my cigarette and disconnected myself from the present. My interaction was neither with her nor with the staff member who was on duty for his two-hour shift, monitoring us incorrigibles. The sun that had caressed me in my room, as I made my way into the bathroom, followed me to the lounge and crept in through the window. It didn't reach me in the chair where I was sitting, but it was there in the room with me just the same, calling attention to dust particles as they danced in its rays. The angry girl, for reasons I never knew, confronted me with words I do not recall. When I stood to defend myself, she hurled her fist into my gut, and then she turned away. In an instant, with no thought to guide me or inhibit me, I flung myself at her and forced my fist into her back, as though I were stabbing her with a blade, deep and penetrating. A shriek, shrill and loud, escaped her as she whirled around in disbelief. Stunned, obviously not accustomed to retaliation, she stood there and eyed me. I stood there and eyed her. For that moment we were alone in the room. The staff member, usually attentive to the needs and behaviors of the patients on the unit, sat seemingly unaware. The angry girl got what she deserved. The staff member knew it. I knew it. She knew it. And so went our day.

SOAP OPERA

*F*reedom, at least in the mind of a person who had come to regard institutional life as normal, only included expectations consistent with the sheltered environment that had become home: at this time, being freed from the locked unit. Back with the general patient population, I slipped into Nancy's bedroom, carrying a hook rug I had been constructing of a dog. Mindless entertainment when we had free time, it kept my hands busy and my mind distracted. Sitting on her bed, Nancy greeted me with a broad smile and a tone of excitement.

"Lee!"

"Nancy!"

"Hey, baby. Come in. Hook rugging?"

I laughed.

"Yeah, hook rugging."

"Come, baby. Sit."

Nancy's warmth elicited a sense of security, safety and acceptance, true love from my true friend, swaddling me in understanding and empathy. I could be myself, and she could be herself, fulfilling a need of total security. I loved Nancy, and I shared with Nancy. Enticing her curiosity, wetting her palate, I spoke.

"Guess what I have."

"What?"

"Something special. Guess."

"Uh, let me see…a bag of potato chips?"

"No."

"Uh, let me see…a bag of Chips Ahoy?"

"Nooooo."

"Uh, let me see…How about you tell me?"

When Nancy chuckled it was real. It came from deep down and pushed through her like a bubbly burst of joy. Her laughter danced around me and beckoned me to reveal my surprise. I dug deep into my pocket, my cheeks tight with excitement and anticipation, both for what I had and for with whom I got to share it. Digging around, I pulled out and produced my surprise.

"Look. What do you think?"

Her eyes widened, and her smile stretched.

"Oh, yeah. Nice."

"You wanna do it now?"

"Yeah."

Brushing away any dust that lay intrusively on the desk in Nancy's room, I prepared my workstation. Nancy ripped a piece of paper and rolled it into a straw. The preparation almost more exciting than the event, I opened the bag and spilled out the white powdery substance that would tickle my nose and elevate my mood, my self-esteem, my sense of self-worth. Talking over each other, barely perceptible as to whose words were whose, we were in a frenzied excitement.

"Oh, my God. I love this. Me too. You wanna go first? No, babe, you brought it—you go. OK, I can't believe we have this! I'm so psyched! This is so cool."

The chatter continued as I laid out the lines of meth I had acquired while on a pass. Silence came only when we inhaled our excitement through the well-rolled paper straw Nancy so skillfully had made.

The delightful anticipation of the effects of the drugs was exhilarating. We sat on Nancy's bed and waited happily, my hook rug taking on even more importance, as everything now seemed to have a positive purpose.

"I love you, babe."

"Me too. You know what I want to do now?"

"What?"

"I shared my speed. Now you share some love."

Nancy seemed to know her preferences. My sense of self was so broken by ravines of lost time that a clear notion of what I wanted was as fragmented and broken as my spirit. My desires became a question that I needed someone else to answer. With this important person standing before me, I was able to borrow something she appeared to securely embrace: her sexuality.

"Come on. Let's go into the bathroom.

Nancy smiled.

"OK, let's go into the bathroom."

Talking rapidly as the effects of the drug began to infuse us, carried readily through our bloodstream and into our brains, we rushed into the bathroom with meth-induced excitement. Nancy flipped the light switch as I jumped up and sat on the counter, my back to the mirror. The bright institutional lighting reflected on Nancy. A big breath allowed me to suck in the attention that was directed only for me. I felt the warmth and softness of Nancy's hands as she cradled my face. The cold atmosphere of the bathroom, its off-white counter, white walls, and white towels were replaced with a warmth provided by security and connection. She held my face, our actions mimicked in the mirror.

When it was time to go to dinner, Nancy and I headed up to the Main House, where the dining room was. I was now allowed off the unit accompanied by staff. Tables of four or six were scattered in a random yet thought-out pattern across the dining room. Nancy and I chose a table for four. We ordered our dinner so as not to cause suspicion from the watchful eyes of our keepers, but still enjoying the delightful effects of the meth I had procured and shared, we played with it instead of eating it, replacing opening our mouths to receive nourishment with the contradictory motion of clenching our jaws and of course chatting endlessly.

Unit life in the evening consisted of television in the lounge, music, with several record choices, in the rec room, downtime in your bedroom to read or just have time to yourself, or the mandatory nightly contact with staff to talk about your feelings, your trauma, your addictions, your relationships, your cutting, your behavior, or anything else that crossed your mind as being relevant to your treatment. On this night I chose to hang out in my room, alone, feeling the withdrawal from my euphoria.

The only light I had on was on my nightstand as I settled into the warm, soft atmosphere of my institutional bedroom. I sat on the floor, listening to The Kinks' *Soap Opera*, an obscure tape by a popular group singing about the mundane life of the average person, working from nine to five. Each word and its accompanying notes hammered me deeper into despair. It wasn't different than the everyday pain I experienced, but the drug that had brought me up so high was now dropping me so low, too low, hard and fast, falling, pain washing over me, saturating me with hurt. It dropped me lower than my everyday pain, equal in torment yet more profound in its intensity. A beastly sense of hideousness overcame me, and I knew I had to hide away to protect others, and myself, from the reality of my existence. My escape lasted hour after hour, as I sat listening to my music, until my door swung open.

"Lee?"

It was Steve Bayer.

"Lee?"

Carefully concealed on the floor between my bed and the wall, I did not answer.

"Lee?"

He entered the room, walked past the closets and bathroom and around the corner, and was confronted by my monstrous appearance as I tried in desperation to sequester myself, to conceal the ugliness that oozed from my pores.

"There you are. You need to come out of your room."

"No."

"You've been in here all evening, and we need you out on the unit. Come on."

"No. I'm not going out there. I wanna be alone."

"That's not a choice. Come on."

"Leave me the fuck alone!"

The softness of his voice cracked ever so slightly with irritation.

"That's not a choice. Come on."

"No!"

Steve walked over to me, gently, slowly, with the same staunch patience he always had. His demeanor now back in check—soft, even, reliable, predictable—made me feel a sense of safety that was so comforting every time I saw him. My dependency on him, like an addiction, pulled me through my days. When he was with me, my feelings became encased within the protective sheath his presence provided, an emotional container. My fragility so palpable, I felt as if his leaving would cause me to crumble, taking with him my definition and my security. He walked to me, leaned over, and took my arm, gently helping me rise to my feet, and together, with just enough resistance on my part to communicate my disapproval, we walked out of my room.

The contrast of the soft, dim lighting in my room to the brighter overhead lighting of the hallway was an insult to my eyes. My body supported by the wall, my head dropped, and there I froze. My sanctuary was locked, and I was forced to mingle with the natives. Panic washed over me at the dysmorphic thoughts of my ugliness out on the unit, exposed for all to see.

What was left of the evening I spent in the lounge, sitting on one of the big comfortable chairs. I sat with the protection of my legs keeping the world at bay, pulled up tightly, arms embracing them, with just enough space for me to peer over my knees. Anyone who passed me I attacked with my glare, firing ammunition of intimidation, the words *"Leave me alone!"* finding their mark. As the evening came to an end, two female staff members approached me, just as they had one week earlier while I sat on my bed during my confinement on the locked unit. Their approach was goal oriented, with intent and determination in their unified step.

"We need you to come with us."

"Why?"

"We need to do a strip search."

Though the answer was as obvious as their presence, a feigned ignorance was my only source for stalling.

"Why?"

"We need to see if you've been cutting."

My mind drifted back, panicked at the discovery that was sure to happen, to a week earlier when coping with the mortification of the search for self-injury was aided by...self-injury. Days after its occurrence, as thoughts of the humiliation continued to swirl in my head, several more private encounters with glass and flesh had been necessary, allowing me to progress up a level and off the unit. But now I was about to get caught. I brainstormed for a solution, an escape. I had betrayed myself in an attempt to regulate an emotional flame ignited by the degrading actions brought about by the treatment team assigned to keep me safe, aid in my recovery, facilitate my care, and resurrect my emotional stability.

"I haven't been cutting."

"Can you come on your own, or do we need to get some help?"

And so the story went.

During the days that I had been out of the locked unit, as I'd progressed in my behavior, I had cut to protect myself, I had cut to contain myself, I had cut to validate myself, I had cut, and now I was about to get caught. I was trapped in my own mind between panic and excitement. My one extreme—to be perceived as all good, healthy, normal, average—had me desperate for an escape. Anticipating the response once my cutting was discovered, fearing the loss of privilege and the judgment, sent anxious ripples running down my spine. My other extreme—dependent, sick, special within my illness, cared for, and controlled—wanted to get caught and nurtured. My progress since leaving the locked unit had been rapid, and the expectation of pleasure and pride gave way to panic and rejection. Progress held a deeper meaning that was not always consistent with its definition. Fears of abandonment from the community I so greatly needed—the community that fed my dependency, fed my illness, and kept the rupture inside me from ripping apart altogether—was too great.

"Lee, you've been cutting."

"So?"

"You need to stop this manipulation."

"I'm not manipulating."

A word that was tossed around like a football in a field, *manipulation*, was thrown my way with great frequency. The accusation of manipulation was often hurled at me, the definition of the word not. I had no idea what *manipulation* meant. What I did understand was that I was in intense emotional pain and had no idea how to make it stop, except for cutting (and drugs and acting out and shoplifting...). And it worked.

As I sat at the nurses' station awaiting the staff conference regarding what to do with me next, Steve and Ryan approached me. "We have to search your room" was the next obvious and predictable step: Search the body; search the room. Take my dignity. Take my privacy. As instructed, I followed them into my bedroom. The bathroom light remained on, a memory of what had taken place about fifteen minutes before. Helplessly awaiting the discovery of my stash, I sat down on the end of my bed and watched, powerless to stop them. A search of my room brought about feelings that swam through my body like sharks feeding on prey—anger at the violation of my privacy, anxiety over the repercussions for what they would inevitably find, helplessness and powerlessness over their authority and their control over my life.

After asking me to move, they searched under my mattress, in my pillow, their hands rummaging through my sheets. Steve and Ryan opened my drawers, pulling out clothes, neatly and respectfully, and putting them back in, moving papers and books, searching the bathroom and closet. They searched dutifully and diligently. Kept neatly hidden under a pile of sweaters were several pieces of shattered glass. With a mocking smile, proud of the find, holding it up like a prized trophy, Steve spoke.

"Lee, we found what we were looking for. Where did you get this?"

I responded with a shrug.

"Where?"

I shrugged.

"You're testing my limits. I need to know where you got this."

Testing the limits. This phrase also was thrown out with great frequency, a go-to for frustrated staff members unable to view things from the perspective of the emotionally distraught victim of illness and institutionalization. What was manipulation or testing in their eyes was survival in mine. I did not manipulate; I did not test. I navigated. I navigated through shark-infested waters on the darkest of nights in the smallest of boats, ready to capsize. Fearing the rise in tension coming from Steve and Ryan, I responded.

"Outside."

Satisfied with my response and not requiring further elaboration, Steve barked out his next command.

"OK, let's go."

"I wanna stay in my room."

"That's not a choice."

The power he held in those words pushed an intense anger through me that was quick as lightning.

"I don't fucking care. I wanna stay in my room!"

Steve and Ryan stood patiently as I vented my anger. They knew they had the control, the power in their hands, and with appropriate timing, they could alter the situation. I could yell, fight, threaten, struggle, resist, rebel, rebuff, refuse, but in the end, when the time was right, they would prevail. That time was now.

"Get away! Get the fuck away!"

Slowly the distance dividing them and me lessened. The air between us compressed, anxiety suffocating me.

"Get away! Get away! Leave me alone! Get away from me!"

My trips to seclusion were plentiful. My nights restrained to a bed were plentiful. The Hospital based its approach to treatment on behavioral techniques, the use of aversion to extinguish the unwanted. Oddly the technique appeared to have a reverse effect on my highly reactive system.

As with most of my experiences in seclusion, I was left alone, locked in to dwell on my pain and feelings of abandonment that always seemed to accompany me to this isolating room. The very fears The Hospital's environment was intended to help us learn to cope with were triggered regularly by the treatment that had been put in place for us to understand the fears in the first place. On every other occasion, once I endured the evening and the night, I was released in the morning and allowed back on the unit. Though I do not know, nor will I ever know, what happened behind the scenes as psychiatrist and staff talked and planned the next course of my treatment, I do know that this occasion was different.

As morning came and went, I found myself still encaged in the brutally isolating room. When human contact finally was made, my expectations for freedom were shattered. The only thing they took out of the room was the bed frame. Though unrestrained, I was left alone again with only a mattress, a pillow, sheets, and a blanket. The day passed slowly. I slept. I woke up. I slept. I woke up. No distractions, no entertainment, only my thoughts and pain, an archaic form of torture. As I was ill equipped, due to the emptiness of the room and the emptiness of my soul, self-soothing came only through drastic means. My head was throbbing with thoughts that could not be quieted. The hard stucco wall was the perfect recipient for my frustration. As I punched my fist against the wall, over and over and over, the physical pain became an acceptable replacement for the emotional anguish. Physical pain was real—concrete and tangible.

Eventually the sound, echoing through the halls of The Hospital, met the ears of staff, split in their understanding of my motivations. Some were concerned, as their ability to experience my perspective perhaps was not so threatening, while others were angered by my behavior, as their own feelings of competency came into question due to their inability to redirect my behavior. Suddenly the door opened, and four staff members charged in, carrying the bed frame they had carried out hours before, and their controlling devices, leather restraints.

As I lay there alone again, tethered, the fluorescent light mocked me. Though not obvious during the day, once night fell, the light screamed out with a shrillness that disturbed my senses. For more than twenty-four hours, I had been made to endure the bright light of isolation.

Battling boredom and rising anxiety, I set a goal of freeing myself of the leather binding, taking back the control they had stripped from me. This was a frequent goal and one I usually achieved with moderate success. As I lay there, I began to work my hand methodically, repetitively, side to side, twisting and turning, slowly and with great patience, all the time squeezing my fingers together and bringing my thumb across my palm. Methodically, repetitively, side to side, twisting and turning, slowly and with great patience, my hand slipped out of the restraint, offering some mobility and accompanying comfort. Now the other side.

As I began to work my left hand free, the jingle of keys and the clicking of the lock stopped me from achieving my goal. Steve entered the room, bringing me a sense of security. His presence, human contact, became a container for the endless feelings of loneliness, boredom, and anxiety. My thoughts had left my freed hand, now hiding beneath the blanket, as I focused on Steve.

"Hey, Lee. How're you doing?"

With a shrug I communicated my disapproval of my predicament. I was pulled by the desire for him to stay, to relieve the loneliness that came with seclusion, and the desire for him to leave, so I could continue to free myself and achieve the physical comfort I had been working toward. Slowly Steve approached the side of the bed and smiling, as though he had caught the cat that had caught the mouse, he spoke.

"I'm going to check and make sure the restraints aren't too tight."

After making his way around the bed, he lifted the blanket and fit two fingers in the restraint on the side of me that actually was bound, satisfying his obligation to ensure my circulation wasn't being constricted. My heart began to beat heavily, the fear of being caught dictating my emotions. As I had no choice but to lie helplessly, he eventually lifted the blanket on the other side, exposing my free hand. There was no doubt in my mind that Steve knew exactly what he was doing and what he was going to find as checking for tightness was something that had never been done before. Saving that side for last, forcing me into the anxiety of anticipation, he was teaching me a lesson. Stating the obvious, Steve spoke.

"You got yourself out."

"So? Leave me alone. Please."

"I can't do that."

"Yes, you can. You can do whatever you want. I'm not comfortable."

"You don't have a choice."

Making me aware of my lack of choices was the disempowering maneuver of a powerless staff, powerless in their lack of understanding of motivating factors in pathological human behavior.

"Can't you just leave this one hand out? It's more comfortable. I'm not doing anything."

"That's the problem: You're not doing anything. You're not doing what you need to do to stay out of restraints and out of seclusion."

My pleas for freedom from the claustrophobic binding were in vain, but perhaps a request for darkness so sleep could push through the discomfort might be heard.

"Steve, can you turn off the light?"

"No."

"Why? It's hard to sleep. I need it dark."

"No. If I turn it off, we'll have to flip it back on every fifteen minutes when we check on you. That'll disturb your sleep more than if we leave it on and give you the chance to adjust to it."

"I'd still rather have it off. It's too bright."

"We're going to leave it on."

The decision was finalized by an irrational bid for control.

To sleep or not to sleep: That was the only choice at that point that no one could take away from me, except my own exhaustion. I fought it until the weight of fatigue devoured me.

I woke to the sun shining in, beating down on me, as the bed stood directly in front of the big window that took up a good portion of the wall, forcing me awake to face yet another day of pain. But it also brought the hope of release from restraints and seclusion and boredom. I didn't have to wait long before a staff member came in to make the first contact of the day, with fifteen-minute checks standard practice.

"Good morning, Lee."

"Are you gonna take these off?"

I gestured to the restraints with my head and moved my arms as much as I could just to be sure there was no miscommunication.

"No. Not yet."

A lightning bolt of confusion ripped through my brain, and my heart sunk like a concrete block hurled into the river.

"*What?* Why not? I haven't done anything! I've been sleeping!"

"It hasn't been decided yet. For now you have to stay as you are."

Pleading over and over, "I haven't done anything!" was met only with sympathetic eyes and the repetitive comment "It hasn't been decided yet."

As the messenger of bad news left the room, locking the door behind him, with the wretched sound of metal to metal as the bolt slid into place, I realized I was being punished. No longer was the physical constraint put in place to keep me safe, as it had been twelve hours earlier, but rather as a psychological deterrent for unwanted behavior, past or future. A warning. A threat.

I was once again left in the chamber of horrors, tethered and immobile for the better part of the day, until I had a visitor.

"Lee, we're going to take you out of the restraints for now. Your mother is here to see you."

Not the visitor I necessarily wanted, as I lay helpless in the room that screamed, *You're out of control!* but still, the visit brought me my temporary release from immobilization as well as a store-bought coffee cake. I assume, to protect my mother from the barbarity of institutional life, and the institution from accusations of cruel and unusual punishment, I was brought out of seclusion to have my visit. We sat around the table at the nurses' station. As we talked, and I pushed through half a pack of my Marlboro Reds, Steve approached my mother and asked to speak with her privately. When my mother returned, she looked pale and shaken, her hazel eyes oozing with pity and fear.

Once the visit ended, I was returned to seclusion, along with my coffee cake, and suspected that my mother had been shown the empty bed, restraints dangling from each corner. Intimidation most likely was used to manipulate her into the belief that incarceration was the only secure means to ensure the safety of her daughter.

Alone in the room, I sat on the floor with the store-bought coffee cake in front of me. I lived my life in extremes, with an impulsive need for immediate gratification. My only choices were to eat none of it or all of it, so I opened the box and devoured my pain.

Once my binge was over, feeling disgust regarding my lack of control and a dysmorphic sense of obesity, I pushed myself off the floor and sat on the edge of the bed. My wallowing in self-loathing was suddenly interrupted by Dr. Bennett's presence. Dragging behind him was one of the plastic chairs found around the unit. He placed it next to the bed and sat down.

"OK, Lee. This is how we're going to do it. You can stay out of restraints as long as you're doing something."

"What do you mean 'doing something'? Why do I have to be doing something? I just want to be out."

"That's not the option I'm giving you. You can be out of them as long as you're engaged. You can draw or read or whatever, but you have to be doing something. You can't just be sitting in here."

"I don't want it that way. I just wanna be out. I've been out for a couple of hours, and I haven't done anything. Why can't I just stay out? I don't get it."

"Well, since that's not a choice…"

Not a choice.

"…what are you going to do?"

"I'm not doing anything!"

"Then you're going back in restraints."

The power struggle between Dr. Bennett and me would inevitably end in his favor. As I argued my point, staff came in as though telepathically messaged. The restraints were still on the bed from before. They knew my release had been a temporary reprieve for my mother's visit.

"*Get the fuck off me!*"

In the end, but for the short reprieve, I spent three afternoons, evenings, and nights bound in the mouth of the demon.

LAST CHANCE

*M*y eyes flew open. I had been yanked from my sleep and thrown mercilessly into my past. I gripped the present, terrified of plunging off the cliff. Focusing on sounds in my bedroom to keep myself grounded, I listened to my sleeping husband's breathing, slow and steady, a disturbing irritation passing through me. So powerful was the pull, my grip finally weakened, that I slid into memories of my institutional past, where I'd spent the better part of my late adolescence and early young adulthood caught in the revolving door of psychiatric inpatient care: in for a year, out, in for three months, out, in for a month, out, in for six months, out, in for eight months, out, in for a year. How many more times in between, I do not recall. As I relived the vivid memories, my mind drifted to the reminders I am left with today, the scars from self-injury that riddle my body. A sudden burst of tears, unexpected, pushed through me, and I sobbed, moisture cascading down my cheeks, as quietly as I could until sleep once again greeted me with its releasing powers.

The escape of sleep lasted only until the brutal awakening by my alarm clock. Lurking in the first minutes of wakefulness was a feeling of desperate dread coming from the depths of my soul, so far out of reach that words could not define it or explain it. I tried to remind myself that a hot shower was usually effective in erasing the intensity of my morning emotional greeting. I awoke trapped in one emotion, unable to remember that I had ever felt any other way.

I pried myself out of bed and staggered into the bathroom. Standing in the flood of warmth as the water washed away the morning dread I thought about that day's mission, to get in touch with another important person from my incarcerated past. It had become an obsession of sorts, to reconnect with as many people as I could remember from that period in my life, an obsession fueled by disconnection, loneliness, and an insatiable need to remember as much as I could.

I was determined to find out what had happened during my blackout—the night I had been sitting on the table at the nurses' station one minute and lying on the floor being bound the next, the night that staff from all the units had been called in to assist, the night that I had been tethered to the bed in the most restricted fashion in all my time institutionalized. Ethan Maloney was the person I hoped would have answers. He was the staff member I had spent time with that evening. He was the one who sensed the severity of my situation, the one who took charge and made the decisions. I needed to find Ethan Maloney.

Again I embarked on an Internet journey, this time into Ethan's world. I typed in his name, and instantly he came up. Not only did his name come up but also his picture. I sat at my computer and gazed at the image of this man—important during a horrifying episode that had taken place during a horrifying period—who was now thirty years older. I gazed at his picture, and I saw him, the Ethan Maloney I knew before, the Ethan Maloney of my youth, the Ethan Maloney who was there that night and could tell me what had happened, filling in blanks that left me questioning.

He was living in a different part of the country. He had moved and become important in research, publishing books on his findings. After a little more searching, I found his contact information. Heart racing, pounding as though desperate for release, my stomach knotted so tightly I could barely breathe, I pushed in the numbers provided. Relief and disappointment rushed through me as a voice mail invited me to leave a message.

The next day I had the opportunity once again to talk with someone I hoped held memories that I did not. He greeted me with an unexpected warmth. Pleased and confused, I took his kindness as my opportunity to ask my questions.

"Ethan, do you remember that night when you and I were sitting in my room talking? I must have been depressed or something because I threw my cigarettes at you, and you handed them back to me. That wasn't typical for you because you used to rip them in half when I did that."

He remained silent but attentive with the occasional "hmm" or "uh-huh" when I paused but obviously was not done.

"When we were done talking, you asked me to go out to the nurses' station. Meg sat with me, and you went into the office with the rest of the staff who were on that night. Meg asked me a question: "Why are you breathing so hard?" The next thing I remember, I was on the floor, being wrestled by adolescent-unit staff and adult-unit staff. Once I was in seclusion, you guys shot me twice—Thorazine—and tied me to the bed like I was a rabid animal. It was different from the other times. Do you remember?"

"I'm sorry, Talya. I don't remember that night specifically" was enough to drop my heart like a bolder off the edge of a cliff.

"We put you in restraints a lot and kept you at the nurses' station a lot. It was our way of keeping you safe."

Disappointment covered me like a blanket, wet with foul marsh water. I was powerless in a sea of lost memories with a desperate desire to remember, to know.

"Yeah, that makes sense. I was just hoping you would remember that night in particular because it had such an impact on me that I think about it a lot. It wakes me up at night, haunting me, you know."

"I wish I could remember. I wish I could help you out, but I don't. I'm sorry."

He paused, waiting for me to respond or searching his mind one last time, and when I did not speak, sadness stealing my words, he continued.

"Is there anything else you want to talk about? Can I help you out with anything else?"

I did not want to end the call. I wanted to keep this piece of my past on the phone as long as I could, but I felt an unsettled awkwardness while talking with Ethan. It was thirty years later, and I had nothing more to say.

"No, Ethan. I guess not. It was just such a weird time—traumatic, you know. I'm just trying to make sense of it."

"I can understand that."

"Well, thanks for taking my call. I appreciate it very much."

"You're welcome, Talya."

And there we said our good-byes.

With the end of the call came an end of an opportunity. With the end of the opportunity came the will, strong and overpowering, to go back to The Hospital, to walk the grounds, the place where I had lived for most of my late adolescence and early young adulthood. My "home."

"HOME"

As I sat with Meredith, the lights turned down to a soft glow, I told her of my next plan to step back in time, not through flashbacks, dreams, or calling people from my old treatment team, but this time through a more hands-on approach to regulating the flood of emotions that were drowning me as I ruminated on my past.

"Meredith, I have to go back."

"Go back?"

"Yeah. I have to go back to The Hospital. I have to walk around the grounds, see the place, feel it, you know?"

My decision to visit The Hospital came from a place deep inside, a drive to reshape, understand, and in essence, relive my past. I needed to feel what I felt then, see again now what I saw then.

I sat quietly in the chair after saying my piece and distracted myself from any eye contact with Meredith, knowing she would not approve. With spring upon us, the weather warmer, I no longer wore my scarf for protection and distraction, so I nervously spun my wedding ring and its accompanying engagement ring around and around. Meredith hadn't approved of my contacting Todd and Ethan, of my launching myself into my past and digging up roots laid deeply and securely in the dirt. I anticipated her response before she even began to speak.

"Talya, I don't think it's such a good idea. I don't think you should be going back there. It has the potential of being very triggering, and there's no telling what might happen. If you become overwhelmed, and someone sees it, they'll have to respond."

"Respond? What do you think they'll do? What do you think *I'm* going to do?"

Meredith answered first with a shrug then with her words.

"I don't know."

I knew what I needed to do and had nothing much more to say. My silence was long enough to pressure Meredith to speak.

"Why don't I go with you? We'll drive out, and that way if it becomes difficult for you to handle, I'll be there."

I looked at Meredith but only for a moment, dropping my gaze quickly. I was relieved to think of her coming with me to that terrifying period of my life, journeying back in time as a companion to my pain. Yet a sense of shame, of obligation for the kindness she was exhibiting toward me became just as powerful as the relief.

"You would do that?"

I was overwhelmed by her kindness, but the desire to push her away and a conflicting need for her presence competed for my attention. I fluctuated from the internal chaos and the external connection. I continued.

"I don't know. It makes me feel bad, your having to go out of your way for me. I don't know if I can handle that."

"I offered because I wanted to. I'm OK with it, or I wouldn't have."

Again my eyes dropped to my rings, reminders of the love that awaited me at home. A smile quickly took over my face, expressing both warmth for her concern and nervousness at the thought. I was still split in confusion between conflicting emotions.

"OK, Meredith. Thanks. Are you sure?"

"Yes. We could meet, and I could drive us out."

"I'd rather drive."

Knowing my tendency for assertive driving, Meredith quickly responded.

"I think it would be better if I drove."

We made plans, and though I felt dependent and helpless at the thought of Meredith coming with me, driving me, caring for me as though I were unable to handle the job myself, I also felt a sense of reassurance and security. She knew the dark anguish that took up residence in my memories, the ghosts of my past that haunted my present. Her gesture showed me she cared, or so I thought.

It was the night before I was to go on my expedition, and I had not heard from Meredith. Wrestling with anxiety, I waited for her to contact me as a sign that her offer was sincere. As the evening passed, I became consumed with the thought that she may have been deceiving me. Was she offering to go with me hoping I wouldn't make the gesture to remind her? I scrolled through my phone contacts and stopped at her name, Meredith Barner. My heart raced because, though she had given me her cell-phone number, I always felt as though I were stepping into her personal life, into her home, whenever I called it.

"Hello?"

"Hi, Meredith. It's Talya."

"Hi, Talya. I was just about to call you."

"Oh, OK. Well, what do we do about tomorrow?"

There was a pause, long enough to send the message that Meredith was having second thoughts, reservations, and regrets about the commitment she had blurted out to me during our session several days before. The pause finally broken, Meredith spoke.

"Well, my brother's in town. He got here yesterday, and I'm not going to be able to come with you."

The second lull was heavier in content, weighed down with meaning and difficult to break through. The nervousness that had accompanied me during the making of the phone call was now quickly pushed aside by rage. I searched for words but found none. Meredith continued.

"He needs me to do some things with him tomorrow. Maybe we can go to The Hospital some other day, or you can go alone and call me if you need me."

Finding a way around the dense wall of anger, I responded to Meredith, offering her cold undertones to match her unemotional delivery and lack of responsibility.

"Right, Meredith. Some other time. Enjoy your brother."

As I hung up the phone, a surge of anger, hurt, and confusion erupted in my chest. Thoughts raced through my head as I tried to make sense of and defend against the unexpected yet anticipated betrayal. *I didn't really want her to come anyway...The thought of her coming made me feel vulnerable, like a child...When was she going to tell me?...Her brother came yesterday?... Didn't she know yesterday?...Was she really ever going to call me, or was she going to stand me up?...Is her brother really even in town?...Did she make something up because she made an offer she really didn't want to make?...Why is she doing this?...It was her suggestion...I never would have asked her to come with me...It was her idea...She knows how hard rejection is for me...She knows this, and she did it anyway.*

I sat listlessly on my bed, fearing movement would disrupt the emotions that were brewing inside me. I held it at bay for as long as I could, and then it broke through. Tears made up of a concoction of anger, hurt, and rejection streamed down my face, my thoughts racing as my emotions tried desperately to keep up. The next day, Saturday, I planned to go to The Hospital. Alone.

Morning came too quickly. I showered, ruminating over what lay ahead of me. After putting on comfortable clothes, feeling safe and warm, I got into my car, leaving my husband with our three children, and drove out to a place where I had been admitted and committed, terrified and alone, to serve out a psychiatric sentence. I was terrified. I was determined. I had to relive and remember.

It was cool out, early spring, but the sun was shining, covering me with warmth as it filtered through the windshield of my car. I drove the distance from my house to The Hospital listening to a CD that would remind me of this day as time passed on. As the music lulled me into a numb state of distraction, lost in thought, I suddenly realized I had made a wrong turn. I turned around and went back, only to turn yet again, around and around, until I spotted a police car idling in a small parking lot. Pulling my car close but facing the opposite direction, so our driver's-side windows were face-to-face, I spoke.

"Excuse me. Can you tell me how to get to The Hospital?"

As I asked I made a distinct effort to maintain a composed demeanor, lest he look inside me and know where I had come from and why I was going where I was going.

"Yeah. You're on the right road. Just keep going straight. You'll get to a traffic light, and The Hospital will be on the corner. You'll see the sign."

"Thank you."

It was ten a.m. when I saw the entry, just as I had remembered it from decades before. Nothing had changed. Static. The long driveway was lined on either side with tall, thick trees barren of leaves, the spring buds yet to emerge. Sucked in as if by a vacuum, I was pulled relentlessly into the foreboding realm of anguished memories of adolescence and events that had taken place right where I was sitting now. I stopped my car and set it in park.

Arriving at school on a clear sunny morning, temperatures warming as the sun beat down on the acres of grass and blacktop driveways that made up the grounds of the state hospital that hosted my school,

I walked into the building, down the stairs, and straight for the bathroom. I closed the door and reached into my pocket, excitedly pulling out three blue Valiums, ten milligrams each. I turned on the faucet, popped them into my mouth, cupped my hands under the stream of yellowish water that ran from the old spigot, and drank, swallowing my prize to take away my anguish.

As I sat with my class of ten or twelve emotionally hopeless students, the drug slowly started to take its desired effect. A warm feeling spread softly inside me, welcoming and peaceful, caressing my soul. Suddenly freed from the weight of painful feelings, a brilliant idea took hold: I was going to bolt. I sat patiently, relishing the excitement of the drug and the anticipation, until half the class was instructed to go to the other room for history. As part of the group going next door to learn about our country's past, I walked with the others as we passed the stairs that led to the outside and made my escape.

As I walked to the main entrance, toward the iron gates, as beautiful as they were ominous, I wondered whether my teachers had noticed that one of their students was missing. Heading across the street and into the neighborhood that surrounded the state hospital, I reveled in the excitement that always nestled inside me whenever I tried to run from my captors. Whether I was running from The Hospital (incarceration) or from my school (warehousing), there was always an excitement, a thrill so deep it made my heart palpitate—intense feelings I could tolerate. Off the grounds I felt a sense of accomplishment, something I rarely experienced by more conventional means. This sense of accomplishment was juxtaposed with a sense of fear and abandonment. As irrational as the thoughts may have been, they came to me readily and with great passion: *Did they not notice I was gone? Did they notice when I was there? Do they care?* As I walked aimlessly, pushing through my combating feelings, I noticed a state hospital security vehicle make its way toward me. I walked into a small parking lot and scurried behind a building to hide myself. The bright white of the cement, with the sun reflecting warm and hard, made me squint to protect my eyes from the burning rays. The effects of the drugs taking away my reasoning, I walked out on the other side of my hiding place, thinking that whoever was in the car approaching and searching for me would think I had disappeared in a warped universe behind the building. Then suddenly I found myself face-to-face with one of my teachers and a security guard.

"Lee, come on. It's time to go back to school."

They approached me slowly, as one would do with a stray dog that may either attack or flee.

"I'm not going back to school. I'm going home."

My speech and reason were compromised by the influence of drugs. With my eyelids heavy, my reflexes slowed, it took little for my teacher and the security guard to size up their prey.

"Lee, it's time to go back to school. Come on. Let's go."

Finding humor in their ridiculous request, I laughed and again responded.

"I'm not going back to school. I'm going home."

Both arms seized, I succumbed readily, as the tranquilizers softened my resistance. Guided into the backseat of the security vehicle, I sat imprisoned behind doors that did not open from the inside. As the car made its way back, I looked out the window, seeing the trees move past, the little house that had been made into a restaurant, mostly patronized by hospital staff, the brick wall that bordered either side of the entry to the grounds with the iron gates. I sat defeated.

"OK, Lee. Here we are. Let's go."

In front of building X, I leaned against the door of the car to heave my drugged body out, letting my teacher hold me for support and listening to her talk in a soft tone.

"We're going to sit in the office and wait for your mother. She's on her way."

With an instant strike to the gut, a piercing scream filled my brain: *The Bitch! My Mother!* Nothing infuriated me more than my mother seeing me vulnerable and sick. This was *my* life, *my* illness, *my* nightmare—Mine!

I did not want her to be a part of it! Anger coursed through me, fast and furious, rushing and hot, spinning and swirling, over and over, around and around, as anxiety built, trying to push its way up fast and hard... until I slowly slid my hand into my pocket and found more Valiums, the blue precious drug, small and irresistible, and ingested them. As small as they were, I didn't need water. I ingested them quickly, quietly, privately.

"Why did you call my mother? I don't want her here!"

"She needs to come, Lee."

"I'm out of here."

Again I made my way for the door, ready for another escape. As I moved I anxiously anticipated the effects of the second dose of Valium, which had brought my consumption up to an impressive fifty milligrams for my small frame. I waited for deliverance from the hell of my emotions, which yet again had spiked to intolerable levels. As I staggered toward the stairs, a hand rested on my shoulder.

"Stop."

Pulling away, I was unable to shake the hand and the repeated word coming from its owner.

"Stop."

I dropped to the concrete stairs, sitting in a puddle of powerlessness. Over and over I hit my head against the cold, light-green, glazed ceramic tiles that lined the walls, attempting to rid my mind of the high emotions that mixed and swirled together. In a moment of compassion, the teacher sitting with me put her hand between my head and the wall. My mother, arriving like an apparition out of nowhere, was now sitting on the step next to my teacher. Her presence molested my mind and filled it with fury. Every organ within me constricted and pulsated, until slowly the effects of the second dose of drugs consumed me more and more, embracing me in calmness.

"It's OK, Lee. You need to stop."

And so I did.

"Your mother and I are going to take you to The Hospital now."

I spat pleas of resistance, the usual "What? I don't want to go! Please, please, no, no, no, no, no, I don't want to go!" and received the usual response, "You need to be there. It's not a choice."

It's not a choice.

My listless body shuffled along between my teacher and my mother. I plopped into the backseat and was instantly imprisoned as we made our journey back to The Hospital in my teacher's two-door coupe.

Admissions was expecting me. I sat. I waited. I escaped.

I made my way down the long driveway that led to the street and freedom. It stretched its reach from the Main House to the boundaries of The Hospital, lined by trees barren of leaves, lacking life, the spring buds yet to emerge. I made my way, walking on the border of tarred pavement and manicured lawn, weighed down by the benzodiazepines that were still affecting my reason and reflexes. As I walked, the sound of an engine came slowly from behind, growing louder with its approach. The pickup truck slowed as it neared, then stopped by my side. Sarge, one of the head nurses from the adolescent unit—the nickname suiting her demeanor—climbed out. The pickup that delivered her to my side belonged to one of the landscapers whose duty it was to keep the grounds as pristine as those of a country club. It was a small pickup, with two doors and only a front seat for its passengers. Slowly, so as not to trigger my urge to flee, Sarge approached me.

"Lee, it's time to go back."

Her few words were accompanied by action as she took me by the arm and gently led me into the truck, trapping me between the landscaper and herself, preventing further opportunity for escape. To avoid more physical confrontations with this woman, whose presence threatened to push a deafening rage into the quiet calm induced by my Valium and whose intimidating demeanor was not lost on me, I cooperated.

My escape offered me the first-class privilege of dodging the admissions process and going directly to the adolescent unit behind locked doors, where the welcoming words from the staff revealed their intent.

"We're going to put you in seclusion. You can come out in the morning."

"Why?" was my shocked retort.

"You're high. You can sleep it off in seclusion and come out in the morning."

As I sat in the same driveway where Sarge and the landscaper had foiled my escape, a thought, thirty years old, passed through my mind, crystal clear, clinging to me still today: *What a drag. I have to spend my high in seclusion.*

With a deep breath, I reoriented myself, shaking the memories off as a dog shakes water off its wet fur, then put my car in gear and drove up to the parking lot. As my car idled in a parking space, my tears flowed while I listened to the music on the CD player.

Trapped in a moment where I could not quite grasp if it was the here and now or the there and then, I sat frozen in time and place. Once I was able to release myself from the captivity of my mind, I opened my car door and was met with the cool, crisp, early-spring air. The smell of suburban springtime was familiar as I climbed out of my car, placing my feet on the grounds for the first time in twenty-five years—grounds where I had walked with friends, run from staff, and lived within my pain, terrified of illness, terrified of recovery.

I got out of my car as though stepping on hallowed ground—sacred ground—my feet glued to the pavement. Standing frozen, I looked ahead, eyes fixed on the building in front of me. The red door bellowed at me, a visual reminder of an outstanding memory, the entrance to each building as red now as they were then. I fixated on the red door until suddenly, unexpectedly, pulling me out of my trance, it opened, and out came a group of patients with a staff member to have their cigarette break. How times have changed. I remembered smoking *on* the unit, both the adult unit *and* the adolescent unit.

I watched them quietly for a moment then walked away, ready to remember. I made my way to the front of the Main House, unnoticed by the employees and patients of The Hospital. Standing several feet back so I could take it all in, I gazed at the facade. Memories and feelings began to flood me, so strong they felt as though they belonged to my world today. The feeling of the sun on my skin, the smell of early spring, the sounds of birds and wind—they all belonged to the past, only visiting my present with intoxicating power. I scanned the facade and was able to identify the window where Dr. Bennett's office used to be. Behind that window lay memories, some of which I can grasp, most of which are hidden deep in my mind and out of reach. I stared at the window and felt the eeriness of a supernatural experience: the ghosts of the past, sitting in the office, experiencing life as it was, unaware that time had passed. As the feeling rushed through me, I turned away, the only thing I could do to shake it.

Time was suspended, hours passing outside of my awareness, as I walked every inch of the grounds. Approaching the adolescent unit, I noticed the red door stood open, luring me in. I scanned my surroundings. With no one in sight, I slipped into the waiting room. Instantly, like running into a brick wall, I was confronted by the smell of institutional cleaning supplies, so familiar, hitting the olfactory region of my brain like a locomotive engine going full speed. It shot fast to the emotional center, as memories ripped through me: strip searches in the bathroom, seclusion, restraints, incarceration, powerlessness, fear, anguish.

With all the courage I could summon, fearing being caught trespassing, I stole my way through the waiting room to the inside door of the unit and peered in through the window. The change was small. The carpeting had been removed, leaving the unit with a cold, impersonal feel rather than the warm, homey atmosphere from my youth, and the large table, maybe five feet by ten feet, gone. Overtaken by emotions, I leaned against the wall and slowly slid to the floor. Squatting, covering my face with my hands, I smelled the air circling in my nostrils. The olfactory memory was powerful, reminding me clearly and distinctly where I was and where I had been. I don't know how much time elapsed, but eventually I stood up and left. Walking down the path, away from the unit, I turned around for another look, another blast of memories.

I expected to see the images in my mind unfold before me. I expected to see myself, sixteen years old, being guided onto the unit, Bruce linking his fingers through mine, walking with me side by side up the path I was now free to leave. I wanted what I expected, but it did not happen. Finally, with all my might, I pulled myself away and left the adolescent unit again.

As I walked from unit to unit, across the grounds, through the Main House, remembering and feeling, overwhelmed with emotion, unable to break free, time passed. Suddenly it was one p.m. Panicked by the time, I broke free from the dazed bubble that had surrounded me for the past three hours, suspending me between the past and the present. I looked around. The grass was shimmering in the sun. The smell of springtime reminded me that warm weather was on the horizon. It gave me hope, hope that I had been losing sight of as I'd walked the grounds of the institution that once had been my home. I knew I needed to leave. I got into my car, put my key into the ignition, and started the engine. Songs that I'd listened to on the way over that morning now linked the past with the present, the present with the past.

I sat again, paralyzed, consumed by the music, and wept. Weeping turned to sobbing. I beat the steering wheel as the pain pushed through my fists.

"Why?"

I sobbed.

"Why did this happen?"

I sobbed.

"Why did I end up here?"

I sobbed. Calling out to no one. Calling out to my past.

"Why was this my fucking life? I don't get it. Why? Why? Oh, my God. Why? I didn't wanna be here! I didn't wanna stay. I told Bennett. I fucking told him! I would've been OK. I knew it. Why?"

The ringing of my cell phone suddenly distracted me from my relentless grief. Seeing my husband's name on the screen, I answered.

"Talya?"

Hysterical sobbing.

"Talya."

"I can't leave. I can't. I can't. I can't. I can't leave. I don't wanna leave. I'm stuck here. I can't get out. I'm stuck!"

"I can help you. I can talk to you."

My husband. My love, my life, my friend talked to me as I drove away, leaving The Hospital behind but taking all the memories and torment with me. They followed me home like a group of ducklings imprinted on my brain.

PHOTOGRAPHS

*M*y daily mission was to search the Internet for any staff whose names I could recall. I was able to find quite a few people, some who would meet with me readily and some who would avoid me at all costs, a split between the good and the evil. The joy I felt for those who understood the need to connect with a traumatic past kept me searching. The deep, personal hurt that was triggered by those who did not eroded my confidence, making me doubt my right to encroach upon their lives. During this period, I vacillated between joy and disappointment, as some of those I reached out to met with me readily, while others refused, dodging my calls or making excuses. After visiting The Hospital, I became consumed by the idea of finding the most important person from those dark days. His influence, his memory, for better or worse, devoured my waking hours. I became fixated on the idea of finding Dr. Bennett.

Though my trust in Meredith had begun to shift dramatically, I continued to confide in her. I had told her I was going to begin to search for my former psychiatrist and, once again against her advice, I sat at my computer and typed in "Leslie Bennett, MD." My eyes fixed firmly on his name in the search box. Anticipation sent a tingling sensation through my limbs. Dr. Bennett, the man on whom I'd focused much of my anger, at night, in my bed, tears rushing down my face as memories pushed their way up. Dr. Bennett. Thoughts raced in my mind. I knew he was no longer a young man, already in his forties when I was sixteen. Could he be dead? I entered what I knew of him, and holding my breath, in a motion that almost seemed to belong to someone else, I clicked the "enter" button.

Pulled from the inner recesses of my mind, Dr. Bennett stood before me. To me, in the transference, he had been a father—an authoritarian, controlling father to be feared, yet the consistency with which he had been available was ongoing and continual, wanted or not.

As I aged out of the adolescent unit, those with whom I had formed bonds were lost. The new unit required that new bonds be formed and fostered, and eventually lost as well. When I wasn't living behind institutional walls, but at home, spending my days attending the structured two-room high school on the grounds of the state hospital, there were yet again new connections, school connections. Who was in my life was changing, and at times unpredictable, except for Dr. Bennett. He followed me. He was there, always and everywhere on both units, adolescent or adult, unending and predictable. When I was not incarcerated, Dr. Bennett, yet again, was there, seeing me, treating me, talking with me, medicating me, exerting his terrifying power over me, mocking me, and threatening me. A consistent element in my inconsistent life, Dr. Bennett was there, predictable in his unpredictability. His importance in my life—in my mind—was huge. I loved him. I hated him. He was the doctor who had changed the course of my life.

On the first day I had met Dr. Bennett—sitting in paralyzed horror with my hands, tightly fisted, pulled up inside my coat sleeves, cocooned for safety—I made a plea on deaf ears: "Let me go home." I believe I would have been different. I believe I wouldn't have spent so many precious years in an institution. I believe I would have survived.

I was driven by anger and longing, competing energies that fueled my search for Dr. Bennett and the opportunity to search his mind for answers. As these thoughts swam inside me, I wondered about him. With a deep breath, I contained myself and remembered where I was, what

I was doing, my mission. Redirecting what I was seeing from inside my head to the screen in front of me, I looked to see what I had found.

And there it was, on the screen staring back at me—Dr. Leslie Bennett, MD. He was a brilliant man, doing something that set him apart, creating a niche, making him easily found. Alone in my home, my children in school, my husband at work, I was free to immerse myself in the experience of being flooded with my past. With flutters in my chest, I clicked on the link, my face flushed as the heat of anticipation rose. When I clicked a website came up. My eyes fixed to the screen, absorbing all that was written. I searched for a phone number. Moving down on the page, I saw it.

"Oh, my God."

The tears flowed from my shock. I put my face in my hands, as if to protect myself from what lay before me on the screen, something too unbearable to face. Before me were two photographs, one of Dr. Bennett, as alive and real as in my imagination, and the other of Steve Bayer. Side by side with my psychiatrist—my incarcerator, my demon, my obsession—was Steve, one of my favorite staff members from the adult unit.

Steve was an easygoing guy, laidback, nonjudgmental, and aware. He seemed to care, genuinely, for those of us incarcerated. Even when I was at my worst, which was most of the time, I never saw his temper. He never belittled me, mocked me, or ridiculed me. He was among a handful of helpers from those terrifying years who had made me feel safe.

Their pictures stared back at me as if they knew I was there. It unnerved me and ungrounded me. My body shook, as tears tore down my cheeks, until I was able to rip myself away from the computer. The shock, now purged from my body, left me both refreshed and drained. Developing in its place was a dilemma: *How do I contact Dr. Bennett?* First I spent some time trying to find out what else he was up to.

To settle the overwhelming fear that he would reject me, I looked for a back door through his professional activities. I happened upon a website for a local university where he was going to be lecturing in a couple of months. I found my safety line: If he would not return my call, I would go to this seminar and surprise the illustrious Dr. Bennett. With this ammunition in hand, I made the call.

As though I were preparing for the most important role of my life, I rehearsed over and over what I was going to say to whoever answered the phone. Then, accompanied by the same palpitations to which I had become accustomed, I dialed the number. A woman answered, his secretary I presumed. She sounded suspicious of me. Whether it was projection or reality, it was disquieting. She took my name and number. Now I had to wait.

Three days had passed. I was at home with my kids, who were muddling through their homework, when a sudden ringing disturbed whatever serenity after-school work brings. I answered. The voice on the other end of the line had an instantaneous impact on me. I hung on to my equilibrium with white knuckles.

"Is this Talya?"

"Yes."

"This is Dr. Bennett. I saw that you called me. I was very surprised."

As he spoke I was aware of a halting quality to his speech. I questioned him.

"Do you remember me?"

"Yes, I do now. At first I was a bit confused. I thought you were your sister, but this is Lee, isn't it?"

A chill quickly ran from my neck down my spine. With everyone else I spoke to from my past, I used the name they would recognize, Lee. When I had called Dr. Bennett, I had failed to do so. A Freudian slip? A test? Hearing him use my nickname ushered in a chilling sense of familiarity. I took the phone and sequestered myself in another room, squatting on the floor, hunkering down for privacy.

"Yes, this is Lee, but I don't use that name anymore. I go by 'Talya' now. It's weird to hear people use that name. So you were confused? You thought I was my sister?"

"Yes. I remembered that she had an unusual name, and I thought she was calling to tell me something."

I did not pursue where his imagination had taken him. I was sure he thought she was calling to report my death.

"Well, no, it's me. I just needed to get in touch with you. I know this is weird, out of the blue and all, but I've been having this need to touch base with some of the people from The Hospital. I'm still kind of traumatized by my time there. It haunts me at night. I wake up a lot in the middle of the night, thinking about it, and then I cry until I fall back to sleep, so I thought it was time to confront it, you know?"

He responded with his phone diagnosis.

"It sounds like you're experiencing PTSD."

I could not debate his assessment.

"Yeah, I suppose."

The point of the call was to meet with him, to be in the same room as this man who had held such power, to master the emotions elicited by my relationship with Dr. Bennett. Together, he and I would take a journey in the time machine of our minds. I needed to see him, but I was terrified to ask. What if he said no? What if he rejected me, my request, my need, my desire, so deep that it was embedded in my core? Ruminating on this possibility, I spat out the words before I changed my mind.

"I need to see you."

NANCY

Each time I made the call, the phone rang and rang until the answering machine came on—"You have reached..."—and left me feeling disappointed. The hope that had carried me in my quest for connections—my quest to quench the loneliness from my past—was squelched. I didn't want to leave a message for fear that switching the hands of power would leave me waiting indefinitely. I didn't even know if she was the right one.

Sitting snuggly in my car, watching my daughters become skilled equestrians from a safe distance, I was lulled by the hum of the engine. Though idling is not good for the environment, I kept the motor running for the heat that protected me from the early-morning cold and for the radio that distracted me from my thoughts. I watched my daughters, and with a clenched stomach, I reached for my phone. Anticipating disappointment I dialed the number and listened to the ringing, waiting for the inevitable "You have reached..."

"Hello?"

A voice, a human voice. Jolted, I spoke.

"Hi. I'm trying to find someone I knew from my past. I know this seems weird, but I'm looking for a Nancy Chapin."

"Nancy? Yeah, there's a Nancy who lives here."

"Wow, OK. Can you tell me around how old she is? It would help me know if it's the right Nancy. I knew her when we were around nineteen or twenty."

"Well, I don't know. I guess she's around forty something. I'm just her roommate. What do want again?"

"I'm looking for a Nancy I knew a long time ago. I know this seems weird, but I don't know any other way of doing it. Is she there?"

"Well, what's your name?"

"Now my name is Talya Lewis, but then she would have known as me as Lee."

"Lee?"

"Yeah."

"Oh, my God, Lee? Lee? Oh, my God, it's me, Lee. I can't believe it! Lee?"

Instantly confused with whom I was speaking, I sat stunned. I was unaware that the phone had changed hands and that I was speaking with someone else now.

"Nancy, is that you?"

"Lee, yeah, it's me. Oh, my God. What're doing? I can't believe you called me."

"Nancy? I can't believe it. Is it you? Is it really you? Oh, my God, I can't believe it!"

"Yeah, girl, it's me. How are you? What're doing? How did you find me?"

A sun-shower of emotions poured over me. Success! I had managed to find my comrade, my partner in crime, my dear friend who had witnessed and participated in so many of my experiences. We shared memories of trauma and treatment, and treatment that had caused trauma. Our shared experience and our shared perspective bound us tightly.

"I Googled you. There were three Nancy Chapins. You know, when you Google someone, their age comes up. One of them was thirty-something, and one was ninety-something. And then there was you. Right age, right Nancy! I can't believe I found you!"

"Do you remember I found *you*, like, eighteen years ago?"

A flash of memory ran through my mind: lying on my bed in the apartment I shared with my new husband, the early-morning sun shining through, talking on the phone with a part of my past I did not want to remember, not yet.

"Oh, my God, yeah. You called me, didn't you?"

"Yeah, but you blew me off."

"What?"

"Yeah. You blew me off. You said, 'I'm married now, and nobody knows about my past. Nobody knows what I went through. And nobody calls me Lee.' You asked me not to call you anymore. I was hurt, but I understood. What I didn't get was how you could start a marriage without telling your husband what you went through. But I figured in time, when you were ready, you would."

"Wow, Nancy. I did that? I remember lying on my bed and talking with you, but I don't remember telling you not to call me. I'm sorry."

"Don't worry about it. I knew it wasn't the end. I knew you'd come around. Hey, didn't your husband want to know where the scars came from? Wasn't he curious?"

"Not really. He always knew, like you, that I would tell him when I was ready. I just can't believe I blew you off like that. I'm sorry."

"It's OK. You're calling me now, babe. You're calling me now."

"Oh, my God, I can't believe I found you. I can't believe it."

With a switching of gears, a more somber moment, I asked the question that linked us.

"Hey, do you remember The Hospital?"

"Do I remember it? Oh, God, yeah, I remember it."

Nancy laughed and continued.

"I remember it, the seclusion room, the restraints, all that."

Her words held an undertone of anxiety. Together we began to reminisce about our mischievous adventures.

"Hey, Nancy. Let's have fun tonight."

"OK. What do you wanna to do?"

"Let's run away, bolt."

"Yeah. We can get totally fucked up somewhere."

Sitting together, plotting and planning, giggling with excitement and anticipation, we built upon our friendship. For better or worse, good or bad, virtuous or evil, we had a great time together, Nancy and I.

"Hey, a trip's going out tonight. You know what we could do?"

"*Whaaat?*"

"We could sneak into the van before it leaves. We'll duck down in the back, and when it gets to the mall and everyone gets out, we'll sneak back out of the van and be free."

"Lee, that's great. That's also impossible."

"Why?"

"Van's locked."

"Shit. OK then, tonight, after the trip is out, and less staff is there, we'll take off then."

"Oh, yeah. I can't wait."

The anticipation, the excitement of freedom, of rebellion, of defiance tingled up and down my body, like a shower of invigorating water penetrating my pores and cleansing my soul. On our way up to the dining room, Nancy and I walked slowly together. We were allowed to walk from the unit to activities or the dining room for meals with a chaperone. With this small amount of freedom, we walked together slowly, out of earshot of the staff. Once in the dining room, we found a table for four: Nancy, two of our peers, and me. We talked but not of our excursion planned for later that evening. Instead the chatter was what one would expect from four institutionalized young adult girls, feigning normalcy in the abnormal.

With mealtime over, the evening dragged on as our anticipation built. Community meeting was the next hurtle before we implemented our plan. This was a long, boring meeting in which the whole unit— twenty-four young adult and adult patients, staff and the psychiatrist in charge, Dr. Bennett—converged in the lounge to discuss events that affected the population as a whole. This could range from trips planned for the week to the latest outburst, from disruptive behavior or act of suicide or self-injury to a fellow inmate needing confrontation and interrogation from peers. As a concept, community meeting was an integrative session to keep all the patients in the loop. In reality it was dull and long, and had an expectation of caring, which I lacked, and especially on this night—the night of the planned escape to freedom and fun—this drawn-out meeting seemed to last an eternity. The clock ticked slowly: tick, tick, tick, tick, tick. On a normal night, my eyes would fight me as I tried to hold them open, but on this night, my excitement held them open until I finally heard: "Meeting over."

Some patients scurried quickly out of the lounge to ready themselves for the mall trip, others to stake claim on the stereo and Ping-Pong table in the rec room. Others lingered, lighting cigarettes on the wall grid and making themselves comfortable on chairs to talk or watch TV. Nancy and I dashed out with a mission—to prepare for our clandestine excursion, our well-deserved evening of fun. We waited for quiet from the excited hustle and bustle of the level-four patients, who were huddled by the door, waiting for staff to escort them out of the building and to the mall. Finally, as the rest of the patients left behind settled in for the evening, Nancy and I were ready to make our escape, the fear of punishment not a concern (or perhaps it was even part of the exhilaration).

"Ready?"

"Ready."

Hearts racing with anticipation and excitement, Nancy and I strolled as naturally as possible to the door, which unlike that of the adolescent unit, remained unlocked until ten p.m. under the watchful eyes of the staff, with the nurses' station window positioned just right for the job. At this moment it was not so secure. The door that would bring us immediately off the unit led to a waiting area from which a red door would lead us to the outside—the door to freedom, unmonitored and ready for access.

We moved stealthily, the ninjas that we were, eyes focused on our goal, avoiding looking toward the nurses' station, where our gaze would cut through the air, tap staff on the shoulder, and force them to look our way. Holding our breath to control the anxiety, anticipating detection with each step, we continued, directed, focused, out the front door, listening for the yell from staff. Not a sound. Darkness surrounded us with the crisp air of a fall evening, and we were free.

"Oh, my God, girl, we did it. *Run!*"

Laughing hard, our sides aching with giddiness, like two children who had successfully stolen a stash of candy, we ran across the parking area to the lawn, down the driveway, which was long and dark, lined by trees losing their leaves in preparation for the long, cold winter. Nancy and I ran and ran and ran.

Sweat running down my forehead, despite the cold, I leaned over and put my hands on my knees, as I breathed in the air hard, filling my lungs back to their capacity after having expended so much energy.

"Whew. Stop. I'm so out of breath. I can't run any more."

"Me neither, but we're safe. I think we did it. I can't believe it. Shit, this is going to be so much fun."

"Let's go to a bar. Let's get drunk."

"I hope we can get served."

"Served? Of course we can. We just have to be creative."

We headed toward a bar that was a couple of blocks from The Hospital. Walking in, I was instantly hit with the smell of alcohol and cigarettes. The atmosphere was typical for a corner tavern: dim lights, TV humming, jukebox singing, and only a few people sitting around the bar counter. The wood floor was sticky under my feet as we made our way deeper into the establishment, trying not to appear conspicuous.

"Is it possible, just maybe, that there is a sign on each of our foreheads that reads, JUST ESCAPED FROM A MENTAL HOSPITAL?"

We looked at each other and giggled at our inside joke.

"See those three guys? Let's ask them to buy us some booze."

"OK. You do it."

"Yeah. You do it."

Again we giggled with excitement and nervousness, the thrill of the forbidden.

"Let's go. We'll both do it. Shit, this is so cool."

Together we approached the three guys sitting huddled over the bar, drinking beers and talking. We interrupted.

"Hi."

They responded.

"Hi."

We flirted.

"We're thirsty."

They responded.

"Want a drink?"

"OK."

"How about we get some drinks to go?"

Nancy and I exchanged subtle glances. Given our particular situation—being mental hospital escapees, residents of a boom boom retreat on an unexcused excursion—perhaps to-go cups were a good idea.

"OK. Where are we gonna go?"

"We can go to our apartment."

Two of them nodded to each other, leaving us to understand that they were roommates, the third a friend in tow.

Outside Nancy and I piled into the back of a pickup truck, with the third guy our companion. With the cool wind hitting us as we drove, we warmed our insides with the beer purchased by our new friends. We wound through back roads, illuminated by the moon, until we arrived at a garage. A side door brought us to an upstairs apartment furnished with a beat-up sofa and a couple of armchairs surrounding an old coffee table, all resting on a ratty rug. We settled in and continued our evening of drinking and laughing.

"You guys want to do some lines?"

Nancy and I answered in perfect harmony.

"Absolutely."

My mouth watered as he pulled out his bag of beautiful, delicate, white powder—the mirror and razor as enticing as the drug itself. I watched patiently with a feeling that produced its own high...anticipation. Once the lines were laid out, we moved in.

"Here's a bill."

"Thanks."

I rolled the dollar bill into a cylinder. Holding my breath so as not to exhale, which would cause the powdery substance to scatter, I leaned over the mirror. Gently I glided the dollar bill along the white line, inhaling deeply. The burn caused a painful sensation that I greeted lovingly, like an old friend with whom I had been reunited. I snorted the next line and handed the dollar bill, still in a perfect cylinder, to Nancy, who was waiting with bated breath.

"Thanks, Lee."

I watched Nancy as I waited for the effects to hit me, to take control of my body and my emotions, changing my perspective from hopeless anguish to confident power over my life and my world.

The evening continued, with cocaine and beer, until Nancy and I brought it to an end.

"We gotta go."

"Why?"

"We have to get back."

"Aren't you guys too old for a curfew?"

Uncontrolled laughter emerged from Nancy and me, a reflection of the nervousness that accompanied the question. Nancy spoke.

"We don't really live at home."

"Where do you live?"

With the giggling still serving as camouflage, I answered.

"A boom boom retreat."

Brows furrowed in confusion, the boys responded together.

"What?"

"A boom boom retreat."

Glances ricocheted around the room like a pinball in a machine, bouncing from one of our new never-to-be-seen-again friends to the next.

"What? What's that?"

"A psych hospital. You know, for crazy people."

"You guys live in a psych hospital?"

"Yeah. Crazy, huh?"

"Yeah. Why do you guys live there?"

"Because we have fucked-up families. Fucked-up families make fucked-up kids. Fucked-up kids end up in fucked-up places."

With that Nancy and I made our exit. That night we may have left behind our virtue, our morals, our dignity, our honor, our self-respect. I do not know. I do not recall, but somehow I feel we did not. What I do remember is that once we were outside—alone, fucked up, and giddy—we had to devise a plan to break back into the very place from which we had escaped. As we contemplated the issue, a van approached us slowly and stopped. In disbelief we watched the door open as Ryan Hayes, another favorite staff member, emerged, with Steve Bayer in the driver's seat.

Through Ryan's particular way of talking, low and halting, he made his command.

"Lee, Nancy, come on."

A stir of contradictory emotions brewed inside me. They cared enough to come find us but were ruining an evening of entertaining freedom. Nancy and I locked eyes and, in unison, shared our sentiment.

"Oh, shit."

"Come on. In the van."

Again we responded in perfect harmony.

"Fuck you."

"In The Van!"

The stern retort from Ryan, not something we were used to coming from him, left us wordless. Nancy and I stepped into the van—incarceration again.

How they'd found us I will never know.

Once we were back at The Hospital, Nancy was escorted to the locked unit. I was restricted to my room. As I lay there alone and abandoned, the anticlimactic emotional barrage hit me with a vengeance. I'd had a night out, blatantly broken the rules, escaped, then caught and brought back, only to be left alone. Anguished emotions swelled by the minute, becoming more intolerable, leaving me feeling hopelessly desperate and unable to cope. I was in dire need of relief. Rendered helpless in the face of emotional distress, unable to look within to find an appropriate means of relief, I punched—over and over, harder and harder—the headboard, the wall, whatever was hard enough to punch me in return. Eventually the noise made its way to Steve and Ryan. I jumped off my bed, startled by their presence as they stood before me, and found myself trapped between the wall, the bed, and them.

Regardless of whether or not I meant it, the only power I possessed was to yell at them.

"Get the fuck out of my room!"

"We can't."

I yelled again.

"Get the fuck out of my room!"

"You need to come with us."

"*No*! Get the fuck out!"

The dialogue of horror, obscenities, and temper continued until I spotted my escape. Next to me was an orange plastic chair that was lighter than it looked with its aluminum frame. I reached for it. Trapped by my conflicting desires to be rescued *and* taken care of *and* left alone, I grabbed the chair and held it in a threatening pose, followed by threatening words.

"If you come toward me, I'm going to throw this chair at you. Stay away. I mean it. Stay away!"

"Lee, put the chair down. Nobody needs to get hurt."

"Back off! Just back the fuck off!"

With the uncontrollable, violent tornado swirling through me, fiercely reaping havoc, I realized I was alone, and would always be alone, within my experience, within my mind, within my body. No human was able to save me, bond with me, attach to me enough to give me the ability to pull myself out of my torment. The knowledge of the sheer isolation that embraced me held me more captive than any locked door. As anger, despair, and aloneness penetrated me deeper and deeper, Ryan moved. In an instant, with no thought attached, I threw the chair at him. A harmless person with a bark much larger than my bite, I did not want to hurt him. My throw was weak, more of a statement than an act of violence. The chair landed clumsily at his ankles.

As I stood unarmed and helpless, except for my verbal expression of anguish, Ryan and Steve approached me. My voice was my most powerful tool. Letting out shrill screams, I pleaded against the inevitable: a gaggle of staff tethering the wildly out-of-control young woman to the bed.

My coconspirator, Nancy, already occupied the seclusion room, so they placed a bed in the vestibule between the two sets of locked and secured doors that led outside. They succeeded, as always, with a speed and care that left me unsure as to whether the event had ever happened in the first place. The only proof was spelled out by the fact that I was unable to move.

All quiet on the locked unit, I called out to Nancy just across the hall in seclusion.

"Nancy? Are you there?"

"Lee, I'm here."

As the evening progressed, staff changed shifts, and every two hours, someone new stood guard in the locked unit. During Ryan's shift, the phone in the back rang. The last thing I heard that night was, "Yes, it's quiet back here now. They've calmed down."

Slowly I drifted. Finally I slept.

THE NOTICE

The next day I finally was released from my overnight immobilization and was free to roam the locked unit. Struggling to outrun
the bombardment of invading emotions, and making the only decision I
had any control over, I signed a seventy-two-hour notice, a contract that
detained an individual for three days, with an immediate release there-
after if no threat to self or others could be proven. The hitch was that
Dr. Bennett had warned my parents of the dangers in letting me come
home. He had not, however, warned my friend's mother.

Rose and I knew each other from outside The Hospital. She was a
friend with whom I had a good relationship and who knew my situation—institutionalization. Her mother, appalled by my plight, supported our friendship and supported my signing a notice, having offered
in the past to take me home should I ever decide to do so. She offered,
I presume, because she felt she could give me what I was lacking in my
own home, in The Hospital, in my head, in my reality. She offered, and
naturally I accepted.

During the course of the seventy-two hours, Dr. Bennett and the
staff repeatedly warned me of their plan to attempt to obtain a court
commitment if I chose not to rescind the notice. Their warnings fell on
deaf ears. Certain, within a mind that chose to see and understand only
what it wanted to see and understand, I was sure that their warnings

were idle threats to intimidate, that in the end I would be released into the care of Rose's mother. I ignored their warnings. I yelled at their warnings. I mocked their warnings.

"Lee, if you don't rescind the notice, we'll have to proceed with a commitment."

"You have no grounds. I don't care what you wanna do—you don't have grounds."

"We do."

"Yeah? What are they?"

"You're a danger to yourself, *and* you're a danger to others."

"Right. How?"

"Well, you repeatedly hit your hand, and you threw a chair at Ryan."

"You know I didn't mean that. I wasn't gonna hurt him. And punching a wall isn't hurting myself."

"No?"

"*No!*"

Enraged I continued.

"I can't believe you! I can't believe you would do this to me. Hitting my hand! So What! Well, you know what? Try to stop me! *It won't work!*"

Pulled between conflicting wants, needs, thoughts, and feelings— split and fragmented—I was torn to shreds in a confused attempt to grip one and stick with it. *What if I can't leave? What if I can? I want them to stop me. I want them to let me. I want to be free. I'm terrified of being abandoned.* I desperately wanted to leave, to be normal, to be like everyone else, with freedom and independence. But I also wanted to avoid abandonment.

Nancy had been released from the locked unit and was back with the general population. I was serving out my seventy-two-hour sentence behind locked doors. Sitting alone in my room, I had little to do and few with whom to communicate. Steve came in and asked to talk.

"So you're leaving?"

"Yeah. I have somewhere to go, and I'm going."

"Your friend's house?"

"Yup."

"Well, we're following through with our plan."

As if I were unaware of their plan, which they'd clearly stated during my three days of waiting, I responded with shocked horror.

"What do you mean 'your plan'? My friend's mom is getting me, and I'm leaving."

"I don't think so. You need to pack some clothes. You're being picked up at six p.m. and taken to the state hospital. You still have time to rescind your notice."

"I don't care. You can't commit me 'cause I haven't done anything."

"Yes, you have—punching walls and throwing a chair. Pack your things. Let us know if you change your mind and want to rescind the notice."

"Yeah, right. I don't think so. I didn't throw a chair *at* anyone, and I wasn't hurting anyone!"

I watched Steve leave. A minute ago there had been a certain sense of containment, with Steve's presence holding my emotions. Now there was simply emptiness, chaotic emptiness. Ready to play whatever game they were playing, I packed some clothes then sat on the bed and waited. I did not know what to expect. The fear of the unknown turned my stomach into knots. A fog clouded my mind protecting me from a reality with which I could not cope. Deep in the haze, Steve's voice reached in and grabbed me.

"It's time to go."

I stood on numb legs and followed him to the back door, where we could bypass the curiosity of dying-to-know patients and strategically prevent contagious copycat behavior. Outside, the engine of an ambulance was humming, the transportation of choice from hospital to hospital. Two technicians greeted me, both exhibiting little emotion, like Swiss guards, there to do their job with no expression and no connection.

As I walked from the unit to the ambulance, pink clouds held the reflection of the setting sun. The trees were beginning to darken as dusk transformed their branches into silhouettes against an orange sky. Silenced by fear I pulled myself up into the back of the ambulance. During the drive the sky shifted from orange to a dark-night blue, with millions of stars dotting the suburban sky. Once we arrived I was escorted into a waiting room by the poker-faced, wordless Swiss guards, and there I was left, alone and waiting.

DR. BENNETT

I had made a statement to Dr. Bennett that left me open for potential rejection—"I need to see you"—and he was leaving enough space between my asking and his answering to make me certain of the outcome. Finally he responded.

"If we meet it would have to be here in my office."

A sense of relief washed over me. With a quiet sigh, I exhaled the breath I'd been holding, not wanting him to become aware of the impact of his answer.

"OK. That's fine."

He then asked a question I would only expect from someone who knew me then but did *not* know me now.

"Lee, are you going to kill yourself after our meeting?"

His question came from his image of me as an adolescent and young adult, consumed by the highly suicidal behaviors that marked the illness I had struggled with. Hearing it now, so long into my recovery, left me feeling angry at a question that no longer had a place in my life. I could not interpret it as a display of caring concern but only as an off-putting assumption of his importance.

"No. Why would I kill myself?"

Satisfied by my response, he agreed to meet me, so his secretary put me in the book.

The outfit I chose to wear was well thought out, to portray me as the confident and refined woman I now was. My recovery was something I was concerned he would miss if his view were blocked by his image of my youth. Looking in the mirror, I was pleased with my reflection. I grabbed my handbag and the list of questions I'd been ruminating over for two and a half decades. These questions needed answering. After folding it neatly and placing it in my purse, I made my way out of the house and headed for my meeting with Dr. Bennett.

Again my journey to the past began with a long car ride, the sun shining warmly through the windshield and music playing from a CD. My stomach was full of butterflies, my heart pumping rapidly. I sang to the music, distracting myself from the drive, until I knew I was close. My past was a wall that lay ahead of me, and I was about to slam into it yet again.

As I pulled into the driveway of a large, sprawling apartment complex, I noticed a house that fit the description given by the secretary who made the appointment. Driving slowly past the front, I saw a sign that clearly displayed the names of the doctors that had offices inside, the top one reading, DR. BENNETT. His name shot at me like a bullet to the chest. I fixated on it for a moment, taking in the name, thirsty for connection. Pulling myself back to the present, I drove into the lot and slipped into an open parking space. With ten minutes to spare, I decided to begin the journey to the past in my car, playing music from Eric Clapton: "Cocaine" and "Let It Grow," two songs indelibly linked to my youth. As the music caressed my ears, I slipped back, gliding down the slope of my memory. Motion from outside, another car pulling into one of the parking spaces, jarred me back to the moment, and I noticed the time. I turned off the engine, losing the music and my link to the past.

Tingling with numbness, my heart beating rapidly, I walked slowly to the front door of the house. The copper knob felt cold in my hand as I slowly turned it, pushing the heavy door until there was room enough for me to fit through. The interior was warm, with an oriental rug covering dark hardwood floors, original to the 1930s structure, and a desk directly ahead, with a warm smile coming from the woman behind it.

"Hi. I'm Talya Lewis. I'm here to see Dr. Bennett."

Obviously expecting me, the woman nodded.

"Yes. Hi. My name's Penny. Dr. Bennett is in a meeting, but he won't be too much longer. Come with me, and I'll take you the waiting room."

As we walked through the halls, I was acutely aware of the smell in the air, uncannily similar to the smell of his office at The Hospital. In that moment I realized I was going to have an olfactory memory of the new office of my former psychiatrist, jailor, pseudo father. I stayed on Penny's heels as we passed through an open area with offices and desks, phones ringing and voices murmuring. This space was not adorned with oriental rugs but cream-colored, wall-to-wall, industrial carpeting. We then made our way down a few stairs to an isolated area with two chairs, an end table with some magazines, and a lamp. She motioned for me to sit.

"Dr. Bennett will be with you soon. Can I get you anything? Would like some coffee?"

"Oh, no. Thank you. I'm fine."

Penny was very warm and friendly, trained well to interact with anyone who may walk through the front door of the main office of a therapeutic facility. She nodded, smiled, and left. I sat in one of the chairs and gazed out the window at the sunny day, the green lawn hosting a few birds and two squirrels chasing each other. I glanced through some magazines, feeling desperate to distract myself from the thoughts that were beginning to disturb any semblance of peace the quiet waiting area was providing. *What am I doing here? This is ridiculous. What was I thinking?*

The *Reader's Digest* hid my uneasiness from anyone passing by. I read short articles written by average people, until I heard a familiar voice, one that jolted me to my core. It had not changed in tone, quality, tenor, or pitch. Dr. Bennett stood before me.

In a cheerful manner, head tilted slightly to one side with a smile of dubious intent, Dr. Bennett addressed me by my old name.

"Lee?"

"Dr. Bennett. Oh, my God, you haven't changed. This is weird."

Out of nervousness and out of the social etiquette to match his, a smile rushed across my face.

"Come on. Let's go to my office. You look great."

"Thanks. So do you."

I wanted to say as little as possible as we made our way into the privacy of his office. It was a bright room with a big window that looked out to the parking area, a couch backed up against the window, and two chairs on either side, making a cozy meeting space. Everything looked pristine, not a thing out of place, not a dust particle lingering on the end tables, the fireplace free of debris. The contrast to Meredith's office was extreme.

I sat in one of the chairs, and Dr. Bennett took the one directly across. For a moment I just looked at him, deep and hard, searching for elements that were familiar from so many years ago. He had changed little. His hair was now white. Back then it was gray. Wrinkles were now present in places they hadn't been before. His body was thinner, somewhat fragile with age. Despite these changes he was the same Dr. Bennett from then sitting with me now. I began.

"I have a lot of questions I want to ask you. Is that OK?"

There it was again, the familiar tilt of his head, the smile, the charm.

"What kind of questions do you have?"

I reached over and dug through my handbag.

"Let me get them. I wrote them down. I didn't want to forget anything."

With each passing minute, I feared the end of our meeting. Somehow, being in his presence brought me a degree of protection from the loneliness that lingered from my past. There I was, sitting with someone who had been there then. Yet the feeling of protection was being overshadowed by anger, longing, fear, and rejection. Slowly I unfolded the paper with the questions for Dr. Bennett. With a deep breath, setting some of the internal pressure free, I began.

"OK, I have a lot of questions. I'm kind of confused about that time in my life, not to mention angry, sad, traumatized, and whatever else you want to tack on. So I have to try to figure it out, you know? Why it happened, what it meant, that kind of thing."

Dr. Bennett sat with an uncharacteristic silence.

"The first thing I need to know is whether you cared about me—really cared about me?"

"Yes. I cared about you very much."

"I'm in therapy again because I'm trying to work past what I went through. Ironic, therapy to deal with the trauma of therapy. Anyway, there's something I've always wanted to know. Why did you make me stay? On that first day I promised you I wouldn't hurt myself if you let me go home. I was so scared that I wouldn't have done anything to end up back in a place like that. It's kind of like those 'scared straight' programs. You know, when they bring at-risk kids into a prison and let the inmates scare them crazy so they won't commit any crimes and end up incarcerated? Well, that's what it was like for me, like being scared straight. I was terrified. I wouldn't have done anything else to hurt myself. My suicide attempt was just a cry for help anyway."

"And I answered it. I had to keep you in The Hospital. You were in no position to go home. I couldn't have let you go."

Dr. Bennett spoke with a fierce confidence that left me little room for argument, his matter-of-fact tone forcing me to leave it unchallenged. I saw his thinking in mathematical terms, the simplest way to break down his rigid logic: Psychiatrist plus suicidal teenager equaled institutionalization. After I had been treated over the course of several years, and once my life had been forever changed and my adolescence and early young adulthood dirtied with incarceration, they had set me free.

Dr. Bennett quietly watched me.

"OK. Well, here's my next question."

A smile took over my face, a camouflage for my anxiety.

"Did you diagnose me correctly? Did I really have borderline personality disorder?"

"Yes. You did."

"You know, they use that diagnosis pretty freely. If someone cuts, is suicidal and is difficult to treat, and God forbid is a female, they slap the 'borderline' label on them. It's the wastebasket diagnosis. Isn't that what they call it? Is that what you did with me, or did I really have it?"

"You really had it."

His head shifted slightly, centering himself. His smile left, though a softness remained as he began to talk.

"I can always guess when someone has borderline personality disorder before I even meet them. All the staff is converged in the office, and they're discussing someone on the unit. The staff is split. Half of them are very sympathetic to this patient. They'll see her as someone who is genuinely in extreme emotional pain and can benefit greatly from the structure and support of the hospital. They see the person as being sincerely distressed and in need of nurturance. The other half of the staff sees this person as being manipulative, angry, difficult to deal with, and unable to benefit from treatment. They're not pleased with having to handle the behaviors she's exhibited in the short time she's been there. There's a real and obvious split between the staff. I listen then I announce, 'You're all right; we have someone with borderline personality disorder.' When I meet the person, I'm able to confirm the diagnosis."

Mesmerized by his simple description of a complex illness, I was left speechless and could summon only an "oh" to confirm I had been listening. I looked down at my hands and played with my rings, my usual distraction. As he spoke I was thrust back to the adolescent unit, to the nurses' station, to all the people, the sounds, the smells, the staff splitting over me. I looked back up at him, and with a confident and somewhat accusatory tone, I spoke.

"So is that what it was like with me?"

He smiled, sending me a clear message with no words.

"OK then, if I really had borderline disorder, how did I get better without dialectical behavior therapy? I mean, isn't that the new therapy for people with borderline? Isn't it impossible for people to get better without it?"

The smile from earlier turned into a more robust version of itself as he let out a chuckle, though there was no great humor in what I had said.

"You would make a great advertisement for dialectical behavior therapy."

"Well, that's the impression nowadays."

"It's a good therapy. It's an effective one. It's not the only one."

I shrugged, really not knowing enough to debate the issue either way.

"All right, I'll buy that. Then here's my next question. I thought people with borderline disorder could never be cured. So do you think I'm cured? If I am, how could I really ever have had the disorder?"

In a baffling, tongue-twisting retort, Dr. Bennett responded with another undebatable assurance.

"It's pretty typical for someone with borderline to use the word *cure* as opposed to *recovery*. It always has to be one extreme or the other, *cured* or *sick*, not just *recovering* and *maintaining*."

He tilted his head again, looking at me as though to say, "What do you think about that?" to which I thought a lot but said nothing. Ideas moved through my mind as I searched for the message he was sending. Did he think I was still diagnosable? Did he see my put-together and confident demeanor as a facade? I once again dropped my eye contact with Dr. Bennett and focused on my rings, spinning them around on my finger. They were my connection to the present, to home, to those who loved me, to my health and happiness. Though he was talking, I lost myself in a moment of remembering as I sat with the man for whom I held so much anger, whom I held responsible for my incarceration. Sitting in the same room with him validated my past and all that I had gone through. I was lost in the moment, his words not as important to me as his presence.

Suddenly my phone's ringtone called out from deep inside my handbag. My heart plummeted, as I was sure this would remind Dr. Bennett of the time and the scheduled ending of our meeting. Sure enough, he spoke the very words I feared.

"Oh, it's twelve thirty. I have a lunch appointment with my son."

Feeling utterly alone with my memories, I replied.

"Sorry. I didn't mean to keep you so long."

My tone was sincere, yet it was more a matter of politeness. I would have hung on to our meeting for an infinite number of minutes. As he stood I folded up my list of questions, most of which had gone unasked after the hour and a half, and put them back into my handbag. Once we were out the door of his office, he turned to me and spoke.

"You can look me up again in six months. Maybe I'll see you again for free."

With this he left. I stood paralyzed, reeling with emotions violently exploding within me. I was nothing more than a minute, insignificant particle standing alone, as imploding forces tried to take me down. Despair surfaced, as though a steel door holding back the flood of dirty water had opened, letting muck and grime spill out, soiling everything around it with debris—wet, dirty debris. Walking slowly so as not to allow any of the internal mess to spill out, I made my way out to my car.

The air had warmed since I'd first arrived, the sun high. It was springtime, a time of new beginnings. I unlocked my door and slid in, put the key into the ignition, and started the engine. Immediately I was greeted by the music I'd been listening to when I'd arrived. The Eric Clapton song picked up where it left off, both in my memories and in my present.

I sat in my car, frozen. Time became an experience in contradictions, standing still and racing ahead. Flashbacks of The Hospital danced in my mind like ghosts forced to experience a moment in time over and over. Suddenly I was jarred from my thoughts by an internal panic. I had been sitting in his parking lot, engine running and music playing, for an hour. With willpower and perseverance, like pushing through thick molasses, I put my car into drive and slid out of the parking space I had slid into a few hours earlier. In an attempt to outrun the hands of my torment as they reached out and tried to pull me back, I raced away quickly, my wheels screeching as they skidded over the tarred road. Racing away, I spied through my rearview mirror the house I had just come from getting smaller and smaller, leaving behind a connection so important that I could not let it go.

Neither of us upheld the six-month moratorium on meeting again. What was important for him about our chats I do not know. What was important for me was the connection to my past implanted in my present, like an old piece of skin grafted onto a new one. Yet it was still not enough.

Eventually I mustered the courage to call Steve Bayer, the man whose photograph stood side by side with Dr. Bennett's. After one meeting with him, he became a part of our little tête-à-têtes, where once every few months I was given the opportunity to reshape my thoughts and perceptions from my traumatizing past.

During this period of resurrecting old relationships, Meredith eventually became unable to tolerate my pain, and I felt as though she began to toy with my vulnerabilities. Ultimately she stood me up for an important session, and therapy dissolved in an instant. Before this she had been pressuring me to try medication to ease some of that pain and had referred me to a psychiatrist. Ironically the psychiatrist turned out to be an amazing, compassionate therapist and was there to pick up the pieces after Meredith had dropped the ball. With him my journey became one of healing—no longer the journey of borderline personality disorder, as I was at that point well into recovery, but a journey that led me out of the trauma of my treatment.

KEYS

*A*t this point my memories were coming frequently. It didn't matter if I were sitting in the office of a therapist, at the dinner table with my parents, or alone—lying in bed, driving my car, walking down the street. They invaded my thoughts regularly, pulling my attention away from whatever task was at hand. A breeze carrying a scent, a song, a program on television—I was easily reminded of the events from my treatment, helplessly dragged wherever they brought me.

"Sit here. Someone's gonna come out and get you in a minute."

The ambulance technicians who had brought me to the state hospital emergency unit turned on their heels and left, their duty done. Terrified, I sat and waited. Within minutes I heard a voice.

"Lee?"

With my eyes pulled to the floor, I made a safe retreat into split-off regions of my mind, detaching myself from my surroundings. I did not engage with the owner of the voice, my lack of cooperation the only element of control left to me. Motionless, I sat in silence.

"Lee, I'm the doctor. I'm going to examine you then bring you on the ward. Come on."

Visibly unmoved by my fear and exuding little sympathy toward this frightened young woman, he guided me into an examination room. He spoke in a commanding tone.

"Up on the table, and unbutton your shirt, but don't take it off."

"Why do I have to unbutton my shirt?"

"I have to examine you."

"I'm fine. Why do you have to do that?"

"We examine everyone who comes in."

With the wearing down of his patience evident in his voice, he made one last plea: "Please cooperate."

Intimidation, not cooperation, got me up on the table. My goal was to convince this doctor that The Hospital had made a horrible mistake by sending me there. I attempted to present as an adjusted, healthy young adult who had been wrongly accused of illness and subsequently incarcerated. Sitting with a posture fit for royalty, my voice clean and clear, I spoke.

"I don't need to be here. I really am fine. They misunderstood my intentions at The Hospital. I have a friend whose mother wants to take me home. I know I'll be fine. Can I go?"

I found my false demeanor and my argument quite reasonable. I was certain he would agree that it had been an egregious decision to send someone like me to the state hospital to be court committed. Again, in his affectively challenged tone, he responded.

"No. That's not an option."

I continued in my plea to convince him.

"I know they said I wasn't safe, but I am. I feel much better now. I know I'll be fine. Please give me a chance. If it doesn't work out, I can always go back."

Ignoring my petition, the doctor listened to my heart, took my blood pressure, looked in my mouth as I said "aah," and had me breathe deeply as he listened to my lungs. I felt like nothing more than an object before him. His exam complete, he looked at me.

"You can button your shirt. I'm going to bring you on the ward."

"But I really want to go home. I promise I'll be fine."

"The only option you have right now is to stay here for an evaluation. You aren't going anywhere."

I realized the terrifying truth—the possibility of release never had existed. With a commanding grip, the doctor walked me toward a set of glass doors, as I relentlessly plead along the way.

He reached into his pocket, his keys jingling as he pulled them out. The sound penetrated my brain as a symbol of my helplessness. He took them in his hand as though to flaunt his power and slowly guided one of them into the keyhole.

The state hospital, founded in 1880, was reminiscent of its era. The building was damp, with institutional tile flooring and bare walls. The doors were thick and sturdy, the air stagnant and musty. Overhead were the standard ubiquitous fluorescent lights. My bedroom was the first on the right. It had blue walls, the paint chipping in the corners. There were four wire-framed beds with thin mattresses, each one pushed into a corner. In the unit, past my room, were the cafeteria, the nurses' station, and the bathrooms, which had no locks and no shower curtains. On the far side were the boys. There was a transitional feeling. No one stayed for more than a week or so while waiting for court hearings that would decide their fate. No one bonded—not with staff, not with each other. Instead we passed our time in sheer boredom in this unstructured holding station.

On my second day in this old asylum building, I met with my caseworker. As we sat facing each other at one of the tables in the cafeteria, he placed his keys in the center and spoke.

"I know you want the privilege of going outside with staff."

As we talked, I unwittingly took the bait and began to play with his keys.

"Yeah, I'd like that because it's pretty boring in here. We just sit around all day, maybe watch some TV."

"Have you been eating?"

"I've been drinking milk."

Both to regulate my emotions and as a protest against my circumstances, I refused solid food but took great pleasure from the milk dispenser that was available at all times in the cafeteria, delivering a deliciously cold glass at the flip of a lever.

"No eating, just milk?"

"I'm not hungry."

We continued our conversation for a period, keys jingling between my fingers, until he got all he needed to know.

"OK, hang tight. I'm going to go make some notes, and I'll catch up with you later, see how you're doing."

He reached for his keys and made his exit, never to be seen again.

Later that afternoon, as staff gathered a group of patients to go out and walk the grounds, I waited in anticipation to be approached. It was a familiar scene—patients standing at a locked door, waiting for their escorts to take them out for some short-lived freedom, with me looking on in vain. Stunned, I called out.

"Why can't I go?"

An anonymous voice answered.

"Your caseworker wasn't comfortable letting you out."

"Why? I was supposed to be allowed to go for a walk today. That's what they told me. Why can't I go? What the fuck did I do?"

"He feels you're at risk for running."

"What? I never said I was going to run!"

"He just feels you're at risk for running."

And that was that.

As I relived that day, I imagined being a caseworker employed by a state hospital with the mundane duty of overseeing severely symptomatic, transient patients in one-time assessments. In retrospect I

realized what he had done. He had set me up—the strategic place-
ment of his keys, interpreted from his perspective but not explored
from mine.

THE HEARING

My time on the crisis unit at the state hospital was six long, torturously boring days blending one into the next. Finally a diversion! A staff member entered my room.

"I need you to come with me."

"Where're we going?"

"It's time for your hearing."

A moment of hope and relief burst through the air.

"They'd better let me go home. I haven't done anything they can keep me for. Will I be able to leave today?"

Either out of rudeness or out of ignorance, he did not respond.

A set of doors led us off the unit and to a staircase. As we walked, with my head weighed down, I dragged my feet with an apprehensive shuffle as panic rippled beneath my skin. When we reached the second floor, I looked up and took in the space. The hallway stretched from one end of the building to the other, lined with offices and hearing rooms. The carpeting was a golden yellow, the color striking. My pace slowed as we approached our door.

"Come on, Lee. Let's go."

"I don't want to."

"You have to. Anyway, it'll be over fast."

"How do you know?"

"I see these hearings all the time. I know."

My head began to spin. As the dark clouds of anguish thickened I felt the fog build, severing my mind from my body, hiding my emotions from my awareness. I walked into the room and looked around. The golden-yellow carpeting ended at the door. The hearing room was carpeted in a dark orange, adding warmth to the room that held my fate. There was a large wooden desk, suggesting power. The man sitting behind it had a round, stern, dispassionate face. This man was just another state hospital employee with the mundane task of committing the mentally ill, day in and day out—unchanging repetition, no challenge, no excitement.

In front of the desk were simple aluminum-and-pleather chairs, three on one side of the room and two on the other. I sat with my mother and the lawyer who had been appointed to "represent" me. On the opposing team, across the room, were Steve and Ryan, who had been summoned as witnesses to support The Hospital's request to commit me.

I sat guarded, my crossed arms protecting my heart from bursting, my head dropped with the weight of worry. I hated my mother being there. I hated the pity—for me, for herself. I was vacillating between dependency upon my captors and the idea of freedom, which elicited a deep humiliation. The torturous contradictions were splitting me into irreparable pieces. My glare ricocheted through the room, piercing as deeply as it could all who were present. The magistrate overseeing my case, silhouetted by the sun as he sat behind his big wooden desk, finally spoke.

"Miss Wasserman, during this hearing you will sit quietly. You will not speak unless your public defender requests that you do. Do you understand?"

Eyes glaring, arms crossed, anger dripping from my brow, I shrugged, unwilling to give him the satisfaction of complying yet aware that the choice was not mine.

"We are here today for commitment proceedings for Talya Wasserman. Can each person please state their name and relationship to the patient?"

Each person stated his or her name, as well as his or her relationship with me and respective role at the hearing. My mother announced herself as "tortured soul"; Steve and Ryan were the voices of The Hospital; my public defender was useless.

"Now we can get started."

The public defender, showing little passion for what he was there to do, spoke first, seemingly more out of a desire to get on with his day than to assist his client.

"It is my understanding that Talya Wasserman, who goes by the name 'Lee,' has been a patient at The Hospital's young adult program for the past seven months. She signed a seventy-two-hour notice, but it is my understanding that her parents are unwilling to accept her into their home at this point in time."

The magistrate looked toward my mother, who responded in a sullen, guilt-laden voice. She was a puppet on a string, with Dr. Bennett's hands manipulating her words.

"Yes. I don't feel as though we can handle her right now."

Silenced during the proceedings, I felt my rage boiling at what to me was misrepresentation. *I am not planning on going home!* I screamed in my head. I was going to my friend's home, where her mother had not been manipulated and terrified by the psychiatric system. As I was powerless to speak, my mind was a place no one could control. It was my own private sanctuary, be it hell or salvation. It was mine, and I could scream within as loud as I wanted, *I have somewhere else to go!* I screamed and screamed, but no one heard.

My public defender and my mother had their opportunity to talk, to hammer the nails in my coffin. The magistrate moved on to Steve and Ryan, who sat skilled and rehearsed, in their chairs.

"Mr. Bayer, can you share your thoughts?"

After clearing his throat, Steve began.

"Yes. We have concerns at The Hospital for Lee's safety, both toward herself and toward others."

"Can you elaborate on that, please?"

"Well, approximately ten days ago, Lee ran away from our facility with another patient. We went out to search for them and were successful in locating them several hours later, and when we did, they were both intoxicated. When we returned to The Hospital, we put Lee in her room while we decided as a team what would be the most appropriate route to ensure her safety and restrict her ability to run away again."

"Go on."

"We heard noises coming from her room, like something being hit. When we went in, we saw Lee punching the headboard of her bed, as well as the wall, as hard as she could over and over. I believe if we didn't stop her, she would have broken her hand."

"You stopped her?"

"Yes. She was very angry and out of control, yelling at us, and at that point, she jumped off her bed and was standing in a corner of the room, screaming at us over and over to get out. We knew she would not be safe, so we couldn't leave her. We tried to talk with her quietly and rationally, but we were unsuccessful, and her anger escalated. At that point she grabbed a chair."

"And what did she do?"

"Well, at first she threatened us, saying that if we didn't leave, she would throw the chair at us."

"Did she throw the chair at any point?"

"Yes."

Passing the storytelling baton, Steve gestured toward Ryan.

"Yes, she threw the chair at me."

"Did it hit you?"

"Yes. It hit my legs."

"Do you concur with the story Mr. Bayer conveyed?"

"Yes, I do."

"Is there anything you would like to add?"

"Yes. I think it's important to be aware that she continued to be uncooperative the rest of the evening. We had to bring her back to our locked unit, and she had to be restrained at that point. She was unable to gain any control, so she remained in restraints throughout the night. She also made threats of suicide."

"OK, gentlemen. Thank you."

Though the story was based in truth, they had greatly exaggerated events to further their cause. By command of the magistrate, I sat mute, helpless to defend myself. My face was scorched, red hot as emotions swirled violently inside me. My fear made it impossible for me to call out in protest.

I watched the face of the powerful man who held my fate in his stubby, chubby, little hands. The magistrate looked through papers on his desk in an attempt to appear as though he were making a decision that, in my mind, had been made before the hearing even had begun. Finally he spoke.

"Thank you all for attending this hearing. Based on the information you all shared, and on the patient's history, I feel it would be in her best interest to receive a thirty-day commitment to be carried out at The Hospital. At the end of that period, if she attempts to leave against medical advice, her case can be reviewed for further commitment."

With his stubby, chubby, little hands, he flipped the folder that lay before him closed, and he glanced around the room, conveying a nonverbal "Case closed."

As others began to rise, gathering their belongings and murmuring quietly to one another, I fled the room in a helpless rage, taking the only route available, back down the stairs to captivity.

BURN

Back at The Hospital, the level of trust staff had in me was minimal. Again I found myself in the locked unit, with every shred of dignity stripped from my being. Their fear of my running was irrational. The doors were bolted, and I had no keys. Still they took my clothes and left me with only a hospital gown in which to dress.

"Why do I have to wear this?" I questioned with shameful indignation.

The response—"To keep you safe"—was intended to squelch the conversation and protect against an argument that might escalate in rocket fashion. Stifled and helpless, humiliated and resigned, I went into the small lounge of the locked unit. I reached for my Marlboro Red pack and slid out a cigarette, placing the filtered end in my mouth and the other end into the wall lighter. As I pushed the button, the grid glowed red and hot. One or two puffs brought the crackling sound of paper and leaves igniting, and in a puff of smoke, I walked to one of the comfortable chairs and sat down. In a numb stupor that shut out the humiliation and feelings of nakedness, I flicked my cigarette's burning ashes onto my skin. The pain was able to override the numbness, the shame, the vulnerable chaos that plagued me. Emotional and physical pain competed for my attention, compromising my sanity with thoughts of despair that spun, taunted, and swirled over and over and over. *Distract. Burn, burn, burn, burn!*

"Lee!"

Lost within myself, his voice pulled me out of my spiral of trying to extinguish my pain.

"Put your cigarette down."

"I'm smoking. I'm allowed to smoke."

"You're allowed to smoke, but you're not allowed to burn yourself. Put your cigarette down."

"Whatever. I'm finished with it anyway."

The next response was to assess the damage, but I had no intention to comply. With the staff member's commanding plea, "Let me see your hand!" and my resounding "No!" I jumped up and turned to leave the lounge. Despite my anxiety, impulsivity lurked behind every corner, grabbing me and holding me with its powerful force. I impetuously had responded, without premeditation, without a plan, without the immediate conscious notion of cause and effect that reigns in human behavior as we weigh the pros and cons of in-the-moment decisions. With my back sending him a clear message, this staff member made his threat.

"You're testing me, Lee. Show me your hand or we can take a trip to seclusion."

"Do whatever you want. You can't tell me what to do."

Effectively disarmed of any control, I managed to find power in my struggles with staff. As my emotions ricocheted, my adamant stance on not cooperating regulated the turmoil. The struggle became physical. One phone call brought a fleet of manpower, equipped with restraints and ready for a fight. The words, the language, the arms and legs flailing were cathartic yet terrifying, bellowing from my core, pushing out the emotional debris that lay in front of it. In the end I found myself in the all-too-familiar compromising position beneath the bright fluorescent light.

"You've burned your hand. We'll talk to you about the consequences later."

Helpless, I remained mute as I watched the posse of staff file out. The sound of the door being shut and locked echoed through the room—bold and harsh, key to metal, metal to metal, the mouth of the demon shut.

As I had yet again been left in a position of total helplessness, the only thing I could control was sleep, whether to allow it or not. Again I fought the exhaustion that draped over me. Each time I drifted into a moment of slumber, I pulled myself out with a jolt. Determined to deprive myself of restful recuperation, I fought unconsciousness until I no longer could.

Warm rays replaced the bright florescence as the morning sun gleamed through the large unbreakable window, pulling me from my sleep and forcing me to face yet another day of anguished existence. As I had little to do but wait, my daydreaming finally was interrupted by the sound of keys. The seclusion door opened, and a staff member entered and freed me from the binding. He offered me a cigarette, which my body was craving. He sat with me as I inhaled deeply, quieting the nicotine withdrawal as we talked.

"Can I come out now?"

"No. We want you to stay in here a little bit longer."

"Why? I'm fine."

"We just want to make sure you can control yourself before you come out."

"I can. Can't you see that?"

After a little more negotiating—a test of our frustration tolerances—the one with the control got up and left, and I was alone yet again. The white walls of seclusion were not going to contain my rapidly escalating emotions. Ignited by the senseless confinement, with no resources at my disposal to calm the rapids that were rushing through me, I relied on the only thing I had—the hospital gown.

Tied in a neat little bow behind my back and behind my neck were the strings to keep the garment from flapping open. Reaching behind my head, I slowly untied the little bow, excitement building from the pit of my stomach and working its way up my spine toward my heart. My thoughts were detached from reason and from consequence, spinning from the rush of adrenaline that my body began to dump as I spurred my plan into action. I felt the strings on the hospital gown with my fingers, the fibers under my tips, the weave of the coarse fabric. Once the bow was released, the strings free and separate, I was able to manipulate them for my benefit, pulling them forward and around my neck, tying them in front. At first I made a loose connection, and then I tightened it, pulling harder, breathing harder, tying it tighter. Then I knotted it.

A sense of helpless excitement brushed over me as I lay in bed. My innate instinct was to try to find my breath and pull in as much air as possible through the small space I had left. My face and lips began to feel swollen, pushing against the strain to breathe. Blue replaced the pink of my skin. My mind danced between panic and exhilaration. Time warped as it shifted from slow motion to rapid speed. The extended struggle to take in air was rapidly replaced with the cold edge of scissors cutting the knot in the ties on the gown that had been provided to ensure my safety. Involuntarily I pulled in a gallon-size breath of air.

Panicked, nonsensical murmuring buzzed about the room. Within minutes I once again was tethered and bound. Ryan pulled up a chair close to the bed, with the scissors-wielding nurse standing over me, and he spoke.

"You're not going to be left alone. We're putting you on suicide precautions, SIP three. There will be a staff member with you at all times, and they'll be no more than an arm's length away."

Ryan settled back in the chair as a sense of calm settled into the seclusion room. At that point I made what to me seemed a reasonable request.

"I have to go to the bathroom."

The scissors-wielding nurse responded without pause.

"I'll be right back to help you with that."

Within minutes she returned, wielding something still more degrading, a bedpan.

"*What?* Are you for real? Why can't I get up? I'm not using that!"

"You don't have a choice. Ryan will leave the room. He'll come back in when you're done."

"Are you for real?"

"Do you have to go?"

"Yes."

"This is it then."

Confronted with the dilemma of my bladder rupturing in an explosive mess or my relieving myself in a degrading, completely unnecessary way pulled me in directions that were met only by sheer humiliation and absolutely no choice in a dehumanizing testament to institutional living.

Eventually I was allowed off the locked unit and allowed to join the community once again, my staff member in tow, no more than an arm's length away.

In a conference with staff, I was told that Nancy and I were no longer allowed in each other's company. No talking, no walking, no eye contact, nothing. My best friend, my support was ripped away like a Band-Aid. We were restricted from each other until further notice. End of story, no discussion.

The notion of an imposed abandonment was devastating, impossible to wrap my head around, impossible to accept, impossible to change. The decision had been made, and staff, like hawks scanning for their prey, watched Nancy and me. The begging and pleading and promises to change were futile. It was a rule we had to adhere to until Nancy's discharge many months

later. Mine soon followed.

THE ROSE GARDEN

By definition of my diagnosis, I was incurable. At the time of my illness, what was known—the experience of the professionals and the research—all pointed to the same conclusion. Borderline personality disorder was not curable, and the likelihood of recovery was slim. Those affected were tolerated at best. Through regimented therapy and strict behavioral techniques, they were taught to manage symptoms *enough* that eventually some—maybe even most—could be fully discharged from the mental health system on which they heavily relied and placed back into the community, where they were expected to perform with some semblance of success, somehow. And so it went for me.

I have a vivid memory of a thought so clear that raced through my mind: *I don't want to be sick anymore.* I wish I could say more: what had gotten me to that point, how long wellness took once that decision had been made, and whether it was really a choice, but I cannot. I can only recount the memory in that moment, my experience. It was as though a switch had flipped, and a decision, previously unavailable to my consciousness, was suddenly accessible.

Once I was deinstitutionalized, my life was filled with flashbacks of the trauma of incarceration and the loss of four and a half years of my life—my adolescence and early young adulthood. Though many memories are still irretrievable, I do recall my transition from relying on my parents to earning a paycheck as I developed a sense of independence and normalcy, reclaiming my young adulthood the best I could.

My poring over the Sunday paper's classified ads at the kitchen table while my parents scanned and devoured the other sections, steaming coffees at each of our places, became our weekend tradition. The routine was relaxing for them. For me the anticipation of potential employment elicited an indescribable anxiety, a much larger and more ominous threat than for most. Perusing the paper made my heart race, my stomach churn, and my limbs tingle as I tried to manage the emotional upheaval of my new life. My exterior demonstrated all my newly learned skills regarding how to maintain my composure, which I accomplished with great success. I circled a few listings and, pleased with my morning's efforts, retreated to my bedroom, coffee in hand, relieved that most employers were closed on Sundays.

My days during that period are a muddled blur. I spent them in reclusive solitude in my bedroom, listening to music, passing Saturday nights with friends, and spending weekdays beating the pavement, riddled with anxiety, handing out a résumé that had been deceptively devised during my incarceration. I was fighting for my life. To succeed I needed to create a garden, beautiful and full of flowers with colors vibrant and radiant, smells that would fill the air, enticing and alluring, trees, tall and protecting, filled with lush green leaves shading me from the harsh sun beating and burning. I needed to fill the garden with soft green grass on which I could lie and sleep and dream of all that I had planted, the roots of my life, a garden I could sustain only in health and normalcy. I set out to plant my garden with courage and terror and strength and will and anger and regret and desire until suddenly, in my life, with my garden, I could no longer rely on incarceration...I simply had too much to lose.

A job in a small, family-run office-supply store in the heart of the business district became my first successful planting. A rich dad had bought his bored son a gift to occupy his time and launch his career in retail. The gift had a trickle-down affect, offering employment to four other people, including me. But with the job came intense levels of panic that invaded my thoughts, my dreams, my days, my nights, with fantasies of the world's collapse through catastrophic means that would render humanity helpless and relieve me of fulfilling my obligation. The panic was so intense that bouts of nausea rushed through me. Hospitalization was no longer an option. I was creating my rose garden.

Though I was abler, stronger, and carried more hope than ever, healthy responses to everyday life were out of my realm of experience. I still relied on self-destructive tendencies to regulate the emotional turmoil that continued to wreak havoc on my still healing internal wounds. I continued to rely on outlets that were easier to hide than the bloodied mess of cutting.

"Talya, are you going to eat?"

"Yes, Mom, I'm going to eat. By myself, though, OK? I have stuff to do, so I'm just going to bring some food up to my room."

Annoyed at the rupture of the seemingly stable state of affairs, she responded with few words.

"I'm making a good dinner, but fine, if that's what you want."

Food to her was love. As she was European not just in roots but also by birth and rearing, food held an important place in the family in terms of community, love, and acceptance. To not appreciate a meal was to not appreciate her. Finishing all our food even when we were satiated, eating what we didn't like so as not to waste, drinking my milk that had been stained with tomato sauce made food an object of control. In either a binge state or a state of starvation, I used food as a tool to master the mayhem.

The night before my first day on the job—with a fear of failure, the unknown, expectations from those around me, and normality after a lifetime of instability—starvation and deprivation appeared to be the only options to control the emotional bombardment that ravaged me from within.

As I sat in my bedroom the television screen became an escape from my world. The lives the actors portrayed, the fantasy, felt safe. I craved to be them and not me. They weren't going to work at the office-supply store. If only I were them. If only I could be an actress. If only I could be the people I was watching on the television, my life would be easy. Though my illness had been replaced with a semblance of sanity, I still didn't understand that others experienced feelings as well, that perhaps those people on television were just as nervous on their first day as I was on mine. So I envied them. I wanted to be them. I saw ease in what they were doing. I saw horror, terror, fear, failure, and panic in what I was doing.

"Talya, are you going to eat?"

I made my way downstairs and found some Weight Watchers low-calorie cheddar cheese. Cutting exactly the serving size recommended on the package, I brought the cheese, a few crackers, and a low-calorie Jell-O up to my room. I sat on the floor and ate slowly, again immersed in the fantasy life of the sitcom.

"Talya, are you going to eat?"

Restricting my daily nutritional intake to a mere five hundred calories helped me contain my emotions. Had anyone noticed, I might have been returned to a life of confinement. But I was in recovery. I was building my rose garden.

THE RISK

A s I struggled to assemble a life for myself, I had to battle the scars
from my past. My arms and legs contained a map of my history, a
window into my life. For the first time since I had begun and ended the
practice of harming my body, I was interacting with people on a daily
basis who were not a part of my past or the psychiatric system or my
illness.

Short sleeves were a must in the sweltering summers. I was beginning to experience a new kind of self-consciousness. I was now acutely
aware of how I held my arms in an effort to keep my scars guarded from
the watchful eyes of others. I wore long pants despite the heat. Only with
the change of seasons was I able to breathe a sigh of relief.

Eventually my job became my routine. I became an expert in self-
camouflage and found unexpected comfort with employment. My eating stabilized to what was normal for me, an alternating pattern of

binging and starving, which balanced itself out. I had begun to give the impression of being a regular person, waking up early, going to work, receiving a paycheck, and going out with friends.

My life seemed to be as normal as that of any other twenty-three-year-old. The people I worked with accepted me, and I began to feel I was fitting into society, developing a sense of security, community, and belonging with my colleagues, all of whom were several years my senior. But there was one person who seemed to sense what others did not—the vulnerability I continued to carry heavily on my back.

Robert Hughes, my manager at the office-supply store, was a small man not much taller than me. Though small, he was tough, with the clichéd Napoleon complex. He was from a rough neighborhood, where he had to survive. Whether it was his intent or my perception, I found Robert Hughes intimidating. Despite his demeanor and my fear of him, I think he liked me. I don't know what he saw, but he treated me as though I had value. The day came when I felt I was due a raise.

"Robert?"

"Yeah, kiddo?"

My words were stymied by my anticipated of the rejection. Eye contact impossible, I gazed across the room and out the big windows as I built the courage to blurt out my words.

"I was wondering if it was time for me to have a raise."

An unreadable expression ran across Robert Hughes's face. The silence seemed to extend for an eternity, his poker face giving me no clues as to what his response would be. Finally he spoke.

"Well, Lee, I think you do deserve a raise. I can't give it to you, though. You have to go to Josh or his dad."

Only slightly encouraged by Robert's assessment, I needed more reassurance.

"What do you think they'll say?"

"I think you deserve it, so I think they will too."

With my store manager's support, I had the courage I needed to ask the rich young man and his rich father whether they valued me as much as Robert Hughes did. Slowly, as though my soft step would increase my chance for a positive outcome, I made my way back to the office where Josh and his dad spent much of their day while the rest of us kept their store running. With a deep breath to slow my racing heart, I knocked twice and awaited a response.

"Yes. Come in."

Slowly turning the knob, I walked in, trying to carry an air of confidence in one hand and a bundle of humility in the other. Both men, sitting at their desks in the small, windowless office, paused and looked up at me.

"What can we do you for you?"

"Well, I was wondering, since I've been working here for six months now, if I could have a raise in my pay. I think I've been doing a good job, and I talked to Robert about it, and he said I deserve one."

The pause was unsettling, and they appeared, by their more readable expressions, less than enthused by my request. They let me know in the simplest of terms.

"No."

As embarrassment rushed through me, starting in my gut and racing up to my face with a speed that sent redness flushing across my cheeks, I stood paralyzed, a hostage to my shame as the rich dad began his explanation as to why I did not deserve a raise.

Like Robert Hughes, the rich father was small, but he was round whereas Robert was slim. His lack of friendliness appeared to be inherent meanness as opposed to a defense learned growing up in a rough neighborhood. Talking to him, respecting him, listening to him explain the rejection took patience and the ability to daydream so as not vomit a barrage of hostile remarks all over his mousy-colored three-piece suit. So there I stood, "listening" patiently while my mind wandered as quickly as possible to a place far from where I was.

His thick lips moved, but my mind refused to listen. Hoping my response made sense, I nodded as his intonation changed. I was hearing something like this: "It's like this, Lee. We're a small store, not a big store. I hired you at a wage I think is fair. Let's stick with that. We can take a look at your pay some other time."

Pleased with his sermon, he paused and looked at me. My breath had stopped, as the rate of inhaling and exhaling was a window into my emotions, a place where he was not welcome. Finally the anger, looming large inside, pushed my first breath out in a gasp. My thoughts raced furiously, screaming, *Fuck you!* at the rich father. *Maybe there won't be another time. I don't want a fucking raise from a bastard like you anyway! I hate you! I hate your son! I hate your store! I want to quit this boring, fucked up job and spit on you!*

"I understand. Thanks anyway."

Through sheer willpower, I held back the flood of tears ready to spill out. I turned my back on the rich father and his silent son and walked quickly into the store as though I could outrun my shame. I stood, silently awaiting my next costumer, when Robert Hughes approached with his yellow-toothed smile and cigarette breath.

"Hey, kid. How'd it go?"

I shrugged, afraid that with words would come tears.

"They turn you down?"

Mustering the anger that sat in my belly, preferring it to the sadness, rejection, criticism, and failure, I answered him.

"Yeah. I can't believe him. He actually turned me down. Don't you think I deserve a raise?"

"Yup. What'd they say?"

"They said something like the store is too small, and they don't have enough money because of that. They think the amount I get now is fair, and we can talk about it some other time. I can't believe it. Don't you think I deserve it?"

"Yeah, I do. Well, sorry 'bout it. You'll try again." And with that Robert Hughes spun coolly on his heels and walked off.

THE GRADUATE

Though I was healthier than I'd ever been in my life, I was still in the process of emerging from the cocoon of mental illness. My job was predictable, offering some semblance of safety in an environment that had initially held a disquieting sense of danger. My coworkers, always the same—no turnover, no shifts—offered a supportive community to which I belonged, allowing me to move farther and farther from my institutionalized past. Today they stand like shadows in my mind as I remember back to those days. All but Robert Hughes—he remains vivid in my memory.

Each Friday Robert would glide smoothly through the store, presenting each employee with an envelope, our weekly reward, however measly in nature. On this particular Friday, he saved me for last. Standing in front of me, he extended his hand, offering me my paycheck, accompanied by a wink. I stood for a confused moment then opened the envelope and glanced at the amount, searching for the meaning of his silent communication. My weekly salary remained unchanged, but a twenty-dollar bill lay folded inside. Looking up, I scanned the store for Robert Hughes, who had disappeared into the back room or to the bank or wherever it is that managers go when you can't find them. I slipped my reward into my pocket.

This continued every week, with every paycheck, in every envelope, until I quit my job.

Oh, I almost forgot...Thank you, Robert Hughes.

Work had become mundane. After more than a year, I decided it was time to do something else.

"I recommend you do not send Lee to college. This is something that would only set her up for disappointment."

I never went to high school really. My education was one hour per day while in The Hospital, and at the Alternative School on the grounds of the state hospital when not, a diploma offered out of pity rather than success. There had been no preparation for higher education, no thought of a career, no guidance for the future. The only expectation had been for me to keep living...until I died.

Though I never took my SATs, not even aware such a thing existed, I managed to get accepted into the continuing education department of a major university through family connections. As I was a nonmatriculating student, they wanted to see a grade point average indicative of bright, creative thinking. I had to be better. I had to be brighter. I had to prove to them that I could succeed, and succeed I did. I became a matriculating student, another planting in my rose garden. Now the only evidence of my disturbing past lay privately in my mind and strategically hidden on my body. Incarceration was an option that no longer belonged in my vocabulary. I had to sustain my new life and mask the fear of failure and the fear of success that plagued me.

It was the proverbial carrot that pulled me along—my carrot: taking methamphetamines and clubbing with my friends. Purchasing on

Thursday secured my weekends and ensured my desire to continue my trek toward normality. Speed was my buoy, my anchor. I enjoyed every weekend with an artificial elation and energy that I couldn't resist. A weekend without speed and without clubs would send me into a fit of temper. Friends and speed made all the struggles of normalcy palatable. The club we went to also became an obsession.

"Does anyone wanna come up and pick a song for when we go back on the air?"

The disc jockey threw out a general plea to all the intoxicated costumers. My friends encouraged me to go onstage. The disc jockey's assistant flattered me: "Your eyes are beautiful and your voice—you should be a disc jockey." After my request aired live from the music hall, he expressed his desire to see me again. I thought little of this flirtatious man, until his presence in my dreams replaced the haunting images that usually dwelled there. Overnight I fell in love.

The following weekend my friends and I returned to the club. The disc jockey's assistant threw flirtatious glances out into the crowd, aiming for me, luring me onto the stage. His eyes locked onto mine, then moved toward the stairs.

"Can I have your number, beautiful eyes?"

"OK."

Scribbling on the inside of a matchbook, he wrote down my phone number, my heart throbbing the beat of love. His last words: "I'll call you tomorrow."

Sitting cradled in one of the yellow 1950s-era chairs that balanced my parents' living room with their symmetry, I sobbed the wretched tears of a heartbroken lover. On this night an obsession was born. The rejection held me captive for a love I'd never had in the first place. Driving hopelessly through his neighborhood and religiously attending the Saturday-night dance party, flirting with other men, I hoped to spark his interest again, an interest that was snuffed out before it even began.

I was consumed with obsession, consumed with drugs. My weekend addictions threatened to crumble the rose garden I was building. Had anyone noticed, they would have seen me spiraling toward dangerous waters. Come Monday, coiffed and manicured, I would brush off and struggle through the week. I had gone from a severely emotionally disturbed child to an office-supply-store employee to a college student, from one end of the earth to the other, but my battle was still raging. I had to learn how to be normal, how to manage in a world of expectations for success.

Fleeing the country, leaving my addictions behind, I studied abroad for a year. I arrived in Europe equipped with six quaaludes, my replacement for meth. Within the first couple of days, they were gone, not by ingestion but by a pickpocket on a crowded bus. I had no choice so I managed. I made friends. I studied. I worked in the abroad program's library.

After six years, and just about as many majors, I finally triumphed. The hopeless renegade with little chance for normalcy earned a degree in the very field that had held her captive for so many years. I graduated in a small winter ceremony with the other students as well as my husband and my mother-in-law to celebrate my accomplishment. It was my class. This time I belonged. I had a degree I deserved.

NOBODY BUT ME

The first night of institutionalization remains a vivid image, the details clear, down to the red stitching in my pants and the Mickey Mouse T-shirt I was wearing. By sharp contrast, the end is a fog. The last months of incarceration have been ripped from my awareness by an amnesiac cloud. How did I leave? How did I escape institutional living, the revolving door of psychiatric care? Dr. Bennett, the man who had been there from the beginning, who, as far as I was concerned, was seemingly intent on keeping me behind locked doors, or perhaps on helping me succeed despite my illness and never give up or give in, was gone. He was no longer in my life.

The need to reconnect with my past continued to apply a relentless pressure. My attempts to remember became the focus of my life. My curiosity allowed me to experience the bizarre workings of memory.

During my stay on the young adult unit, I had a strong connection with a social worker named Carol Larkin. Dr. Bennett encouraged this relationship. She was my sole female attachment. Her medium-length brown hair, bright-blue eyes, and medium stature were etched firmly in mind. I knew what Carol looked like, yet any recollection of the time we spent together—walks or talks, intimate or superficial—were gone, experiences split off from my consciousness.

Just like I'd found the others—on the Internet—I found Carol. Again my past crashed into my present. With shaking hands, I called her and was instantly struck by the recognition of her voice, unchanged over the decades.

During our fairly regular visits together, she shared what she remembered. She shared whatever she could.

"When you left The Hospital, you didn't want to work with Dr. Bennett anymore. Since you still needed outpatient treatment, I took you on as my client."

"Why didn't I want to see Dr. Bennett anymore?"

"I'm not sure. You had a hard time with him. You butted heads a lot."

"He scared me. Maybe that's why. His power. His control."

Holding a cup of hot green tea between my hands, I dropped my eyes to the soothing liquid. Memories, reinforced by the presence of Carol, pushed through. In that moment I felt the fear I had of Dr. Bennett, his powerful authority from which I could not hide. Carol continued, pulling me back to the present.

"Anyway, I took you on as my client, and that worked out at first. Dr. Bennett agreed to it, and he saw it as a step-down process. You basically went from seeing him, the doctor, to seeing me, a social worker. It was a step down, not as intense."

"How long did I see you? What happened?"

Whenever I lunched with Carol, sitting across from her, drinking in all she had to tell me, my body would lean forward in an expression of wanting it all, more. I devoured every word, every memory Carol had for me.

"Well, during the time I saw you, there was an issue with your frequently calling me feeling very suicidal. You would call me at all hours, even late at night, and tell me you were going to kill yourself."

"Oh, my God, Carol! At all hours? Even at night?"

"Yes, even at night. You actually would call my home."

"How did I get your home phone number?"

"I don't really remember. I may have given it to you in case you needed something urgently. Well, you would use it. You would call me, and the urgency was your suicidal feelings. One time you called me from a bridge."

Decades later I could not think of myself as the type to call from a bridge. Shock ran through me like a gulp of hot tea, unexpected and scorching.

"I called you from a bridge? Why?"

"You called me from a bridge, telling me you were going to jump. I was caught. I was caught between wanting to help you and watching you die, and I didn't want to watch you die. I didn't want to be a part of your death. I was getting supervision for myself because I needed someone else to help me keep my perspective. It was recommended that I have you agree to a safety contract in order for us to continue. I agreed with this suggestion because I wasn't going to just watch you die, Talya, and that's where you were heading."

"What if I didn't agree to the contract?"

"I presented you with a choice, so it was in your hands. Either you'd agree to the contract for your safety, or I would have to discontinue our work together. You were pretty stubborn, you know."

Old feelings were rising, overwhelming emotions twenty-five years old. I searched inside myself to try to see the incident, to try to see Carol back then, to try to remember. The fact was that I did not remember. I did not remember seeing Carol as my outpatient therapist, calling her, pulling her down into my suicidal underworld of demons and torture and pain and suffering.

"What happened then?"

"I can't remember exactly. You refused to sign the contract. I can't imagine I would have just left you. My guess is that you didn't want another therapist. I told Dr. Bennett, and he was disappointed at what had happened. You were pretty much on your own at that point."

I began to imagine the darkness that must have encased me. A dream I'd had came to mind—alone in an ocean, young and child-like, helpless, without the aid of a lifeguard to pull me up as I almost drowned. Nobody could see me. Nobody could save me. Nobody but me.

MY LAST JOURNEY

I sat in my car trying to reach a man I had heard was slippery to nail down. My need to bring closure to my journey, my last stop on the road to my past, motivated me to keep trying, no matter how many meetings he was in or how many unreturned messages I had to endure.

"Hi. My name is Talya Lewis. I'm calling because I'm interested in getting into two of the buildings on the grounds of the state hospital."

"You realize that many of them are abandoned."

"Yes."

"Which buildings are you interested in going into?"

"Buildings X and IX.

"The person you need to talk to is Mark Anderson. Let me see if he's available."

The wait seemed endless—no music, just silence. I prepared myself for the disappointment I was sure to feel when the voice returned. I also battled the feeling that I was doing something wrong, as though making my request was somehow inviting others to see what I had been trying to keep hidden for so many years.

"Hello. This is Mark Anderson."

Startled, both by the voice and by the fact that I had nailed down the slippery man on my first attempt, I spoke cautiously.

"Hi, Mr. Anderson? My name is Talya Lewis, and well, I'm calling to see if there's any way for me to get in to see two of the buildings on the grounds of the state hospital."

"To see two of the buildings, inside?"

"Yes."

"What's your interest?"

"I'm writing a book. I would like to see the state hospital before I can feel it's complete."

What I wasn't expecting, but was quite relieved to find, was no curiosity from Mark Anderson, just a warning.

"Well, you need to realize what these buildings are like. They're cold and damp. If it's cold outside, they're colder inside. If it's wet outside, they're wetter inside. There's no life left in these buildings. They're abandoned."

It was unseasonably warm, with temperatures in the high forties. The sun was strong, taming the usual frigid temperatures expected for this time of the year. Mark and I agreed that if the weather were too cold or if there were snow, we would reschedule. I had anticipated disappointment, so the relief was that much greater. Though he had told me that walking through some of the buildings wasn't an option, the day was suitable for the agreed-upon visit.

The driveway was a photograph into the past, so familiar, unchanged in any way. Agitated voices seemed to call out in the breeze, the air carrying all the emotions from those anguished days, residual hauntings from my past. I sat frozen in my car as I gathered the presence of mind necessary to present myself as a curious member of society rather than a former captive resident. Entering the office, I was greeted by a security guard.

"Can I help you?"

"Hi. Yeah. I'm here to meet with Mark Anderson."

"Your name?"

"Talya Lewis. He's expecting me."

The security guard dropped his head and glanced at an appointment book that rested on the desk in front of him.

"Yes. I see here. Daniel Freeze and Sandra Herman are going to take you through the buildings you asked to see. Just sit down and make yourself comfortable, and they'll be right out."

"Thank you."

Disappointed that Mark was missing this important day, I had to remind myself that rejection was no longer part of the equation. I sat as a healthy researcher on a personal assignment for the closure of my memoir. Waiting for my escorts to guide me through the condemned buildings, I braided the tassels of my scarf.

"You have an interesting name. How do you spell it?"

I glanced up, locking eyes with the security guard, his teeth white against his dark skin. It was a question I had heard many times, one that touched a nerve.

"It's spelled T-a-l-y-a. I know. It's a weird name. My parents were having a bad day when I was born. I would have preferred being Mary or Jane."

"Or Carol?"

I smiled back at him, assuming the name held some meaning for him, and nodded. "Or Carol."

Eventually a man appeared, a female not far behind. Flashlights in hand, they approached, and I stood.

"Hi. My name's Dan."

Smiling, he gestured toward the woman.

"And this is Sandy. We're going to bring you through building X."

"Great! It's nice to meet you. There's just one thing. When I talked to Mark, I asked him if I could see building IX as well. He said that would be OK."

"That's fine. We can do them both."

A momentary roller-coaster ride from panic to relief, and we were on our way.

I followed Dan and Sandy out the door and into the mild winter air. The breeze had a familiar smell that awakened feelings and thoughts from the days I'd spent there, when I was young, alone, frightened, fighting for my life. Pulling myself back to the present, I remembered the conversation I'd had with Mark Anderson, words that had sent a chill through me one month before: *You have to realize these buildings are not like they used to be. They're abandoned and falling apart. There's no life left in them.* Over and over, my mind replayed what he'd said.

There is no life left.

"OK, here we are, building X."

As we stopped in front of building X, the enormity of its facade was striking. The building was an eerie juxtaposition between beautiful and terrifying, the energy from the anguish not yet dissipated but hanging heavily in the air. Many of the buildings on the grounds of the state hospital were condemned, too much in need of repair to save. They carried a sadness as they awaited demolition.

"Can we go in through that door?"

I gestured toward the thick metal door I had walked through every morning of high school, the warehouse for the emotionally hopeless.

"No, that door is nailed shut from the inside."

My heart sank. I had been warned about access to the inside of the buildings. A rush of disappointment washed over me. Dan continued.

"We have to go in the front, but then we can walk down to the rooms you want to see."

My heart began to beat again, in relief and anticipation, slamming against my chest. I mumbled quietly to myself, reassuring myself of the time, the place, and who I was. *Breathe. It's OK. It's now, not then.*

Dan inserted his key and slowly pushed the heavy front door open. Inside it was dead.

"Wow. It's creepy in here."

Dan and Sandy looked at me. They shone their flashlights down a long tunnel to our right as we descended the stairs. It was dark, except for whatever sun seeped through the few unboarded windows. The smell was musty and dirty, old and abandoned. Paint was chipping away from the walls and the ceiling. Some of the pipes were dripping, making an eerie, penetrating sound. There was no life left.

Walking to the left, I recognized the first of the two rooms that had made up my high school. Dan turned the knob, but the door did not budge. He pushed with his weight but to no effect. Time had sealed the room. Once again I was awash with disappointment. The loud sound of banging replaced the weighted emotion with a reflexive startle as Dan began to kick.

"Go, Dan!"

He kicked.

"Go, Dan!"

He kicked...and kicked...and with each kick the door moved a little more, and with each kick, I had hope and the door moved more, and with this final kick...it opened. Dan's voice echoed in the damp room.

"I wonder if we have any electricity in here. Check the light switch, would you?"

I watched Sandy's hand as she reached over, shining her flashlight and flipping the switch, a fluorescent brightness breaking through the darkness.

"So is this the room you remember?"

The orientation of the room, the one I had been locked inside after my escape through the tunnels, was somehow changed, the passage of time playing tricks on my memory. Only the two bay windows were as I recalled them. Taking in every inch of the space, I noticed something on the floor.

"What's that?"

Dan and Sandy turned their heads, Sandy unnecessarily casting her flashlight on the barely identifiable creature. Dan responded in a matter-of-fact tone.

"Looks like a dead animal."

"What do you think it was?"

"Looks like a kitten."

"Do you think it got trapped in here and starved?"

Dan said the words I wanted to hear but didn't really believe.

"I bet something dragged it in here. Probably already dead."

I knew the kitten had found itself in circumstances in which it could not escape, imprisoned in a hell with no one to save it, its death slow and lonely. The kitten, young and helpless, unprotected and alone, served as a chilling metaphor for an anguished childhood.

"So what was your connection with this room anyway?"

It was inevitable. Dan and Sandy had to be curious. They had to wonder why this woman, put together and polite, smiling and cheerful, would be asking for a tour of two abandoned buildings on the grounds of an old state hospital.

"Well, this used to be an old school."

Searching my mind for a way out of the truth, I was going to tell them I had been a teacher there, but given that the school was there in the late 1970s and early 1980s, I was quickly aware, my math savvy in action, of the unrealistic lie this would have been. Taking a spoonful of shame and swallowing it rapidly, so as not to taste it for too long, I blurted out my connection to this condemned, damp, eerie room in the basement of building X.

"This was a school, and I actually went here."

Dan responded with surprise but no judgment.

"Oh, wow. How long did you go here?"

"I was here on and off for eleventh and twelfth grade. Pretty weird, huh? It's amazing what they used to do to kids. I guess they still do. My high school kicked me out, and this was the only place that would take me, I guess."

I paused, waiting for a response, the shame I had swallowed resurfacing. Sandy kept shining her flashlight around the corners of the already lit room. Dan started talking, swooping in to the rescue.

"Boy, when I think of the things I used to do. I eventually went into the military, but some of the things I used to do. Drinking and driving all around. The cops would pull you over and pour out your booze and send you on your way. Not nowadays, no way."

"I know. It's a different world now. Probably better in some ways, more careful."

I was grateful for Dan, whether he knew what he was doing or simply had his own story to share. I asked if we could move on.

"Can we go see the other room? I want to see if I recognize that one. If that room is right, then this one is too, and I'm just not remembering it as it really was."

Dan and Sandy agreed. Taking my lead, we walked out, leaving the light on because we all knew I was going to go back and forth between the rooms a couple of times. We made our way down the hall. I passed the stairs that led to the door I had gone in and out of every day, the stairs where I sat in a puddle of powerlessness, hitting my head over and over against the cold, light-green, glazed, ceramic tiles that lined the walls, the teacher sitting by my side, her hand protecting me.

Slowly I approached the entrance to the main room of my little school, where we spent most of our time. The moment I stepped into the room I was slammed by ghosts from the past. The room had remained eerily unchanged. I stood and stared at the partition that made up the teachers' office, still intact, as though they simply had gathered all their belongings and left for the day. I strained to hear voices, those of the four teachers who were specially trained to work with the hopeless, and of the ten or twelve kids specifically chosen to attend the small school on the grounds of an old asylum. I was struck by chilling memories, sadness and despair, reexperiencing them for a moment, the vision of the room today sending me back to the room as it had been thirty years ago.

As we left building X, the crisp, clear air with the sun shining brightly against the blue sky was a striking contrast to the dark, damp interior of the condemned building of my abandoned school. The next destination was the building where I had been confined for one week while I awaited my hearing. Slowly we made our way up the path to the door of building IX. Dan spoke.

"Mr. Anderson asked that we not walk all the way through this building. It hasn't been occupied in some time, and the floors, especially those upstairs, may not be secure."

Hearing Dan's words, I was doused with disappointment again, a familiar though fleeting feeling on this day. My desire to walk through these buildings had an unquenchable hold on me. I wanted to visually slip back and reexperience the emotions of the six days I'd spent locked behind the doors of a state hospital awaiting my fate. I wanted to see it, to remember it. We walked through the front doors on the first floor.

"Do you remember this lobby?"

My heart stopped dead.

"Yes."

"So this is where you were?"

"Yes."

"Weird for you to be here?"

"Yes."

I looked around and remembered. I was standing in the room where the ambulance drivers had left me and the affect-challenged doctor had admitted me into a week of hell.

"I wish we could walk all the way through. I would love to see more."

I locked eyes with Dan, sending him a plea from my soul. Building IX was marked for death, its demolition absolute. This was my only chance, my last chance, to walk the path of my traumatic past.

"I really wish we could walk through, at least a little bit farther."

I flirted—shameless eye fluttering, my head tilted slightly to one side, my smile coy. Dan finally succumbed to my feminine pressure.

"Well, I suppose we could go a little bit farther."

Once again a sigh escaped as the weight lifted. Slowly we made our way deeper into the ward of the former state hospital's crisis center. We made our way through like ducklings, single file: Dan, me, then Sandy trailing behind us, picking up the rear as though to make sure no ghosts from the past crept up. Once we were all feeling safer, I wandered into the rooms. The first room that caught my attention sucked me in like a vacuum. I scanned the room, the blue walls shedding their paint in disrepair, molting from time, age, and abandon. A strong sense of familiarity hovered around me.

"Oh, my God. This was my room."

Dan turned to me.

"This is where you slept while you were here?"

"Yeah. There were four of us in each in room, if I remember right. It's weird, though. My memory is of the room being much bigger, but this is it. Oh, my God, this is it."

A sinister feeling flooded the room. More than twenty-five years separated the me of today from the me of yesterday. I looked around, touching the walls as though to catch my germs still lingering in the fibers of the paint, something I did as a child as my family and I traipsed through the ruins of ancient civilizations, trying to connect with the long dead. Dan and Sandy stood quietly as I sucked in the memories.

Eventually I made my way out of the room and walked farther into the ward.

"In here. This is where we would watch TV. We never got to pick because someone was always there first."

I turned and faced the length of the long hallway.

"That was the nurses' station. It looks exactly the same, just eerie and lonely now. Nothing's changed. It looks the same."

We walked into what once had been the cafeteria, where I'd sat with the case manager, playing with his keys as a distraction. Signs still hung on the walls, left from a time when life had walked through these rooms.

We walked out, back into the hallway, and passed in front of the nurses' station. The silence of a bygone era lurked in every corner of the building. A chill ran down my spine. I swung like a pendulum from numb ambivalence to deep-seated desperation as I relived my past, my youth, my incarceration.

"Dan, can we go upstairs?"

"The building isn't really structurally sound. Nobody comes in here. Nobody has for decades."

"*Please*, Dan. I really need to see this whole place. Soon it won't be here anymore. This is my only chance."

I smiled at him, head tilted, with one last appeal.

"Pleeease."

"OK. We can go up but under one condition."

"Anything. What is it?"

"You have to stay behind me at all times. If the floor is weak in any section, I'm the one who'll fall through, not you. So stay behind me. Understand?"

That was a condition I was happy to abide by.

"Absolutely. Thanks, Dan. Thank you. Thank you. Thank you."

Slowly we made our way up.

Suddenly I stopped.

Dan stopped.

Sandy stopped.

"I remember these stairs. These are the stairs I ran down after my hearing."

Dan and Sandy stood silent, aware that I was talking more to myself than to them. I caressed the railing under the palm of my hand. I continued to talk.

"I have no idea where I was running to, because there was no place for me to go. I ran down the stairs, I remember, and into my room. I can still see myself."

My silence was Dan's cue to proceed, and we continued to make our way up the stairs to the second floor.

None of the rooms was familiar, none of the rooms except the one where my hearing had taken place.

"I'm pretty sure this is the room where they had the hearings. The room where our fates were decided by some guy who'd never seen us before."

"It's storage now."

"Yeah, I can see. It's strange. This room once held people's fates. Now it holds their belongings. Soon it'll hold nothing. Soon it'll be rubble, an accumulation of bricks."

Since the writing of this book, building IX, a frighteningly beautiful display of nineteenth-century asylum architecture and a monument to my pain, is gone.

RECOVERY TALK

I frequently am asked to share my story of recovery. From all I have learned, due to my history and my unquenchable thirst for knowledge in the field of trauma, I educate students and providers on the experience and treatment of borderline personality disorder. On this day I stood in front of an audience of approximately fifty people in an old church west of the city. I had been asked to speak specifically about my past, my illness, my treatment, my hopes, and my dreams.

"I would like to introduce Talya Lewis. She's here to share with us her story of experiences with borderline personality disorder."

My heart always races, no matter how many times I share my story of recovery with people struggling with symptoms of illness, as well as their family members, or stand before an audience of eager professionals, providing a more clinical workshop. Scanning my audience, with a joke or two to ease the tension, both theirs and mine, I began.

"When I was eight years old I had game. I called it TP, which stood for taking pills...

"At nine years old I hated my two front teeth, so I took a hammer and a screwdriver...

"By eleven years old, I was impulsively shoplifting.

"And by twelve I had my first thoughts of suicide.

"By thirteen I had tried drugs.

"By fourteen the frequency increased dramatically.

"Also by fourteen I was binging and starving.

"And by fifteen I was paranoid and cutting.

"I had intense love-hate relationships.

"My identity was tied into my evil core.

"I was empty.

"Bored.

"Angry.

"Terrified.

"Alone.

"I was sick."

I paused, looked at my audience, and continued.

"At this point in my life, I felt as though I no longer had any options. When I was sixteen years old, I overdosed on a bottle of sleeping pills in the lobby of my high school. That was the beginning of years of long-term confinements in a private psychiatric hospital. It also was the beginning of my having to deal with the diagnosis borderline personality disorder."

As I continued with my story, there was absolute silence in the room. Motionless spectators listened to a story, a journey from illness to recovery. At the end of my thirty minutes, they applauded. They applauded for me. They applauded for my story. They applauded for my recovery.

Made in the USA
Lexington, KY
13 June 2014